NEW CONTEXTS

RE-FRAMING NINETEENTH-CENTURY
IRISH WOMEN'S PROSE

New Contexts:

Re-Framing Nineteenth-Century Irish Women's Prose

EDITED BY HEIDI HANSSON

CORK UNIVERSITY PRESS

First published in 2008 by
Cork University Press
Youngline Industrial Estate
Pouladuff Road, Togher
Cork, Ireland

British Library Cataloguing in Publication Data
A CIP catalogue record for this book is available from the British Library.

ISBN 978-1-85918-4165

Typesetting by Red Barn Publishing, Skeagh, Skibbereen, Co. Cork
Printed by ColourBooks Ltd, Baldoyle, Co. Dublin

Published with the support of the Swedish Research Council

www.corkuniversitypress.com

Contents

Contributors

Dr Jacqueline Belanger is the editor of *Ireland and the Novel in the Nineteenth Century: Facts and Fictions* (2006). She has published essays on nineteenth-century Irish literature and is the co-author of the web database *British fiction, 1800-1829*.

Professor Heidi Hansson lectures in English at Umeå University, Sweden. Her main research interest is women's literature, and she has previously published in the fields of postmodern romance, *Romance Revived: Postmodern Romances and the Tradition* (1998), nineteenth-century women's cross-gendered writing, nineteenth-century travel writing and Irish women's literature. She is the author of a full-length study of the Irish nineteenth-century writer Emily Lawless. Heidi Hansson is also the leader of an interdisciplinary project on foreign travellers to northern Scandinavia in the nineteenth century, and is working on a study of gender and the experience of the North.

Dr Margaret Kelleher is a Senior Lecturer in English at National University of Ireland, Maynooth. She is the author of *The Feminization of Famine: Expressions of the Inexpressible* (1997) and co-editor (with James H. Murphy) of *Gender Perspectives in Nineteenth-Century Ireland* (1997). Her research interests include nineteenth-century Irish literature and culture and the history of Irish women's writings. Most recently, she is co-editor (with Philip O'Leary) of *The Cambridge History of Irish Literature* (2006). She is currently working on a study of Irish reading in the nineteenth century.

Dr Maria Lindgren Leavenworth is a Senior Lecturer in English at Umeå University Sweden. Her doctoral thesis *The Second Journey, Travelling in Literary Footsteps* (2000) focused on how modern travellers use old travelogues as maps to follow. Originality, authenticity and intertextuality were key areas of interest. Her current research focuses on remediated texts, especially film adaptations of literary works. A connected area of interest is how texts are used and interpreted in fan fiction. Maria Lindgren Leavenworth also participates in an interdisciplinary project concerning images of northern Scandinavia in texts by foreign travellers during the nineteenth century.

Dr Riana O'Dwyer is Senior Lecturer in the English Department at National University of Ireland, Galway. She edited the section on 'Women's Narratives 1800-1840' in the *Field Day Anthology of Irish Writing* Vol. 5 and is currently working on a longer study of Irish women's fiction before the famine. She was elected Chair of the International Association for the Study of Irish Literatures [IASIL] for the period 2003-6. She has lectured and published on Joyce, modern Irish drama, Irish studies, and Irish women novelists of the nineteenth century.

Dr Tina O'Toole is a lecturer in English at the Department of Language & Cultural Studies, University of Limerick. Her research interests include nineteenth and twentieth-century literature in Ireland and Britain, and in particular, the 1890s New Woman project and *fin de siècle* culture. She is the general editor and compiler of the *Dictionary of Munster Women Writers 1800-2000* (2005), and she co-authored, with Linda Connolly, an archival study of the Irish Women's Movement, *Documenting Irish Feminisms: The Second Wave* (2005).

Dr Julie Anne Stevens lectures on literature in Trinity College Dublin and St. Patrick's College, Drumcondra, Dublin. She has published articles on nineteenth- and twentieth-century Irish writing. In 2002, she set up an exhibition on the manuscripts and illustrations of Edith Somerville and Martin Ross in Trinity College Library. Her book, *The Irish Scene: Somerville and Ross's Fiction and Illustrations, 1890-1915* (Irish Academic Press) was published in October 2006.

Dr Elisabeth Wennö is Associate Professor of English at Karlstad University, Sweden. She has published articles on modern literature and literary theory, and a book-length study, *Ironic Formula in the Novels of Beryl Bainbridge* (1993). Elisabeth Wennö is also the co-editor of three critical anthologies and co-leader of the Narrativity research group at Karlstad University.

Acknowledgements

This project began in 1999–2000 as a joint Swedish-Irish study of nineteenth-century Irish women's prose. I was fortunate enough to be able to spend a year as a postdoctoral research fellow at the Centre for Irish Literature and Bibliography, University of Ulster, and during that time, I worked closely with Dr Anne McCartney. Together, we devised a research plan to investigate Irish women's writing from the perspectives of our different cultural and national positions. Unfortunately, Dr McCartney left the university before our plans could come to fruition, but the ideas we shared are very much present in this volume. First of all, therefore, I would like to thank Dr Anne McCartney for her valuable contributions in the early stages of the project, as well as for her friendship and hospitality.

I also wish to express my sincere gratitude to the Swedish Research Council for the grant that allowed me to spend a year in Northern Ireland together with my family. The opportunity to develop my knowledge of Irish literature and to spend uninterrupted time doing research was invaluable. I am very grateful to the University of Ulster and the staff at the Centre for Irish Literature and Bibliography for giving me a place among them and making me feel welcome. After I returned home, I received a grant that allowed me to continue working with scholars in Ireland from the Swedish Foundation for International Cooperation in Research and Higher Education. This grant was essential for the final success of the project and I am truly grateful.

Living for a period in a different country is stimulating and exciting in so many ways, but it is not always easy. Therefore I want to especially thank Susan, Joe, Cathy and Conor McReynolds for helping us adapt to life in a new country. I am so grateful to my children, Marit, Nils and Jerker, for agreeing to leave their friends and familiar surroundings for a whole year and come to Northern Ireland. You never cease to impress me. Finally, and always, thank you Per, for believing in me, supporting me and helping me in more ways than I can ever say.

Introduction: Out of Context

Heidi Hansson

Until quite recently, it looked as if women prose writers from the nineteenth century would be completely lost from Irish literary history.[1] This situation has now changed, thanks to a number of works that retrieve forgotten women's voices. The publication of volumes IV and V of the *Field Day Anthology of Irish Writing: Women's Writing and Traditions* (2002) and the *Dictionary of Munster Women Writers 1800–2000* edited by Tina O'Toole (2005), for instance, has laid important foundations for further investigations. The June 2000 issue of the *Colby Quarterly* edited by Anne Fogarty and Kathryn Kirkpatrick's edited collection *Border Crossings: Irish Women Writers and National Identities* from the same year attest to a growing interest in nineteenth-century women's fiction, with articles not only on already acclaimed authors like Maria Edgeworth and Lady Morgan, but also studies of the relatively unknown Charlotte Riddell, George Egerton and Katherine Cecil Thurston. Other writers who have attracted critical attention in recent years are Sydney Owenson/Lady Morgan, Julia Kavanagh and Rosa Mulholland. Books like Lisbet Kickham's *Protestant Women Novelists and Irish Society, 1879–1922* (2003, new ed. 2004), edited collections like Jacqueline Belanger's *The Irish Novel in the Nineteenth Century: Facts and Fictions* (2005), studies of Emily Lawless by Heidi Hansson and of Somerville and Ross by Julie Anne Stevens and books and articles by Margaret Kelleher, James H. Murphy, Claire Connolly and a range of other scholars show that there is vibrant activity in the field. To some extent, however, this movement has arisen from a wish to reclaim the history of women rather than a desire to re-evaluate their texts, and there is sometimes a sense of unease as to the literary importance of women's work. The question that now needs to be addressed is what kind of contexts are appropriate for the study of these recovered works, since it seems clear that the contexts that have governed literary studies so far still manage to exclude women's writing in many ways.

Part of the reason why nineteenth-century women novelists were overlooked so long is the polemical style that has characterized Irish literary studies, where scholars have frequently positioned themselves in opposition to each other. While this combative climate may be positively understood as creating a dynamic environment, 'engaged in a relentless reappraisal of its own fundamental principles, and, moreover, that of the culture of which it is both product and analysis',[2] it has also led to a reactive type of criticism focused on a limited number of writers and texts, which automatically counteracts an expansion of the traditional canon. Critical standards and ideas of aesthetic value have been based on the writings of, primarily, Yeats, Joyce and Beckett, and women have automatically been regarded as lesser writers. The pervasive nature of this form of criticism has meant that even critics advocating further investigation of women's writing are sometimes unable to extricate themselves from its clutches.

Attempts to include women writers in already existing literary canons have been mainly unsuccessful. The 'equality approach' easily effaces women's particularity and does not allow for the possibility that women's writing may be *different* and therefore may require another critical paradigm. Summing up the points of divergence between egalitarian feminism and feminisms of difference, Elizabeth Grosz says:

> The right to equality entails the right to be the same as men, while struggles for autonomy imply the right to either consider oneself equal to another, or reject the terms whereby equality is measured and to define oneself in different terms. It entails the right to be and to act differently.[3]

To be able to define themselves in different terms, women need to change the contexts in which they have been placed. For the analysis of nineteenth-century women's writing, this means a rejection of evaluative criteria emanating from male critical traditions in order to create a theoretical framework that can contextualize and explain the dialogic strategies in much of nineteenth-century women's writing. To compare women's work with that of their male contemporaries, on the other hand, almost inevitably imposes a male-oriented model of criticism where equivocality is too often seen as a defect.

Past and contemporary sexual politics thus partly explain why the Irish literary canon has hitherto included so few women writers. But present-day political considerations also intrude, and a further difficulty when women's works are studied is that the focus on 'national identity' in Irish criticism has made feminist approaches difficult. Even though feminist criticism has moved beyond a simplistic belief in a common experience shared by a unified group of women, communal loyalty has often made it difficult for nationalist women to make women with an Anglo-Irish origin their object of study and vice versa. In such cases, feminist commitments, however theoretical, become tantamount to identity conflict or, at worst, treachery. As Ailbhe Smyth expresses it, for 'Irish women, the anonymity of womanhood has long been overshadowed by the otherness of Ireland, the difficulty of naming ourselves as women complicated by a national history of colonization, deprivation and strife.'[4] Irish feminism may have embraced the theories of fluidity proposed by Luce Irigaray, Hélène Cixous, Judith Butler and Donna Haraway, but the idea that national identity is also indefinable has been much slower to take hold, since to 'admit to more varied, mixed, fluid and relational kinds of identity would advance nobody's territorial claim.'[5] Thus, while Eavan Boland argues that it is necessary for her as a woman poet to repossess the nationalist icons of femininity and restore to them the complexity of real women's experiences, she does not question the idea of the nation to the same extent.[6] The circulation of an essentialist idea of nation means that questions of nationalism and colonialism have become intertwined with feminist issues in an uneasy relationship that has been one of the greatest obstacles to forging a women's tradition in Irish literature. A further problem is the unstable political identity of many nineteenth-century writers such as Lady Morgan, Emily Lawless or Rosa Mulholland. Resistant to political labelling, these women's writing becomes problematic in a critical climate where the predominant questions are those of nationality and cultural identity.

An additional problem is the unadventurous nature of much of nineteenth-century Irish women's prose. For feminist critics, the superficial conventionality of the texts may be as discouraging as their lack of explicit feminist declarations. The search for subversions and transgressions has, as Margaret Kelleher cautions, become 'a new orthodoxy in critical writings',[7] and when this search is fruitless, or at least inconclusive, the result may easily be that a whole body of writing is dismissed because it does not fit the political agenda of the critics. The 'material turn' in criticism offers one way out, since it is a way to deal with history as reflected in literature, and to some extent liberates critics from the necessity of dealing with the writing itself. 'The feminist desire to reclaim women's writing', says Rita Felski, 'can surely only ground itself in a political commitment to recover the lost voices of women rather than in an epistemological claim for the necessary truth that is spoken by such voices.'[8] The point, in other words, is not that women's stories are inherently truer than men's in their representations of women's reality. The point is that they have been missing. Even so, a problem with an approach that considers women's writing primarily as a source of information about women's conditions in the past is that it disregards the possibility that women's works have literary value.

Cultural studies may provide an escape from political positioning as well as from the straitjacket of received aesthetic criteria, but as yet this recent turn in criticism has not succeeded very well in recovering women writers. Studies have mainly been concerned with writers who took part in public debates: university teachers, scholars, priests and other (male) intellectuals. Women's intellectual activities usually took place outside the *Dublin University Magazine*, the Young Ireland movement, medicine, political economy and Celtic studies or the other institutions and scientific fields that shaped Irish culture at the time. Despite its aim to 'resist the rather canonical bent of Irish literary studies by retrieving some minor figures and salvaging some neglected reputations', Terry Eagleton's *Scholars and Rebels in Nineteenth-Century Ireland* (1999), for instance, manages to retrieve almost only male thinkers.[9] So far, this orientation of research has therefore mainly worked to reinstate the dominance and importance of men's cultural activities. Women writers have been censured as being uncommitted to the important questions of the day, while in fact they were engaged with creating a different literary-political scene that included women's private experiences.

A common argument for disregarding women's writing is that it simply is not good enough to merit attention. But the exclusion of women's works on the grounds of a disinterested notion of 'aesthetic quality' is certainly not viable, since aesthetics are shaped by ideological motives, and ideology operates primarily on an unconscious level. In his introduction to *Irish Classics*, Declan Kiberd defines a classic as 'the sort of book that everybody enjoys reading and nobody wants to come to an end.'[10] It is a work that 'owes its reputation, undoubtedly, to its initial impact on its own generation, without which few books ever survive: but after that it displays a capacity to remain forever young and fresh, offering challenges to every succeeding generation.'[11] The problem with this definition is that the 'initial impact' of women's writing *on those in power* was generally slight, not because of its inferior quality but because of women's social situation. As Jacqueline Belanger shows in this collection, Elizabeth Hamilton's *The Cottagers of Glenburnie* (1808) had considerable impact on early nineteenth-century ideas about how to improve the conditions for peasants in Ireland, but the work has nevertheless been forgotten. In a similar manner, the Land War novels discussed by Margaret Kelleher and Heidi Hansson had considerable influence on popular political opinions in both Ireland and England, but since they are also examples of sentimental domestic fiction, their importance has been overlooked. Information about women's reading habits contained in reading databases could significantly change the picture and help rewrite the literary record. Literary value is not intrinsic, but contingent, as Barbara Herrnstein Smith says, and aesthetic criteria are bound up with the historical circumstances in which they are produced.[12]

As the essays in this collection demonstrate, it is not enough to find a place for neglected women writers in an already existing canon of Irish literature, since this might simply assimilate these writers into the ideology of that canon. It is also necessary to examine how, and on what grounds, works and writers are included in and excluded from the canon, to what extent aesthetic judgements are politically biased and whose interests a certain literary ideal might serve. It is necessary to broaden the field of literary studies. The illusory coherence of literary history is after all a product of previous, patriarchal cultural politics, and the very organization of the literary past into periods creates a context that sometimes has no room for women writers, at least not if they wrote in the wrong mode at the wrong time. The view that avant-garde writing is the best expression of the *Zeitgeist* or more politically radical than traditional forms, for example, tends to consign the ostensibly conventional women writers to the background. Stories of man in society are generally seen as more exemplary of realism than stories of private lives, which again is of disservice to women. The principle that good literature should treat universal questions can also easily be recruited to justify women's exclusion from literary history. According to Laurie Finke

> it is a 'fact' of cultural hegemony, part of the logic of margi‑
> nalization, that whatever group is constructed as the 'other', the
> marginal—local colorists, women writers, black writers, third-
> world writers—will always be perceived as writing about less
> universal themes than those of the culturally dominant group.
> This criterion is characteristically evoked as an aesthetic ideal,
> which can then be used to deny marginal groups representation
> in the canon.[13]

If women's writing is construed as personal, local and particular it can comfortably be ignored for allegedly aesthetic reasons, as second-rate literature. The meaning of 'universality', on the other hand, generally goes unexamined.

It has long been recognized that the canon is produced by those with access to the main cultural institutions, such as universities, literary magazines and newspapers. But this does not mean that women's literary production was never valued. As Laurie Finke shows, literary reception is always characterized by a considerable amount of 'noise', with reviews and evaluations that reflect the whole range of 'political, social, cultural, and intellectual ways of viewing the world which exist in dialogical tension with each other' at any given time.[14] It is only later that a certain opinion emerges as authoritative and the narrative achieves coherence. In some cases the 'noise' can be recovered so that the processes of suppression that precede an official view are exposed. Emily Lawless's novels, for instance, were praised by critics from Canada to Allahabad, and in Ireland she was esteemed enough to be given an honorary doctorate at Trinity College Dublin in 1905. For a time, these positive assessments existed in dialogue with negative evaluations in the New York-based Fenian paper the *Nation* or by major cultural figures like W. B. Yeats and J. M. Synge.[15] Because of Yeats's and Synge's status as cultural arbiters and a political situation that could make use of nationalist sentiments like those in *Nation*, the negative criticism proved more lasting, and so the positive 'noise' was gradually repressed to justify

Lawless's exclusion from the canon. The question of literary value has to include the question for whom and in what circumstances a work has value, and the political complexity of Lawless's novels deprived them of worth in the context of the emerging new state.

Unfortunately it is not always possible to retrieve the dialogue that typifies cultural reception. Dialogues, Finke says, are never free and equal:

> Rather, the notion of the dialogic requires precisely an investigation of the power relations that inform and shape any discourse. It calls for an investigation of the social institutions that control who speaks, in what situation and with what force.[16]

With little access to the important cultural institutions of their time, nineteenth-century Irish women's speaking force was limited. Women readers certainly enjoyed and thus conferred value on women's writing, but since their literary consumption took place primarily in their homes, this side of the dialogue never entered the public domain except, perhaps, through sales figures. Because of its ephemeral quality, such cultural 'noise' cannot be cited as evidence of literary value, and what remains is the common devaluation of women's literature–originally only one side of a dialogue, but because the other side has been lost, now masquerading as authoritative monologue.

Canon formation thus has to be recognized as an ideologically charged activity that takes place in the historical now, not by such mysterious organic processes as 'the test of time'. As Eavan Boland notes, a 'society, a nation, a literary heritage is always in danger of making up its communicable heritage from its visible elements. Women, as it happens, are not especially visible in Ireland.'[17] It is a fraught question whether the study of women's literature as a distinct tradition is simply an instance of ghettoization and therefore only manages to establish an alternative, already-depreciated canon. It appears to be the only practical solution, however. Referring to collections of Irish women's poetry, Patricia Boyle Haberstroh comments that what such compilations make clear is that 'outside the mainstream literary tradition, Irish women have been writing for a long time', and even though anthologies and studies exclusively devoted to women's writing may in one sense contribute to the process of marginalization, they are nevertheless necessary if women are to be represented at all.[18] That it is still sometimes necessary to present women writers in an all-female context was an important reason behind volumes IV and V of the *Field Day Anthology of Irish Writing: Women's Writing and Traditions*, published in 2002. Looking exclusively at literature by women is not a relapse into biological essentialism, but a strategic choice, because even though gendered identities may be contingent, this does not cancel *political* differences between men and women, now or historically. A strategic application of essentialist analysis might even present a solution to what Susan Gubar calls the 'current impasse in feminist thinking, namely, the need to employ identity categories for the purposes of political agency versus the fictiveness of those categories as displayed by post-structuralist and postcolonial theorists'.[19]

Important questions are what position nineteenth-century Irish women could speak from and in what contexts their cultural activities took place. The most basic answer is of course Ireland, but nineteenth-century Ireland was not an isolated entity, it was a country under global influence, not least because of the transnational experiences of emigrants and workers who spent part of the year in England, Scotland or other parts of Europe. Intellectual and popular discourses were circulated and exchanged between Ireland and England, the continent and the growing Irish communities in America and Australia. Travel writers like Selina Bunbury, discussed by Maria Lindgren Leavenworth in this collection, spread knowledge about life in other parts of the world. London journals like the *Fortnightly*, the *Cornhill Magazine* or the *Nineteenth Century* were read alongside the *Dublin University Magazine* and the *Nation*; and although Irish publishing revived in the 1820s, after the temporary lull caused by the introduction of English copyright laws following the Union, Irish writers often published in London or Edinburgh. Irish women writers were thus part of a British, and sometimes international, literary establishment as well as an Irish one, and could frequently expect their audience to be unfamiliar with at least some aspects of Irish life. As a consequence, their works regularly negotiate the expectations of different types of audiences, not only in national, but also in gender terms because while their readers may have been mostly female, their critics were still mainly male.

As a rule, women writers speak from the 'counter-public sphere', which is not identical with the 'private sphere', but is a semi- or counter-official position. In the eighteenth century the 'public sphere' was the 'realm of social institutions—clubs, journals, coffee houses, periodicals' in which opinions were exchanged and a middle-class ideology gradually produced.[20] This public sphere reflected popular opinion since it was built on consensus and an equality proceeding from a common investment in rationality. Fringe groups like the dissenting churches, the radical press and, indeed, feminism, could not be successfully integrated, however, and this led to the formation of a 'counter-public sphere', loosely constituted in opposition to official ideology.[21] Partly because of the assault from this counter-public sphere, any sense of consensus had disappeared from the public sphere by the mid-nineteenth century, and in contrast to their predecessors, nineteenth-century critics saw it as their task to form, not to reflect, public opinion. But the idea of public and counter-public spheres still survived, sustained among other things in the prescription of separate spheres for men and women. Insofar as the decree was that women belonged in the home, the very act of writing therefore placed female authors in opposition, no matter how fiercely they may have defended official politics in their works. Some women certainly had a kind of access to the public sphere–Emily Lawless, for instance, published in prestigious journals such as the *Gentleman's Magazine*, the *National Review* and *Belgravia*–but the intellectual woman's dilemma was that, to be taken seriously, she might have to dissociate herself from issues that defined her as oppositional. The apparently anti-feminist sentiments expressed in some nineteenth-century women's works, for example, can to some extent be understood as a strategic move, a negotiation with the patriarchal value system that pervaded the public sphere. New Women writers, on the other hand, can be said to remain in the counter-public sphere and may sometimes even have revelled in being regarded as the opposition. Tina O'Toole's article in this collection shows the subversive nature of writing by New Women like Sarah Grand and George Egerton.

On a more concrete level, the literary space accorded to women writers in nineteenth-century Ireland was primarily in the field of popular literature, and in general, female writers wrote for a predominantly female audience and were expected to deal with private and domestic themes. Biographies and histories introduced previous women writers as inspirational role models, and the studies usually highlighted and praised the domesticity and femininity of these earlier writers.[22] In Julia Kavanagh's *English Women of Letters* (1863) for instance, 'delicacy' emerges as 'the primary standard of literary merit for women writers'.[23] As Riana O'Dwyer's article shows, Lady Blessington's personal life was surrounded by scandal almost from beginning to end, and such a woman would have to be very careful in her writing to counteract the image of indelicacy. There were also financial incentives to avoid supposedly improper areas, since following the moral guidelines of owners of lending libraries like the influential Charles Mudie and W. H. Smith could guarantee success, at least in monetary terms. Women's works were thus generally reviewed in terms of gender, and not really taken seriously as literature.[24] Market forces and cultural ideals combined to produce a clear, though gradually weakened, ban on certain topics as unsuitable for women, which influenced their treatment of social, political and religious themes. To create a space for their work women writers needed–though not necessarily consciously–to negotiate prevalent gender perceptions as well as established critical opinions and aesthetic criteria. Elizabeth Wennö's analysis of Margaret Hungerford's *Molly Bawn* (1878) is a clear demonstration of how humour may function as a method of negotiating conventional and unconventional gender criteria in a text. When reading nineteenth-century Irish women novelists it is vital to remember that the context of their writing always included gender, whereas the various contexts of male writers were perceived as neutral in gender terms.

But despite their exclusion from what remained of the public sphere and their relegation to the popular domain, women in nineteenth-century Ireland normally spoke from a position of privilege. Like most women writers in the past, they were located in the middle of the class structure, enjoying the independence of the middle and upper classes and usually the privilege of English language and culture as members of the Anglo-Irish collective. This is sometimes seen as sufficient motive for ignoring their work since it is easy to see them as simply an extension of the colonial power, if not actively practising colonialism, at least condoning it and enjoying its rewards. Julie Anne Stevens's discussion of the 'fox-hunting fiction' by Somerville and Ross shows a much more complex picture however. Neither cultural nor national identity could be taken for granted in nineteenth-century Ireland, and the Anglo-Irish middle class experienced a deep identity crisis when former certainties were dislodged. Nationalism was the ideology at hand, but this only aggravated the problem for 'the national-minded Anglo-Irish, whose liberal disinterest-edness may have [had] to stretch to the point where they [found] themselves excluded from the very political order they [sought] to establish.'[25] For women the crisis was often even more acute. Lady Wilde–'Speranza'–may have found a place in the Young Ireland movement, but women of the upper classes were not usually part of nationalist groups, at least not before the end of the century. Increasingly, the position of privilege routinely associated with the Ascendancy woman writer was transformed into an experience of displacement. This sense of displacement frequently surfaces as what might be termed 'double voice' in Irish nineteenth-century women's novels.

Obviously literary strategies do not have meaning on their own, but when nineteenth-century women's writing techniques interact or collide with the themes of the work, the result is often that a message is both transmitted and retracted. The resulting ambiguity reflects women's, and particularly Anglo-Irish women's, position as both powerful in terms of class and powerless in terms of gender; their frequently double or torn loyalties to both their native Ireland and the English Crown; the intellectual woman's dilemma as being both inside and outside the cultural institutions of her time; and the conflict between the protection offered by the traditional feminine role and the autonomy promised by the demands for the vote, to name only a few of the problems nineteenth-century women writers needed to negotiate. It seems only logical that such hybrid identities and positions should find textual expression as noise, double voice or dialogue.

When noticed as double voice and not simply dismissed as inferior style, this feature of women's writing has been diversely understood as an expression of unease,[26] as a wish to cater to different audiences,[27] as a two-way relationship between literary and political discourses[28] and as a troubling reply to the imperial narrative.[29] In various ways these interpretations all point to the process of negotiation where the inclusion of opposite points of view and the shifting positions of the negotiators preclude a clear final outcome. Through the means of the double voice, women writers can introduce ideas that contradict or contrast with the ostensible message of the text, and as a result the narrative becomes richer and more complex, but also more unstable. But it is important to recognize that the double voice is not only a subversive strategy, but also a sign of a very real conflict resulting in a process of negotiation where the resolution remains elusive. This 'noise' of apparently irrelevant or contradictory material is a source of information that can rarely be retrieved in a context that privileges clear positioning.

If women indeed write from a 'counter public sphere', 'outside the mainstream' tradition, and frequently employ strategies that make their works ambiguous, it seems clear that a mainstream *critical* tradition will be unable to contain their work. This means that unless new ways of reading emerge, Irish women writers will continue to remain out of context and eventually disappear from the canon altogether. A theoretical approach that highlights elements of dialogue and negotiation has the potential both to escape national/political constrictions and to accommodate the complexity and fluidity of women's work, so that Irish women's fiction can be read on its own terms, instead of according to a critical matrix that excludes it simply because it embodies a different outlook. To achieve a fuller understanding of nineteenth-century Irish women's works, it is therefore necessary to change the contexts in which they have been read. The articles in this collection demonstrate that such a change of context can reveal new layers of meaning and restore value to women's writing.

*

Jacqueline Belanger's article considers the Irish reception of the 1808 novel *The Cottagers of Glenburnie: A Tale for the Farmer's Inglenook*, by the Belfast-born author Elizabeth Hamilton (1758–1816). The novel was phenomenally popular at the time, and tells the story of the attempts by the benevolent Mrs Mason to improve the living conditions of the inhabitants of the Scottish village of Glenburnie. It is not, strictly speaking, an 'Irish text', nor has it been considered as such by recent critics of Hamilton's work. Nevertheless, early nineteenth-century Irish readers and critics readily assimilated *Glenburnie* into their sense of what Irish literature could be, largely because its relevance and applicability to Irish life were recognized almost immediately. An attention to the contemporary reception of texts such as *Glenburnie* points to the limitations of defining a national literature in purely territorial terms. The essay also investigates Hamilton's own flexible approach in claiming various and multiple national identities. Throughout her long career, she presented herself as Irish, Scottish and British, sometimes alternating these identities, sometimes letting them overlap. Her refusal to identify herself with any one national identity enabled her to critique various aspects of English, Scottish and Irish society. This, in turn, enabled Irish and

Scottish readers–as well as a larger British audience–to claim her works as their own.

Riana O'Dwyer's essay on Lady Blessington (1789–1849) shows how she functioned as a subversive Irish influence on the society of early Victorian London, and how her life and works, especially her 'political' novel *Grace Cassidy, or The Repealers*, deliver a complex message that challenges the social mores of her day as well as the current understanding of Irish identity formation in our own. Yet, from the perspective of present-day critical practice, the biography and writings of Lady Blessington pose some problems. From a feminist perspective, she did not resist the roles and expectations of her day, at least not in a radical way, although she was affected by the double standards regarding sexual morality that prevailed at the time. From the viewpoint of post-colonialism, she disregarded her nationality at least some of the time, and her family's religion fairly thoroughly. In addition, she happily transformed herself from the daughter of an Irish country-town gentleman merchant into the fashionable wife of an aristocrat. She was a social chameleon, an outsider resented by many, particularly women, for her success as hostess of a famous London salon. She was a prolific writer from the 1830s onwards, driven by financial necessity, but her writings suffer from the speed with which she produced them, and the inconsistencies of plot and characterization that abound. To resurrect her work means to change the contexts of nineteenth-century women's writing and avoid universalizing frameworks such as feminism, nationalism or aestheticism so that the writer's voice can emerge.

Selina Bunbury (1802–82) is usually dismissed as a conservative hack writer, and her production is rarely seriously discussed and related to other texts of the genres in which she worked. Maria Lindgren Leavenworth, however, analyses three of Bunbury's travel texts, *Evelyn; or a Journey from Stockholm to Rome in 1847–48* (1849), *Life in Sweden; with Excursions in Norway and Denmark* (1853) and *A Summer in Northern Europe, Including Sketches in Sweden, Norway, Finland, the Aland Islands, Gothland, &c.* (1856). Of primary interest are the descriptions of the encountered places, people and customs and how these are presented in contrast to conditions and behaviour in England. Although she was born in Ireland, Bunbury, like Elizabeth Hamilton, claimed an English or British identity as well, and England is her most frequent point of reference. Thus Bunbury used English habits and customs as a yardstick when she criticizes what she encounters, but she also used her new experiences to criticize conditions, practices and behaviour at home—and not infrequently in Ireland. Lindgren Leavenworth's essay also discusses issues connected to truth-claims, originality and the writing process and looks at Bunbury's references to guidebooks and travel in general in order to place her in the tradition of travel writing.

In the last quarter of the nineteenth century, 'the land question' became a very popular subject for writers of Irish fiction. Margaret Kelleher looks specifically at three little-known texts: Letitia McClintock's *A Boycotted Household* (1881), Elizabeth Owens Blackburne's *The Heart of Erin* (1882) and Fannie Gallaher's *Thy Name is Truth* (1884). All three novels deal with the activities of the Irish Land League, founded in 1879, and may be termed 'factual fictions', drawing in detail from recognizably 'real' events and persons, and frequently making use of journalistic representations of these 'facts'. Like many other novels of the period, they employ standard plots from sentimental fiction—social and economic obstacles to lovers' relationships, love triangles, etc.—but in their depiction of contemporary politics they also take on a substantial burden of representation involving political tensions, contemporary class antagonisms and debates regarding gender roles. Yet the significance of these novels is not confined to their historical content, although their value in these respects *is* considerable. To read them only as documentation of contemporary events is to ignore their literary form, their status as novels. A fuller evaluation of their importance will therefore involve a return to long-standing debates about literature as historical source, along with more recent discussions of the function and nature of the Irish nineteenth-century novel.

Margaret Hungerford (1855?–97), or 'The Duchess' as she was sometimes called, was a very popular writer at the end of the nineteenth century. As so often happens, her popularity has meant that critics have too easily dismissed her work as slight and uninteresting. In her essay, however, Elisabeth Wennö shows that Hungerford's novel *Molly Bawn*, disregarded for many years as an example of shallow romantic fiction, deserves attention and a place in literary history. Its alleged lack of guile, consistency and character analysis is not a stylistic flaw, but a significant literary strategy, necessitated by the juxtaposition of comic emplotment and romantic discourse for humorous, ironic, and ultimately, ethical effects, which are designed to reinstate the precedence of social bonds over individual needs. Wennö takes Hungerford's novel out of the context of romantic literature and places it in the context of humorous literature; in so doing she demonstrates how a change of context may alter how the work is understood.

M. E. Francis's (Mary E. Sweetman, later Blundell, 1859–1930) novel *Miss Erin* (1898) can be grouped together with the 'factual fictions' of the Land War that Margaret Kelleher discusses in her essay. However, it is also an exploration of the relations between gender limitations and nationalist commitments and an example of how the rules of the romance genre clash with the conventions of the national tale. The union between Erin and her English suitor can be seen as an allegory of the union of Ireland and Great Britain, but this reading is complicated by the novel's two main intertexts: the story of Joan of Arc and Sophocles's *Antigone*, which both describe the precedence of a cause over personal happiness. Heidi Hansson's article shows how the *Antigone*, in particular, problematizes the surface story and allows Francis both to overcome the limitations of genre and avoid the simplifications of national and romantic writing. Such intertextual readings become possible only if Irish writing is taken out of a limiting national context and seen as interacting with global literary culture.

When literature and culture in the 1890s in Ireland are addressed, the focus tends to be on the Celtic Revival, and the group of writers whose work and politics are associated with it. Although Tina O'Toole's essay examines Irish writing in the 1890s, it does so from the perspective of quite a different cultural and social project, looking at the work of a group of writers at the end of the nineteenth century who problematized the binaries of Irish/British definition by exploring Scandinavian texts, and addressing revolutionary politics in Italy and Poland. These writers deconstructed gender binaries and disrupted the heterosocial economy by opening up subjects such as women's sexual expression and the construction of gender identities in their work. The essay refers to the 'New Woman' project of writers such as George Egerton (Mary Chavelita Dunne, 1859–1945), Sarah Grand (Frances Elizabeth Clarke, later McFall, 1854–1943), 'Iota' (Kathleen Mannington Caffyn, 1853–1926), and E. L. Voynich (Ethel Lillian Boole, 1864–1960). These writers have been almost completely disregarded by Irish literary history in the intervening century, but to draw the conclusion that their work was sub-standard, or obscure and unpopular in its own day, and that this is why we know nothing of them, would be misguided. Apart from being best-selling fiction, 'New Woman' writing was also critically acclaimed at the end of the nineteenth century, and the experimental work of writers such as George Egerton changed the face of writing in the pre-modernist period.

Somerville and Ross (Edith Anne Œnone Somerville, 1858–1949 and Violet Florence Martin, 'Martin Ross', 1862–1915) are among the few nineteenth-century Irish women writers who have received sustained critical attention. Sometimes, however, they have been too easily seen as representatives of the Anglo-Irish upper classes. Julie Anne Stevens takes Somerville and Ross out of the context of 'the hunting-stable tradition' and shows how they treat the fox as the supreme trickster in both politics and art. The essay traces the origins of the writers' use of the fox in their sporting novel, *The Silver Fox* (1898), and in the most political of their three volumes of Irish R. M. stories and their final collaborative work, *In Mr. Knox's Country* (1915). These works draw upon the many aliases of Reynard the Fox in history and literature and produce a complex portrait of the late nineteenth- and early twentieth-century Irish countryside. The focus on Reynard provides an opportunity to demonstrate the significance of both an Anglo-Irish discourse and the broader European tradition of burlesque and beast fable in Irish writing. Even more importantly, the essay argues that the free-flying fox's passage through Somerville and Ross's country, his flight into the earth and his multiple aliases, allow him to act as a vehicle of change. With Reynard it becomes possible to analyse the writers' modernizing treatment of traditional material. The fox's shifting face in Somerville and Ross's novels and stories offers a key to our understanding of the development of Irish fiction.

In different ways these essays bring new critical and theoretical perspectives to bear on Irish nineteenth-century women's writing. They take them out of contexts that have proved too narrow and provide new contexts in which women's work can be more fully understood. Literary value is a concept with many facets, and when only a few criteria are used—whether aesthetic, national-political, feminist or other—too many voices are lost. The essays do not attempt to argue that previous dismissals of some of the writers considered were wrong, within the contexts of the evaluative norms that were used. The argument is instead that there is plenty of room for new, different and less constricting tools of evaluation.

'Improvement is a Nation's Blessing':
Elizabeth Hamilton's
The Cottagers of Glenburnie *in Ireland*

Jacqueline Belanger

In his seminal essay 'What is the History of Books', the cultural historian Robert Darnton calls for a truly interdisciplinary, international study of the history of books, reading and reception. This particular approach is necessary, Darnton observes, because 'books themselves do not respect limits either linguistic or national'.[1] While studies of the book in Ireland are, of course, imbricated in questions of what constitutes Irish literature (as they are in any national context), the vexed nature of this very question has often obscured the influence of 'non-Irish' texts on readers and critics in Ireland. Irish literary historiography's concerns with questions of national identity, and the relationship of Ireland to England, have often taken precedence over interest in Ireland's place within larger Anglophone print networks encompassing not just England, Scotland and Wales, but also continental Europe, North America and, in time, the whole of the British Empire. Recent sociological and historical studies such as Niall Ó Ciosáin's *Print and Popular Culture in Ireland* have begun to broaden our understanding of exactly what sorts of books were available to readers in nineteenth-century Ireland, and pose important questions about how these readers appropriated texts (both Irish and non-Irish) in a variety of creative and unexpected ways.[2]

This essay is concerned with just one book, and with its relatively short journey from Scotland to Ireland: Elizabeth Hamilton's 1808 novel of Scottish peasant life, *The Cottagers of Glenburnie*. It may not quite be the full-scale international study of book history called for by Darnton, but the reception of this important early nineteenth-century novel in Ireland opens up our understanding of how a work such as *Glenburnie*, which seems to bear little connection to Ireland, could be adopted by reformers in order to map a course around the class and sectarian divisions that plagued Anglo-Irish attempts to educate the Irish poor. The history of *Glenburnie* in early nineteenth-century Ireland illustrates how critics and readers such as Maria Edgeworth appropriated this Scottish novel to resolve specifically Irish questions, precisely because it represented an alternative to the fraught political relationships within nineteenth-century Ireland, and between Ireland and England. In doing so, *Glenburnie* forms a crucial link in what Katie Trumpener has called the 'transperipheral literary life' of early nineteenth-century Ireland and Scotland.³ *Glenburnie* provides one important example of how the exchange of books and ideas between Ireland and Scotland can lead us to a more nuanced understanding of nineteenth-century discourses and practices of improvement.

In its own tangential way, this essay is as much about Maria Edgeworth as it is about Belfast-born Elizabeth Hamilton and *The Cottagers of Glenburnie*. In her article 'Irish Culture and Scottish Enlightenment: Maria Edgeworth's histories of the future', Marilyn Butler points out that

> Maria Edgeworth's Irish Tales have not hitherto been considered
> in relation to the Scottish Enlightenment. Indeed, at the present
> time much of the most energised new comment on her comes
> from academic departments that place her in Anglo-Irish or post-
> colonial literature; it is the English connection that is attended to,
> and from a specific point of view.⁴

In attending only to the 'English connection', Butler observes, we overlook the important ways in which Edgeworth's work was influenced by Scottish Enlightenment thinkers such as Adam Smith and Dugald Stewart. Edgeworth's praise of *Glenburnie* marks a point of continuity in her engagement with Scottish thought and culture. Hamilton—herself a friend and correspondent of Dugald Stewart—was, like Edgeworth, indebted to Stewart's philosophy of mind and theories of socio-political progress, and it is certainly no coincidence that one of the model characters in *Glenburnie* is given the name of Stewart. Edgeworth's comments on *Glenburnie*, expressed in her 1816 obituary of Hamilton, represent her ongoing interest in Scottish Enlightenment thought. In particular, her comments make visible the concern—addressed both in her own and Hamilton's work—with Stewart's thinking on the subject of the processes of improvement and reform.

The Cottagers of Glenburnie could be termed the first truly Scottish novel. It was written by an author who identified herself as Scottish (although not exclusively so); its subject matter was thoroughly Scottish; and it was printed and published in Scotland, by the Edinburgh printing firm of John Ballantyne & Co, and by the publishers Manners & Miller.[5] It would be possible to argue that *The Cottagers of Glenburnie* in fact paved the way for Walter Scott's hugely successful and influential series of *Waverley* novels, inaugurated in 1814 with the Scottish historical novel *Waverley*. In his 'Postscript, that should have been a Preface' to *Waverley*, Scott paid tribute to Maria Edgeworth's delineations of Irish manners in works such as *The Absentee*, and to Hamilton's representations of Scotland in *Glenburnie*. What he did not acknowledge was that, beyond her representations of Scottish life and dialect, Hamilton's novel proved that a novel of local colour, published outside London, was a commercially viable prospect, one that helped make possible the publication of his own works in Edinburgh.[6]

The Cottagers of Glenburnie was a phenomenally popular work at the time of its initial publication, running rapidly through five editions in the years 1808–10. Like many works in this didactic strain, *Glenburnie* is a thinly veiled improvement tract that often reads like a household management guide, and indeed some of Hamilton's contemporary critics recognized that this was a work that defied classification along strict generic lines. Signalling that the fictional tale is subordinate to the rendering of Scottish life and to its reforming aims, the *Monthly Review* places *The Cottagers of Glenburnie* under the heading 'Miscellaneous' in its catalogue of notices.[7] The core of *Glenburnie's* fictional narrative tells the story of the attempts of the benevolent protagonist Mrs Mason to improve the living conditions of the inhabitants of the Scottish village of Glenburnie. Mrs Mason retires to her native Scotland to live with her relatives the MacClartys after a long and successful career as a servant with the Longland family on their English estate. In the MacClarty cottage, and in the village generally, Mrs Mason discovers only indolence, dirt, disorder, poor child-rearing practices and an attachment to 'traditional' ways that, in one case at least, results in tragedy for the MacClarty family. Despite Mrs Mason's best efforts to teach the MacClartys the basics of domestic economy, they remain resolutely–defiantly–unreformed. The oft-repeated riposte of the MacClarty family to Mrs Mason's helpful suggestions is that they 'cou'dna be fash'd' (that is, they 'cannot be bothered'), which became a catch phrase of the season amongst the novel's metropolitan readers in London.[8]

Undaunted by her failure to change the ways of the MacClartys, Mrs Mason moves to the home of William and Peggy Morison and transfers her energies to improving the rest of the village. By the close of the novel, Mrs Mason has been instrumental in establishing a successful school for the village children, and has transformed Glenburnie into a model of cleanliness, temperance and industriousness. An inset narrative relates Mrs Mason's own story of self improvement. Designed to illustrate the importance of education, diligence, and a strict moral code, the story details how the young Betty Mason rose from her origins as a destitute and orphaned servant girl to a place as a governess at the centre of Lord Longland's household.

Praised by reviewers for its accurate rendering of Scottish idioms, Francis Jeffrey in the *Edinburgh Review* took a 'sort of malicious pleasure' in noting that the Scottish dialect spoken by the novel's peasant characters ensured that *Glenburnie* is a 'sealed book' to 'Southern readers'.[9] If much of *Glenburnie*, like Thady's speech in Maria Edgeworth's *Castle Rackrent*, was 'untranslatable'[10] to a non-Scottish audience, how then did it translate to Ireland? Unfortunately, we have scant evidence of how the majority of contemporary Irish readers (and readers amongst the intended audience in particular) responded to *Glenburnie*, or, for that matter, to printed material generally. Initially published in a more expensive octavo format at the price of 7s. 6d., *Glenburnie* would have been too expensive for the majority of readers in either Scotland or Ireland to purchase.[11] Like many didactic works of this time, such as Mary Leadbeater's 1811 *Cottage Dialogues*, it appears that *Glenburnie* was initially intended for purchase by landlords or stewards, who could then make the text available to tenants, either through direct distribution or through lending from quasi-libraries. *Glenburnie* was certainly available to middle-class Irish readers to borrow from various circulating libraries. The novel is listed in the 1816 catalogue for the Cork Library Society (which indicates that it holds the fifth edition of the novel, published in 1810), in the 1826 catalogue of the Belfast Library, and in the 1834 catalogue of Gerrard Tyrrell's Public Library in Dublin. *Glenburnie* was also apparently held in the library of Irish works at Lough Fea.[12] The very fact that it was contained in this last collection is indicative not just of the availability of *Glenburnie* in Ireland, but also of the possible willingness to place it within the category of Irish literature.

A cheap edition of *Glenburnie* (in a smaller duodecimo format) was published shortly after its initial appearance, and, according to a comment reported by Hamilton's biographer Elizabeth Benger, it appears to have been read and had its intended effect upon the manners and habits of the Scottish peasantry: 'The cheap edition is to be found in every village library; and Mrs M'Clarty's [*sic*] example has *provoked* many a Scottish housewife into cleanliness and good order.'[13] Such cheap editions would no doubt also have been available in Ireland, but it is a testament to *Glenburnie*'s enduring popularity that an edition was published in Belfast in 1820, and another cheap Irish edition was published as late as 1840.[14] An *Abridgement of the Cottagers of Glenburnie* was published in Belfast by Simms & M'Intyre *c.* 1840, with the stated aim (as given on the title page), 'to instil into the minds of youth, the Advantages of a Tractable Disposition, and habits of attention, Regularity, Cleanliness & Industry'.

While it is difficult to excavate the precise extent of an Irish readership for *Glenburnie*, and the exact nature of readers' responses to this work, critics and authors such as Maria Edgeworth recognized immediately its applicability to Ireland. In his 1812 work *An Account of Ireland, Statistical and Political*, the statistician and philanthropist Edward Wakefield grants *Glenburnie* the status of an honorary Irish text alongside those of Edgeworth and Leadbeater, and points to the usefulness of this particular novel in Ireland. Commenting in a note to an observation on the state of education in Ireland, Wakefield opines that

> A minister, of more than ordinary talent, once declared, that he did not care who made the laws, as long as he wrote the ballads of the nation. Did the government purchase the copy-right of Miss Hamilton's Cottagers of Glenburnie; or Miss Edgeworth's Popular and Rural tales; Mrs. Leadbeater's Cottage Dialogues; and a few more such works, and sell them at a cheap rate, it would save the sheriff the cost of many a halter, and effect more than half the acts of parliament which will be passed in the next

> ten years. Dr Franklin, in the Memoirs of his Life, has described
> the effect which his establishing a book society, had upon the
> American people; a circumstance, recorded by that great man,
> [which] should not pass unheeded by the British statesman.[15]

Although ostensibly aiming to persuade–rather than coerce–the peasantry into reform, Wakefield's comment certainly represents the darker side of the Enlightenment belief in the improving power of print: in Wakefield's rather crude formulation, texts such as *Glenburnie* are deployed as a means of counter-revolutionary social control, diffusing potential threats from peasant insurgency through reform of the Irish 'lower orders'.

Wakefield was not the first to recognize the possibilities for *Glenburnie* in Ireland. Writing in May 1809, a critic in the *Belfast Monthly Magazine* (possibly the editor and former United Irishman, William Drennan) argued that the novel offered equally valuable lessons for the improvement of the Irish counterparts of Hamilton's Scottish peasantry:

> Though the book in question be written purposely for the
> improvement of the Scotch peasantry, yet in many points it will
> be found applicable to ourselves, and if it be again brought
> forward before the public eye for this purpose, and held up in this
> particular point of view, as a means of introducing a system of
> domestic economy among the lower classes in this country, the
> investigation of its merits, though but a repetition of the praises
> it has already so deservedly obtained, will not be without its use.[16]

Such praise for *Glenburnie*'s applicability to Ireland, however, must be seen in the context of wider debates within the *Belfast Monthly Magazine*–and in Irish and British culture generally–about the challenges posed to an enlightenment belief in gradual improvement and reform by an emergent Irish nationalism. Described by Tom Clyde as 'mildly nationalistic' in tone, and having a predominantly Protestant audience, the *Belfast Monthly Magazine* was firmly committed to improvement.[17] Reviewing the translation of Madame Genlis's Irish tale *The Earl of Cork* provides the critic with an opportunity to reiterate this stance: 'We have said, more than once, *Ireland is our station*. We repeat it: we glory in that national feeling, that *amor patriae*, which turns all our thoughts, and bends all our exertions to the improvement of our native land.'[18] This dedication to improvement fundamentally shapes the editorial and reviewing policy of the periodical: literary texts are judged on the premise that the main object of 'every work of imagination' should be 'instruction'.[19] In the *Belfast Monthly Magazine*, texts such as *Glenburnie* (with its specifically Scottish content) and *The Earl of Cork* (an Irish novel by a French author) are enlisted to demonstrate that true *amor patriae* resides in a commitment to instruction and improvement in Ireland, with the result that the category of 'Irish literature' appears open and flexible, not strictly defined by Irishness *per se* but instead by a shared emphasis on the reforming power of fiction.

The dedicatory preface to *Glenburnie* reveals Hamilton, unsurprisingly, to be entirely in step with the patriotic sentiments voiced by the *Magazine*'s critic. Stating that her intended audience is those 'well-wishers to the improvement of their country', Hamilton acknowledges, however, that there are widely divergent views about how an 'attachment' to one's nation ought to be expressed:

> In the opinion of vulgar minds, it ought to produce a blind and indiscriminating partiality for national modes, manners, and customs; and a zeal that kindles into rage at whoever dares to suppose that our country has not in every instance reached perfection. Every hint at the necessity of further improvement is, by such persons, deemed a libel on all that has been already done; and the exposition of what is faulty, though with a view to its amendment, an unpardonable offence. From readers of this description, you will soon perceive, I cannot hope for quarter.[20]

Much of the review of *Glenburnie* in the *Belfast Monthly Magazine* directly echoes these comments by equating patriotism with a desire for gradual reform. However, it is not simply that *Glenburnie*'s emphasis on improvement, with all its connotations of progress and looking to the future, resonates with the political/editorial principles of Drennan and the *Belfast Monthly Magazine*. As the reviewer makes clear, it also provides an ideological counterweight to the proto-nationalism of such works as Sydney Owenson's *The Wild Irish Girl*, published two years earlier than *Glenburnie* in 1806. Not by coincidence, the review of *Glenburnie* appears just two months after a scathing review of Sydney Owenson's *Woman; or Ida of Athens*, and in the same issue as a letter offering a critique of *The*

Wild Irish Girl and *Ida of Athens*. The review of *Glenburnie* begins on a note of slight defensiveness, ('To review a book which has already passed through three large editions with universal approbation, may appear superfluous [. . .]'[21]), but the reason for such a belated notice quickly becomes apparent:

> Let us not be accused of want of patriotism in making such an avowal [of the need for reform of the Irish peasantry]. To see our own faults, and to endeavour to amend them, is real patriotism. Improvement is a nation's blessing; a blessing which can never be duly appreciated until we are conscious of our own wants. And for this reason the writer appears to me much more deserving of his country's thanks, who with the candour and courage of a true friend, points out the defects in hopes of applying a remedy, than he who by fanciful high drawn pictures, flatters it into a false sentiment of ideal superiority; or by incorrect representations of its ancient state, leads us to sigh after a return of those days of splendour, and to prefer a relapse into former barbarism to an exertion at increased improvement. This leads us to confess that another reason for undertaking the present review was that after having expressed ourselves with such severe though necessary reprehension on a writer of our own country, we are glad to seize an excuse for holding up another countrywoman in the light she deserves as one who has really raised the character of her country by her writings.[22]

The review of *Glenburnie* therefore provides the critic with the opportunity to contrast Owenson's proto-nationalism (with its insistence on the romantic and antiquarian, and its concomitant failure to provide practical strategies for the amelioration of Ireland's social and political dilemmas) with the 'true' patriotism of authors such as Hamilton. *Glenburnie* thus serves two functions in Ireland: at its most basic level, the novel provides a template for the reform of the Irish peasantry. On a deeper level, *Glenburnie* provides a strategic vantage point from which to strike out at Owenson, and as such is part of a much larger battle involving Irish cultural nationalism's challenge to the belief that Ireland's progress could be achieved by gradual, reformist measures—and, even more fundamentally, to the notion of what 'progress' itself meant.

To a certain extent, Hamilton's connection to Belfast, and the flexibility of her own national identity, facilitated *Glenburnie*'s strategic appropriation by the *Belfast Monthly Magazine*. The critic in the *Magazine* claims Hamilton as a 'countrywoman',[23] but likewise Hamilton is claimed as 'one of ourselves' in the *Scots Magazine*. The London-based journal, the *British Critic* hedges its bets, stating that, Hamilton is a 'native of the North of Ireland', but that Scotland is her 'adopted country'.[24] It is this last assessment, by the journal that proclaims its Britishness, that is the most accurate. Born in Belfast in 1758 to a Scottish merchant father and an Irish mother, from 1762 Hamilton was raised in Stirlingshire by her Scottish aunt and uncle. While she did not return to Ireland to live for any extended period of time, she visited her sister Katherine there, who settled in Ireland after her marriage. Hamilton lived for a time in London, but spent most of her adult life in Edinburgh, where she became part of the city's thriving early nineteenth-century literary and intellectual scene. Hamilton's brother Charles served in the East India Company under Warren Hastings, and was well known for his translation into English of the Muslim code of laws, the Hedaya. Hamilton's early literary efforts bear the marks of what she learned from her brother's Orientalist researches: her first published novel, *Translations of the Letters of a Hindoo Rajah* (which Hamilton called her 'black baby'[25]), incorporates much of his formal scholarship, as well as material from his letters to Hamilton from India, and is dedicated to Warren Hastings.

During the course of her long and productive life, Hamilton seems to have identified herself with both Scotland and Ireland. Carol Anderson and Aileen M. Riddell, citing evidence from Hamilton's published letters, note that 'as an adult [Hamilton] strongly identified with the Scottish element of her heritage'. As they point out, Hamilton uses the possessive form 'our own country' in talking about Scotland.[26] Yet Hamilton uses the same terms when discussing Ireland. In a letter dated 1780 to her brother Charles, which describes a recent visit to their sister in Ireland, Hamilton writes: '[. . .] I can't help thinking, that in general our country people have a more pleasing manner, and a more liberal, enlarged way of thinking, than those of the same station in this kingdom [. . .].'[27] Hamilton appears to slip effortlessly between British, Scottish, Irish and, indeed, imperial, identities, and it is this negotiable sense of national belonging that enabled her to take up a variety of flexible subject positions vis-à-vis her targets for reform. Hamilton's work is in many ways characterized by a constant willingness to criss-cross cultural and political boundaries, and it is often as difficult to categorize her writings in terms of nation and ideology as it is to place them generically.

Beyond Hamilton's own Belfast links and her ability to think of herself as both Irish and Scottish, *Glenburnie* also encodes specific references that point to potentially local Irish origins. In the chapter 'Concerning the Duties of a Schoolmaster', the benevolent clergyman Mr Gourlay engages in a wide-ranging conversation about education methods with Glenburnie's soon-to-be-schoolmaster William Morison. In the course of the conversation, Gourlay recommends 'a book written by one Mr David Manson, a schoolmaster in the North of Ireland', who pioneered a system of education in which older pupils were involved in tutoring the younger ones.[28] As the reviewer in the *British Critic* notes, in this chapter Hamilton pays tribute to Manson who 'appears to have anticipated not Mr Lancaster only, but even Dr Bell, in some of the most important improvements which they have introduced into the discipline of large schools'.[29] David Manson (1726–92) rose from humble origins (starting out as a servant to an Antrim farmer) to become a well-respected businessman and educationalist. Manson opened his first school after moving to Belfast in 1755; his aim was to develop educational methods that worked 'without the discipline of the rod'.[30] Like the Irish educationalist and inventor par excellence, Richard Lovell Edgeworth, Manson appears to have been an amateur mechanic, designing machines for the amusement of his pupils and inventing a machine for spinning yarn.

While Glenburnie's village school is obviously indebted to Manson's approach to education, this reference to the Irish educationalist carries yet another meaning, one that is based on the very principles exemplified by Manson's life: starting out as a poor servant, Manson raised himself through the social ranks through education and self-improvement. This, as the *Belfast Monthly Magazine* notes, is the real key to the text:

> [. . .] it is not by instilling habits of cleanliness and industry in the lower orders, that this book may be useful. It shows that any person, however humble his original station, may rise to respectability and independence, by the practice of those virtues, the exercise of which is within every body's reach.'[31]

It is the parallel between self-improvement and education of the individual and the improvement of the nation that underwrites *Glenburnie*, but the reference to Manson also makes visible how *Glenburnie* might be inflected by Hamilton's connections to Ireland–it would perhaps not be too fanciful to suggest that dropping the 'n' from Manson's name transforms him from the self-made Mr Manson of Belfast to the self-made Mrs Mason of Glenburnie (who, like Manson, raises herself from humble origins to stand testament to the advantages of education and a useful life). The name Mrs Mason also conjures up intertextual echoes of Mary Wollstonecraft's Mrs Mason, the governess of her *Original Stories* for children, which were written and published upon Wollstonecraft's return to London after a brief stint in Ireland as governess to the children of Lord and Lady Kingsborough.[32]

The importance of the nuanced cultural exchanges between Scotland and Ireland (particularly on the subject of improvement) are clearly evident in Maria Edgeworth's responses to *The Cottagers of Glenburnie*. Marilyn Butler notes that *Glenburnie* was one of Edgeworth's favourite novels, and Edgeworth's private letters reveal her eagerness to obtain a copy, and her satisfaction with the novel once she had read it.[33] Two letters from Maria Edgeworth to Charles Sneyd Edgeworth of December 1808 mention *Glenburnie*, which was specially sent from Hamilton to Edgeworth via Edgeworth's publisher Joseph Johnson. By late December, she had still not received her copy: 'For the soul and body of me I cannot get the Cottagers of Glenburnie. I have some faint hope that papa will bring them [*sic*] with him this day [. . .].'[34] By 2 February 1809, Edgeworth had received and read the work, and was sending it along to her aunt Margaret Ruxton: 'I hasten to send you the Cottagers of Glenburnie which I hope you will like as well as I do. I think it will do a vast deal of good in Ireland & besides it is extremely interesting which all good books are not. It has great powers both comic and tragic.'[35] Like Edward Wakefield and the critic in the *Belfast Monthly Magazine*, Edgeworth signals the hope that *Glenburnie* would prove as useful to the Irish peasantry as to their counterparts in Scotland. From the evidence of her letters, it appears that Edgeworth believed firmly in *Glenburnie*'s potential to improve the habits and customs of the Irish lower classes, and played her own part in the dissemination of the work to those who, in her mind, would benefit most from it. In early February 1809, Edgeworth wrote to Margaret Ruxton that she was sending 'The Cottagers of

Glenburnie & Drogheda edn of Parent's Assistant which two books with your good leave I beg to present with my best wishes for his improvement to your protege Richard'.[36]

It was in fact to Edgeworth that Hamilton was most frequently compared in contemporary reviews and criticism, although critics were also keen to highlight connections between Hamilton's work and that of the English evangelical reformer and author Hannah More. In a review of Hamilton's *Popular Essays*, Hamilton makes up the Scottish third of the United Kingdom's triumvirate of influential 'reforming' women authors, with Edgeworth representing Ireland and Hannah More representing England.[37] While Hamilton acknowledges in the preface to *Glenburnie* her indebtedness to More's *Cheap Repository Tracts*, the comparison with Edgeworth is (at least for my purposes) more apposite: it rested on the basis not only of the depictions of the speech, manners, and customs of the peasantry of their respective nations, but also on the perceived congruence of their ideological principles and methods for reforming society. Edgeworth's and Hamilton's works emphasized the need for gradual improvement and reform of both upper and lower strata of society, accomplished through a diffusion of middle-class virtues of industry, thrift and self-reliance to their counterparts in the classes above and below. The ultimate aim of this drive towards improvement is, as Gary Kelly argues, 'to eliminate social, cultural, and economic disparities that threatened the unity of state and empire'.[38] In such aims, *Glenburnie* was almost certainly influenced by Edgeworth's *Popular Tales* (1804) as well as by More's *Tracts*.

In their views on the subject of improvement, both Edgeworth and Hamilton owed much to their contact with Scottish Enlightenment thinkers and, in particular, with the Edinburgh mathematician and philosopher Dugald Stewart.[39] Stewart had acted as host and tutor to Edgeworth's brothers Henry and Lovell, and, based on their descriptions, Stewart provided the model for Dr Campbell in *Forester*, in Edgeworth's *Moral Tales* (1801).[40] Edgeworth met both Stewart and Hamilton during her trip to Edinburgh in 1803, and she subsequently corresponded with Stewart and Stewart's wife Helen, as well as with Hamilton. Edgeworth later paid tribute to Stewart in her 1808 preface to a revised edition of *An Essay on Irish Bulls*, in which the Scottish Stewart is invoked alongside the English philosopher Locke and the Irishman Edmund Burke.

Hamilton and Stewart were part of the same Edinburgh society that also included Stewart's former pupil Francis Jeffrey, who, as editor of the *Edinburgh Review*, wrote reviews of both Edgeworth's and Hamilton's works (including the review of *Glenburnie*).[41] Hamilton and Stewart corresponded regularly, and her non-fictional works such as *Popular Essays* are heavily indebted to Stewart. While Hamilton's non-fictional works directly acknowledge Stewart's influence, she was more reluctant to connect *Glenburnie* directly with him, perhaps because of a diffidence about the intellectual weightiness of a novel. In a letter from Hamilton to Stewart just after the publication of *Glenburnie*, she is ostensibly self-effacing about her novel, but draws his attention to the 'little work' nonetheless:

> You will see in the newspapers, that I have not been quite idle all the winter; but were you to look into the little work which is now advertised, I am afraid you would think I have been employing myself to very little purpose. Had I thought it worthy of your perusal, I should have sent a copy; but in fact it is intended for a very different order of readers, and was written solely with a view to shame my good country folks into a greater degree of nicety with regard to cleanliness, and to awaken their attention to the source of corruption in the lower orders.[42]

If she did not directly acknowledge Stewart's influence in *Glenburnie*, he is nonetheless present in the figure of Mr Stewart, the steward on the Scottish estate of the Longlands family.

Despite Dugald Stewart's commitment to the concept of improvement, and his 'adherence to a form of intellectual and moral perfectibilism', the historians Collini, Winch and Burrow point out that Stewart 'displays little [. . .] detailed interest in the problems of persuasion and the processes of implementing desirable policies in an imperfect world'.[43] Texts such as *Glenburnie* (along with many of Edgeworth's works, such as the Irish tales *Ennui*, *The Absentee*, and *Ormond*) address this hiatus in Stewart's thinking about improvement. In providing concrete examples in their fictions of the 'processes' of improvement, Edgeworth's and Hamilton's texts represent tangible attempts to put Stewart's 'perfectibilist' theories into practice. They also raise questions about how to achieve effective change in the face of possible resistance on the part of the targets of reform—precisely those 'problems of persuasion' glossed over in Stewart's work.

In Edgeworth's *Ennui* (1809), for example, the ostentatiously benevolent Lord Glenthorn attempts to improve the life of his Irish foster-mother Ellinor by providing her with an new cottage 'fitted [. . .] up in the most elegant style of English cottages'.[44] His endeavours to impose such supposed improvements on Ellinor result in failure, however, largely because of his inability to attend to local contexts and conditions. Similarly, Mrs Mason's attempts to reform the MacClarty home in *Glenburnie* also result in frustration and failure. Although obviously misguided, Mrs MacClarty remains insistently the voice of the local and the particular, opposing Mrs Mason's programme of Enlightenment reform. In answer to one of Mrs Mason's suggestions, Mrs MacClarty responds by pointing out that every place has its own way of doing things, which must be respected: 'Ilka place has just its ain gait [. . .] and ye needna think that ever we'll learn yours.'[45] Ann Jones speculates that if Hamilton's initial plan was to end the text with the complete reform of the MacClarty family, the demands of realism eventually outweighed those of didacticism and the MacClartys were left to their old ways.[46] While Hamilton makes it clear that the MacClartys are left behind when the rest of the village 'progresses', the trace of Mrs MacClarty's resistance cannot be entirely eradicated from the text, and remains to warn of the perils of a blind faith in the inevitability of improvement. Above all else, the failure to reform Mrs MacClarty reveals the fragility of the ideal that individuals can be persuaded to respond rationally and amend their behaviour once their faults have been pointed out to them, and once they are shown that it is in their own (and society's) best interest to change–an ideal fundamental to Enlightenment discourses of improvement.

In their exploration of the processes of improvement, Edgeworth and Hamilton are certainly part of wider cultural trends emerging in late eighteenth and early nineteenth-century Britain and Ireland. In the 1790s, reformers such as Hannah More came to realize that, in order to maintain social order and combat potential radicalism amongst the lower classes, it was necessary to attend as closely to *how* reforming ideas were disseminated, as to the counter-revolutionary principles themselves. As Niall Ó Ciosáin puts it, '[t]he problem was [. . .] not one of simply answering republican arguments but also of infiltrating the channels of communication through which they passed'.[47] From 1795, Hannah More's solution to this problem was the publication of the *Cheap Repository Tracts*. These *Tracts* (published in both London and Dublin) encouraged values of temperance, hard work and piety, and adopted the identical format and style of that popular (and potentially subversive) chapbook-style literature they were designed to replace. This strategy was later adopted in Ireland by the Society for Promoting the Education of the Poor in Ireland, known as the Kildare Place Society, established in 1811. The publications of the Kildare Place Society followed the model of the *Cheap Repository Tracts* in adopting the 'protective mimicry' of cheap, popular literary forms.[48]

One of the most striking features of the early nineteenth-century 'vocabulary of improvement'[49] is how seamlessly it shades into the language of covert operations: popular literature is 'infiltrated' from within by reforming literature masquerading as chapbooks, and even fiction intended to reform the morals of a middle-class readership operates by stealth. In a review of Mary Brunton's 1811 evangelical novel *Self-Control*, a critic in the *Eclectic Review* argues that fiction is a legitimate mode of conveying improving sentiments because 'opposition is not awakened by a covert attack'.[50] The question of how to achieve reform without appearing to patronize or lecture one's audience was obviously not unique to Ireland, yet it was arguably further complicated in Ireland by the intersection of competing sectarian and class interests. Anglo-Irish efforts at reform could often be met with a degree of suspicion, as such attempts were (often legitimately) equated with Protestant proselytizing. Many authors of morally improving didactic fiction, such as Edgeworth and Mary Leadbeater, avoided the subject of religion entirely as a result. In addition to avoiding any imputation of sectarianism in providing useful information to Irish cottagers, Leadbeater was also conscious of the potential dangers of explicitly announcing her work's reforming intentions. Returning the manuscript of Leadbeater's new work, Mrs O'Beirne, the wife of the Bishop of Meath, wrote:

> In all books intended for instruction to the lower classes, care should be taken not to let the title or the preface imply that the book means to point out their faults and apply remedies to them. Their perceiving this intention, until they read the book, I have often known to prevent them from reading it at all; or, at least, to make them so perfectly prejudiced against whatever might be the contents, as to put their being benefited by those contents entirely out of the question.[51]

In light of such views, and on the advice of the Anglican Bishop of Meath himself, Leadbeater decided to give her new work the neutral title *Cottage Dialogues*, so that any readers amongst the Irish peasantry would not be immediately put off the work.

For Maria Edgeworth, it was precisely because *Glenburnie* did not appear to address Irish readers directly that it was so potentially effective in Ireland. The Scottish novel represented just such a 'covert attack' necessary to achieve improvement in Ireland. Writing in an 1816 obituary of Hamilton, Edgeworth offered her most fully articulated rationale for her belief in the improving power of *Glenburnie*:

> It is a proof of the great merit of this book, that it has, in spite of the Scottish dialect with which it abounds, been universally read in England and Ireland, as well as in Scotland. [. . .] In Ireland, in particular, the history of the Cottagers of Glenburnie has been read with peculiar avidity, and it has probably done as much good to the Irish as to the Scotch. While the Irish have seized and enjoyed the opportunity it afforded of a good humoured laugh at their Scotch neighbours, they have secretly seen through shades of difference, a resemblance to themselves, and are conscious that changing the names, the tale might be told of them. In this tale, the difference and the resemblance, between Scottish and Hibernian faults or foibles, are both advantageous to its popularity in Ireland. The difference is sufficient to give an air of novelty that wakens curiosity, while the resemblance fixes attention, and creates a new species of interest. Besides this, the self love of the Hibernian reader, being happily relieved from all apprehension that the lesson was intended for him, his good sense takes and profits by the advice that is offered to another.[52]

The key to *Glenburnie*'s success in Ireland is that it achieves improvement obliquely: the Scottish peasantry of *Glenburnie* is 'foreign', yet not entirely unfamiliar. While Irish readers are granted a degree of superiority over their 'Scotch neighbours', they are also susceptible to its reforming influence because they can recognize themselves in the text. Unlike those works criticized by Mrs O'Beirne that directly 'pointed out the faults' of the peasantry, *Glenburnie* offered readers *themselves* the opportunity to see 'secretly [. . .] through shades of difference' to recognize their own 'faults or foibles' without the intervention of Anglo-Irish reformers. If many attempts to reform were often stymied by resistance to seemingly 'rational' arguments, in Edgeworth's analysis, *Glenburnie* is successful because it gives space to the non-rational–to laughter–while at the same time allowing readers to exercise their reason in discovering and applying its lessons to themselves.

It is also the case that *Glenburnie* offers Edgeworth a model of how national difference could be preserved under the Union. As such, Edgeworth's praise of *Glenburnie* should be seen on a continuum with her earlier efforts to represent English, Irish, Scottish and Welsh distinctiveness in works such as the 1801 *Essay on Irish Bulls*. In many ways, as Marilyn Butler argues, Edgeworth's turn to the model of Scottish thought and culture enabled her to distance herself from England altogether:

> In the *Essay [on Irish Bulls]*, the Union is a fact: it need not mean the absorption of the Irish into the English. Instead the clear focus on the Irish and the Scots brings out the gifts of both, and hints hopefully at a future alliance to provide a counterweight to the centralising impulses of metropolitan England.[53]

The possibility of a productive Scottish-Irish counter-union recurs in *Ennui*, in the figure of the Scottish steward M'Leod, who successfully manages an Irish estate according to principles derived from Adam Smith's *Wealth of Nations*. While Edgeworth's advocacy of a progressivist, reformist model of social, political and economic improvement is often attached to the shorthand designation of 'Anglicization' (in its strictest sense, 'the action or process of making English'), her response to *Glenburnie* instead points, literally, in a different direction–away from England and towards Scotland.

If examining *Glenburnie* in Ireland allows us to see how Edgeworth's views on the novel are part of her overall engagement with a Scottish Enlightenment discourse on improvement, bringing the weight of Irish reception to bear on *Glenburnie* in turn reveals how Hamilton imports into her novel elements of both Irish and Scottish culture. These elements, along with her own negotiable national 'Scotch-Irish' identity, enabled Irish critics to appropriate *Glenburnie* to advance their own political agendas. Of course, it is impossible to know whether *Glenburnie* really did encourage any of Edgeworth's imagined 'Hibernian readers' to adopt Mrs Mason's code of reform. Individual readers may have just as easily appropriated *Glenburnie* for their own ends, enjoying the portrayal of the ramshackle MacClarty household and ignoring the dull didacticism of Mrs Mason. In the absence of such empirical evidence, we must rely largely on what *Glenburnie* represented for élite readers in Ireland. For these readers, it was not just that *Glenburnie* offered a convenient model of improvement that could be transplanted to Ireland; above all else, *Glenburnie* enabled critics to posit an alternative to both Edgeworth's (and Leadbeater's) Anglo-Irishness and to Owenson's Romantic proto-nationalism at a crucial moment in time for Ireland, when an Enlightenment faith in improvement was coming under increasing pressure by an emergent cultural nationalism.

Travels of a Lady of Fashion:
The Literary Career of Lady Blessington (1789–1849)

Riana O'Dwyer

From the horizon of present-day critical practice, the biography and writings of Lady Blessington pose some problems. From a feminist perspective, she did not resist the roles and expectations of her day, at least not in a radical way, although she was affected by the double standards regarding sexual morality that prevailed at the time. From the viewpoint of post-colonialism, she disregarded her nationality at least some of the time, and her family's religion fairly thoroughly. In addition, she happily transformed herself from the daughter of an Irish country-town gentleman merchant into the fashionable wife of an aristocrat. She was a social chameleon, an outsider resented by many, especially women, for her success as the hostess of a famous London salon. She was a prolific writer from the 1830s onwards, driven by financial necessity, but her writings suffer from the speed with which she produced them, and the inconsistencies of plot and characterization that abound. Why then should her work be resurrected at all, and not left to languish in the limbo of nineteenth-century pulp fiction? In her day, Lady Blessington attracted the kind of attention that today is directed by tabloid newspapers towards stars and celebrities, with an ongoing interest in her entertainments and who attended them, what she wore, her reported sayings and doings, and a ready market, stimulated at times by a *frisson* of scandal, for her writings. There is no easy answer to such criticism of Lady Blessington, yet her energy in the face of personal tribulations radiates from her writings and biography, and she emerges as a subversive Irish influence on the society

35

of early Victorian London, somewhat as Oscar Wilde came to be at the end of the nineteenth century. Her biography and her writings, especially her 'political' novel *Grace Cassidy, or, The Repealers*, deliver a complex message, challenging the social mores of her day and the current understanding of Irish identity formation in our own.

Marguerite Power, later Lady Blessington, was a striking figure in the English society of the 1820s and 1830s, as indicated by the title of her biography by J. Fitzgerald Molloy: *The Most Gorgeous Lady Blessington*.[1] Lady Wilde described her as 'brilliant, genial and beautiful', yet also said that 'her life was made up of the most startling contrasts'.[2] The contrasts were political and religious as well as social. The future Lady Blessington (known as Sally to her family) was born at Knockbrit, about two miles from Cashel in County Tipperary, on 1 September, 1789. She was the second of six children. Her grandfather Edmund Sheehy was 'a gentleman of moderate independence, connected with several of the most respectable Catholic families in the county [Tipperary]'.[3] Prior to this, the family had been victimized by accusations of participation in an alleged 'Popish Plot', as a result of which Edmund Sheehy's cousin, Father Nicholas Sheehy, Catholic parish priest of Ballyporeen, was executed. Following the priest's execution on 15 March 1766, convicted as he was on a false charge of treasonable conspiracy and incitement to rebellion, Blessington's grandfather Edmund Sheehy and two other affluent Catholics were also arrested. These three were executed at Clogheen near Clonmel on 3 May 1766. Further attempts were made to implicate Catholic gentlemen, including other members of the Sheehy family and even a relative of Edmund Burke in the alleged plot, but these later attempts failed, and all were acquitted. The accusations seem to have been motivated by sectarian rivalry, at a time when the penal laws against Catholics were still in force, though not always implemented.[4]

Family lore connected the Sheehys with the ancient Gaelic chiefs of Desmond, whose power had waned after the failure of the Munster rebellion in the late seventeenth century, but whose name still evoked the heroic past of the clans. Lady Blessington was proud of her descent from the Desmonds through the Sheehys, and gave an account of her genealogy, handwritten by herself and entitled 'Pedigree of the Sheehy Family', to her friend and biographer Richard Robert Madden. This account traces the origins of her mother Ellen Sheehy's family to a marriage between the daughter of the first Earl of Desmond and Morgan Sheehy.[5]

On the other side, Marguerite's father Edmund Power, a small landowner of Catholic stock, pursued any avenue that would allow him to become upwardly mobile. His family roots were in County Waterford, and he was the son of Michael Power, of Curragheen near Dungarvan. Shortly after his marriage to Ellen Sheehy, he moved to Knockbrit, about two miles from Cashel in County Tipperary, where his elder children were born, and where he lived the life of a country gentleman, 'occupied with field sports and agricultural pursuits'.[6] The family moved to Clonmel about 1796, when Marguerite was about seven years old, and there Power developed business interests as a corn-merchant and butter buyer. Subsequently he became the proprietor of the *Clonmel Gazette or Munster Mercury*. As R. R Madden, the historian and biographer of Lady Blessington has observed: 'The politics of the paper were liberal Catholic politics–Power was a Catholic, though not a very strict or observant one.'[7]

Power also accepted the patronage of Lord Donoughmore, a liberal Protestant with lands in Tipperary, who recommended him for the magistracy of Tipperary and Waterford, which he held during the period of the 1798 Rising. This position provided the prospect of social advancement, rather than financial rewards, although there appear to have been promises of a lucrative sinecure, even of a baronetcy.[8] In the countryside, Power was feared as a brutal and indiscriminate enforcer, riding out personally at night with troops of dragoons, hunting down, beating and arresting those whom he suspected of participation in the Rising. He continued these activities for years, long after the Rising had been suppressed and the Act of Union came into force.[9] In 1807, however, he was tried for the murder of one such 'rebel', an innocent farm-worker who ran away from Power and his mounted patrol and was shot in the back. Although Power was acquitted of murder, he was not allowed to continue as magistrate.[10]

Some aspects of Marguerite's girlhood life in the garrison town of Clonmel were revisited in a nostalgic novel written towards the end of her life, called *Country Quarters* (published posthumously in 1850). It is a light-hearted and rambling fiction depicting flirtations between the local beauties and the lively young officers of the regiments stationed in the area between Waterford and Tipperary, echoes perhaps of the amusements of the young Power daughters in the early years of the century. However, this girlish existence was short lived, since in 1804 Edmund Power arranged the marriage of Marguerite, then aged fourteen, to Captain Maurice St

Leger Farmer, an officer of the 47th Regiment stationed at Clonmel. The marriage took place on 7 March. Farmer was violent and abusive, and after a period of three months the couple lived apart. Marguerite at first returned home to Clonmel, and Farmer, who had gone with his regiment to the Curragh, sold his commission shortly afterwards and went to India.[11] Edmund Power was not pleased with his daughter's return to his house, where several unmarried sisters remained, and made her feel very unwelcome. Eventually, probably in 1807 during the family turmoil of Edmund Power's murder trial, Marguerite left Tipperary with Captain Thomas Jenkins of the 11th Light Dragoons, whom she had got to know at her father's house. The couple may have spent some time in Dublin at first, but 'by the autumn of 1809, Margaret Farmer, just twenty years of age, was happily, if equivocally, established at Jenkins' house in Hampshire'.[12]

Here, in 1814, Charles John Gardiner, Viscount Mountjoy, came to visit Jenkins, his old army friend. Marguerite had met Gardiner in Clonmel a decade earlier when the Tyrone militia, in which he was an officer, was stationed nearby. The friendships were renewed, with visits by Gardiner to Hampshire and in 1816 by Jenkins and Marguerite to Gardiner's estate, Mountjoy Forest in Tyrone. In that year, Gardiner was also created Earl of Blessington.[13] It appears that soon after this an agreement was reached between Gardiner and Jenkins, as a result of which Marguerite moved to Manchester Square in London, supported financially by the new Earl of Blessington and therefore his mistress, although the proprieties were observed to a degree by their separate establishments. Her husband, Captain Farmer, died as a result of a drunken accident in 1817, and in 1818 Marguerite married Blessington, who was a widower with four children from his first marriage.[14] These children did not live with the couple, but remained in Dublin, where they were raised by Blessington's sister, Miss Harriet Gardiner.

The newly-weds set up house in splendid style in London, and Marguerite published her first descriptions of society life: *The Magic Lantern* (1822) and *Sketches and Fragments* (1822).[15] Even at this stage, her cool assessment of the fickleness of fashion, and the precarious nature of friendship and loyalty in the fashionable world is evident in the mildly satirical tone through which she reveals the price paid, especially by women, for social success. This is a central subject of her later novel, *Grace Cassidy, or, The Repealers*. In 1822, the Blessingtons departed for Europe on a tour that was to last for seven years. They were accompanied on their travels by a large party, including Alfred, Count d'Orsay, a dispossessed French aristocrat and sculptor. In 1823, following the death of his only legitimate son and heir, Luke Wellington Gardiner, not yet ten years of age, the Earl of Blessington made an extraordinary set of family arrangements, which were to have long-term consequences for all concerned. He arranged that d'Orsay should marry his legitimate daughter from his first marriage, Lady Harriet Gardiner, only eleven at the time and living in Dublin. He also settled a large fortune on Harriet and d'Orsay, in a codicil to his will which caused lengthy family litigation later. The marriage took place in Italy in 1827, and was never a success.

In 1829 the party began a leisurely journey home, pausing in Paris, where the Blessingtons acquired a large house and began renovations, as they intended to remain there for some time. In April, Blessington travelled from Paris to London to support the Catholic Emancipation Bill, which was introduced in the House of Lords by the Duke of Wellington. Having voted in favour, he returned to Paris.[16] He did not long survive this intervention in Irish affairs, as on 23 May he suffered a stroke from which he died on 25 May, without regaining consciousness. He was just a few weeks from his forty-seventh birthday. Marguerite was left with a relatively modest income of £2,000 per annum, on which to support an expensive lifestyle, a large household and dependent relatives in Ireland. She returned to London in 1831, and established herself as a fashionable hostess, most notably at Gore House, Kensington.

This was a period of rapid development in publishing and journalism as newspapers and periodicals were established to serve the many interests of the new literate public. It was also a period of intense social and cultural competition, with rival factions seeking to become the arbiters of fashion. London society soon speculated that Lady Blessington's son-in-law, the Count d'Orsay, was also her lover, although the two did not live in the same house until after the formal separation of the Count and Harriet in 1838. Nonetheless, the suspected liaison was considered scandalous, and Lady Blessington was shunned by respectable society. In an effort to supplement her income, Lady Blessington began to write, producing novels, sketches, travel accounts and satires upon the society that both ostracized and was fascinated by her. She took advantage of the fashion for magazines and annuals, and edited *The Keepsake* and *The Book of Beauty* for many years. Mrs Samuel Carter Hall, well-known for her own stories and travel books about Ireland, contributed to some of these and said of her: '[Her beauty] was charming in its autumn time; and the Irish accent, and soft sweet Irish laugh, used to make my heart beat with the pleasures of memory.'[17] The Annuals were published as suitable gifts for Christmas, and were small, elegant volumes, attractively bound, with a frontispiece on which the donor could write a greeting. The text consisted of sentimental poems and short stories, some of which referred to the engravings of notable, and usually titled, ladies that were also a feature of the volumes. These publications appealed to the developing middle classes; the attraction was access to the faces and styles of 'society', and to the literary efforts of the fashionable. While some contributions were by the famous authors of the day, many were offered by young ladies who wanted to appear in print. The business end, printing, binding and marketing, was managed by the publishers, but the contributions were commissioned by the editors, such as Lady Blessington, who needed to have access to a steady stream of voluntary and eligible writers. The publishers paid for the services of the editor, and perhaps one important author who would appeal to the public, but the contributions were mostly given free; the authors, especially the young ladies, were rewarded only by the gratification of seeing their work in print. Lady Blessington was also able to command contributions from many of the important writers of the day, whose only reward was entry to her sociable drawing-room. Her nieces, living in her extended household, are frequently noted as contributors, earning their keep by filling up the necessary quota of pages. Lady Wilde remarked scornfully:

> a titled editress was indispensable as nurse to the small literary buds of fashion that lisped their pretty twaddle in gilded annuals, while the lady herself loved celebrities and display; and this occupation brought her into contact with almost every literary man of eminence in the kingdom. [. . .] The whole system of the annuals was, in fact, a speculation based upon personal vanity.[18]

For some years, Lady Blessington's literary activities produced a considerable income, estimated by her niece Miss Power to amount to an average of £1,000 a year, and by the editor of the *Literary Gazette* to be between £2,000–£3,000 in the years when the Annuals were doing well.[19]

However, the Deed of Family Arrangement of 1838, which was made necessary by the legal separation of the Count D'Orsay and his wife Harriet Gardiner, left the extravagant Count almost totally dependent on Lady Blessington, who was also supporting several members of her own family. She paid a quarterly pension to her father and mother for many years before they died, and helped to educate the children of her siblings. She gave a permanent home to two of her brother's daughters, who were living with her when she died, and also provided for her sisters at various times.[20]

The Count had raised extensive loans on the expectations of his marriage property, which he was then totally unable to repay, and from 1841 until he fled to France in 1849, he was a virtual prisoner in Gore House, unable to leave the house except at night and on Sundays, in order to avoid being imprisoned for debt.[21] For some years Lady Blessington managed to keep the establishment going, becoming in effect a professional, if part-time, writer and editor. Even her evening salons contributed to her income as she used the lubrication of sociability to coax contributions for the Annuals from her literary visitors, and to flatter editors and publishing people with access to 'society'. The Count infuriated his creditors with his apparent invulnerability, while he made some contribution to the household by establishing a studio at home and painting society portraits. The famine in Ireland was the proximate cause of the collapse of this house of cards. The annuities from the estate of Lord Blessington dwindled as the rents could no longer be paid, and in 1849 the Count was forced to flee to France to avoid arrest. Lady Blessington soon followed, leaving Gore House and its contents to be sold, in one of the most spectacular bankruptcies of the time. William Thackeray attended the pre-auction viewing, and wrote to a friend: 'I have just come away from a dismal sight, Gore House full of snobs looking at the furniture [. . .] Ah it was a strange sad picture of Wanaty Fair [*sic*].'[22] To the moralists, it appeared that the wheel of fortune had turned, and a life founded on scandal and opportunism had ended as it should, a striking example of Vanity Fair. However, irrepressible as ever, Lady Blessington began to make plans for more books, a new home, a fresh start, but all came to a sudden end on 4 June 1849, when she died of a heart attack in her sixtieth year. She was buried at Chambourcy, in a vault designed for her by the Count d'Orsay. He died on 4 August 1852, and was interred with her.

*

Editor, journalist, travel-writer, pulp-fiction producer–how may we assess Lady Blessington's writing's career today? Margaret Kelleher, considering the impact of the writings published in the *Field Day Anthology*, volumes IV and V, suggests that it 'is time to look at their contents again in the wider tradition from whence they came and to study how the tradition changes with their return to view'.[23] In many ways, Blessington was a figure ahead of her time, who would be perfectly at home in the current media world, and is best considered in that context. She wrote travel books, short satirical sketches and stories, light verse and twelve novels (most of them in three or four volumes) between her return to London in 1831 and her death in 1849, a prodigious output especially considering that her time was also occupied with her evening entertainments and many visitors.[24] Her earliest writings were lightly satirical short pieces, 'sketches' written to amuse her friends in the early days of her marriage in London. Novel writing was one of her sources of income when she returned to England later on, and she began and ended her career as a novelist with narratives set in Ireland: *Grace Cassidy, or, The Repealers* published in 1833, and *Country Quarters* published posthumously in 1850. In between these novels she published ten others, such as *The Victims of Society* (1837) and *The Governess* (1839). She also began to publish travel writings, based on journals she had kept when travelling with her husband, and which provided the basic material for publications such as *The Idler in Italy* (1839) and *The Idler in France* (1841). Her most enduring publication, also based on her journals, was *Conversations of Lord Byron with the Countess of Blessington* (1834). More detailed consideration will now be given to this text, and also to her first Irish novel, *Grace Cassidy, or, The Repealers*.

Only one of Lady Blessington's works, *Conversations of Lord Byron*, has been republished since the nineteenth century.[25] Her modern editor, Ernest Lovell, a Byron scholar, weighs up her account against those of other contemporaries. Reviews and reactions at the time of the serial publication in *The New Monthly Magazine and Literary Journal* between July 1832 and December 1833 (single volume publication by Bentley for Colburn followed in 1834), were coloured by the relationships of the commentators with Lady Blessington, whether friendly or inimical. Ernest Lovell, in his introduction, recounts how twentieth-century accounts of

Byron relied on her material, and credits it with being based on reality, not the product of invention, as contemporary opponents suggested.[26] He concludes that at best, 'her insights into Byron's character are often impressive and convincing', and that 'her book is an important record of her impressions, distilled over a decade, cast into dramatic form, and greatly enriched by her association over the years with many of Byron's friends, acquaintances and enemies'.[27]

The Blessingtons stayed in Genoa from 31 March to 2 June 1823, and met Byron almost immediately. They met about twenty times during the visit, including seven dinners or formal calls, and several casual encounters during walks or rides.[28] Lady Blessington's account of their friendship is vivid and persuasive, even today. Its immediacy is accounted for by her habit of making notes in her journal as soon as possible after encounters or conversations. These journals proved to be her capital in her later years of financial struggle, furnishing, in addition to the *Conversations*, two further publications, *The Idler in Italy* (1839) and *The Idler in France* (1841). She defends Byron against common charges, such as that of being irreligious: 'he is sceptical, but not unbelieving' or that of being haughty and distant: 'Byron never makes light of the griefs of others, but shows commiseration and kindness'.[29] Lovell also argues that Lady Blessington identified with Byron to a great extent: both 'had begun life in simplicity and goodness of heart, had become the victims of envy and jealousy in a hypocritical society, ever ready to attack persons of superior talent, had suffered bitterly from this, and had become disillusioned upon the loss of supposed friends'.[30]

Lady Blessington, therefore, was uniquely positioned to interpret the personality of Byron. She had the ability to encourage conversation, to draw out opinions and to challenge them tactfully. Today she might have been a talk-show host; in Victorian London she employed her talents in her sociable drawing-room. In Genoa in the company of Byron, she and her husband entertained the poet with anecdotes of his English friends and acquaintances, and together they discussed many subjects, the nature of true friendship being a recurrent topic and differences in national character such as those between the English and the Italian or Irish being another. Of Shelley, Byron said:

> You should have known Shelley to feel how much I must regret him. He was the most gentle, most amiable, and *least* worldly-

minded person I ever met; full of delicacy, disinterested beyond all other men, and possessing a degree of genius, joined to a simplicity, as rare as it is admirable [. . .] I have seen nothing like him, and never shall again, I am certain.[31]

Some of Byron's remarks about Lady Blessington in his letters of this period are not flattering, though they vary depending on how he thinks his correspondent of the moment regards the Blessingtons.[32] He appears to have liked Lord Blessington and been intrigued by the Count d'Orsay, who made sketches of him.[33] While they were neighbours, they fell into companionship, but once they had gone their separate ways, Byron did not make any effort to keep in touch. Whether for this reason, or because some of his negative remarks came to her ears in the ten years that passed before she prepared her *Conversations* for publication, even her friend and biographer Madden noticed 'some secret feeling of pique and sense of annoyance' in her tone, especially towards the end of her account.[34] Her sense of vulnerability emerges in such comments as the following:

[His remarks] were sufficiently severe to make me feel that there was no safety with him, and that in five minutes after one's quitting him on terms of friendship, he could not resist the temptation of showing one up, either in conversation or by letter, though in half an hour after he would put himself to personal inconvenience to render a kindness to the person so shown up.[35]

While her husband was alive, Lady Blessington was protected from the snobbery and scorn that her origins and reputation engendered in the competitive and ruthless society of the day. Once he was dead, she was fully exposed to the judgements of 'society', and the arbiters of social opinion did not spare her.

In her later years, Lady Blessington had ample opportunity to experience the cruelties of social ostracism in London. The ambiguity with which she was regarded, and the complexity which she represented, is well expressed by Jane Francesca Wilde, Speranza, in her *Notes on Men, Women and Books* (1891). She wrote:

Though born and reared a Roman Catholic, yet she talks of herself on one occasion as 'a stern Protestant,' merely because those around her were so; and she forgot for the moment exactly what she believed. Another time, with the same comprehensive sympathy, she speaks of her 'proud feelings as an Englishwoman,' quite oblivious of Tipperary and the murdered Sheehys; though when writing to Dr. Madden, her love for 'her poor country' is ardently expressed.[36]

It appears that Marguerite Power survived by adopting a complex series of roles: society bride, cultivated traveller and friend of Byron, hostess of an intellectual salon. The role of Irishwoman was left behind in Ireland, together with the religion of her youth, as Lady Wilde observed.

These ambiguities are present in her Irish novel of 1833, *Grace Cassidy, or, The Repealers*, in which we can detect an uneasy exploration of the stresses involved in the relationship between Ireland and England in the decades after the Union. Ostensibly written from the viewpoint of fashionable society, *Grace Cassidy* reveals the fissures and insecurities implicit in the uneasy social and political compromises that prevailed in the early nineteenth century. The plot was in part a vehicle for considering the relationship between landlords and their tenants in Ireland at a time when the political desire for repeal of the Union was expressed in secret societies and agrarian movements. It also included consideration of how Irish landlord families related to England after the Union, what their social status was, and how they negotiated the complexities of politics and economics. The novel had to acknowledge the friction created by the inequality of these relationships, and sought to lubricate this by means of the idealized character of Grace Cassidy and her actions. While this device is not successful as a narrative strategy, the novel is nonetheless interesting as an exploration of the tensions generated by the Irish question in the London of the 1830s, as seen from the perspective of an expatriate Irishwoman brought up decades earlier in strife-ridden Tipperary.

*

The novel *Grace Cassidy, or, The Repealers* is set in 1832, and opens in a rural district of County Waterford with a description of the cottage and domestic situation of the eponymous Grace Cassidy and her husband Jim. The nearby Big House, Springmount, is the home of the Desmond family: husband, wife and daughter Frances. The surname was carefully chosen, referring to the cherished connection between Lady Blessington's family and the aristocratic Munster Desmonds.[37] The action of the first volume of the three-decker novel concerns the political and personal concerns of these two families. In the cottage, Grace tries to dissuade her husband Jim from getting involved with politics in general and the Repealers in particular. In the Big House, the family is mainly occupied with the courtship and marriage of Frances to Colonel Forrester, commanding officer of the local garrison. Grace is also shown visiting Springmount, bringing honey, eggs and cream cheese, and being warmly greeted by Mrs Desmond and Frances. These early chapters include discussions between Grace and her husband on Repeal, the nature of liberty and the controversial tithes, still a legal requirement even after Catholic Emancipation. However, volume one is a preamble to the plot development of the subsequent two volumes, which are mainly set in England and concern the upper-class characters. Ireland returns to central focus only at the end of volume three.

At the end of volume one, a subplot emerges concerning the social disgrace of Colonel Forrester's married sister Lady Oriel, who has become involved in a flirtation with the villain of the novel, Lord Delmore, in London. This becomes the central narrative interest of volume two, while the Irish issues continue in some chapters only. Checking the chapters by content shows that in volumes two and three, fourteen chapters narrate the cottage incidents and concerns, while the remaining twenty-nine chapters concern the progress of events in high society. Included in the latter chapters, however, are some concerned with Irish affairs from the perspective of the society characters.

The cottiers are the stable centre of the novel geographically, confined to their land and locality, and not travelling far from their homes in the course of the novel. The gentry, on the other hand, constantly move. Mr Desmond goes to Dublin to discuss the land agitation with the Lord Lieutenant. His entire family travels to England and visits London and the country. His English friends in their turn come to Ireland. Mobility, whether for business or pleasure, is one of the indicators of social position in the novel, since the transfer of Irish political representation to London as a result of the Union has resulted in a corresponding movement of people in both directions, though mainly from Ireland to England. In writing about the social consequences of journeys, Lady Blessington is drawing on her personal knowledge of the advantages and pitfalls of geographical mobility as a means to social mobility. Among the consequences of the political union and the economic expansion that empire was already encouraging, was the fact that social position was no longer such a firm category as it had been in earlier generations, an ambiguity of which Lady Blessington could take advantage for a time, but which failed her in the end.

In her depiction of the lives of the cottiers, especially the Cassidy couple, Blessington is less sure. She is relying on memories of Ireland from almost twenty years earlier, although the setting of the novel's action is just the year before publication. Therefore her attempts at 'brogue' are exaggerated and unconvincing, and are in fact quietly abandoned as the novel progresses. She includes a few words of Irish, such as 'my colleen dhas', 'na bochlish' [*ná bac leis*] and 'cuishlamachree', which indicate that she has some recollection of phrases heard when she lived in the Tipperary countryside as a child.[38] Grace Cassidy is the natural heroine, represented as possessing inherently the same qualities of gentleness, industry and intelligence which are to be found in the respectable ladies of high society. Her housekeeping is praised by the ladies of the Big House. Her cottage and that of her friend are examples fit to be compared with the cottages of England:

> Grace Cassidy and Mary Mahoney profited by the countenance and support which they received. Their cottages were as clean and tidily kept as in England, their gardens as redolent of flowers, and there was even a spirit of coquetry in the care bestowed on the decoration, particularly by Grace, who, having no children to occupy her time, had more leisure than Mary. The fresh nosegays ranged on the dresser as white as unsunned snow, and on which a goodly show of pewter and delf was set out; the brick floor, cleanly swept, and as red as a cherry; the windows rubbed bright, and all the rustic furniture shining from the efforts of Grace's hands–all showed the tasteful care, as well as cleanly habits of the tidy housewife; and her person was as well attended to as her house.[39]

Grace disapproves of her husband's drinking, and his involvement with the Repealers, but he is to her 'the misguided but still dearly beloved husband' (vol. 1, 76). She tricks the Repealers into sparing the Big House but suffers the burning of her own cottage. Though Blessington idealizes Grace for the benefit of her English readers, many of the descriptions of country pursuits ring true, recollections of an Edenic country girlhood the sudden end of which was traumatic for her. Her niece and companion recalled:

> Gathering a handful of flowers to keep in memory of the place, yet fearing the ridicule of the other members of the family, she carefully concealed them in her pocket; and with many tears and bitter regrets, was at last driven from Knockbrit, where, as it seemed to her, she left all happiness behind her.[40]

The central concern of volumes two and three of the novel, however, is the negotiation necessary to gain and maintain a place in English society. This aspect of the plot centres on the social exclusion of Lady Oriel, when her flirtation with Lord Delmore has become public. Blessington is at pains to emphasize that the flirtation was thoughtless, not culpable, and that Lady Oriel has infringed the codes of discretion, not of morality. The novel castigates the hypocrisy of self-styled arbiters of fashionable conduct, such as the Patronesses of Almack's (a fashionable venue for balls), who decide who may attend and who shall be excluded.[41] One of these patronesses criticizes Lady Oriel for herself being too inclusive, particularly because 'she opposed herself to cutting or leaving off people' (vol. 2, 291), an essential part of the social control which the patronesses wished to exercise. An alternative social circle, more concerned with true worth than with appearances, is mobilized to reinforce Lady Oriel's rehabilitation:

> This circle is a kind of oasis in the desert of the vast metropolis, refreshing to all who approach it, and where politics, that powerful leveller, has no influence [. . .] The females who adorn this high and pure aristocracy [. . .] are neither patronesses of Almack's, nor obstinate sticklers for any system of exclusiveness excepting that which regards moral character. (vol. 2, 128)

Most of the originals of this circle are identified in a 'Key to The Repealers.'[42] The nominal disguises are easily penetrated, the Marchioness of Glanricarde for the Marchioness of Clanricarde, for example, and as Blessington's biographer Sadleir remarks: 'not surprisingly the persons thus avowedly introduced are described with a facile flattery which precludes characterization.'⁴³ This alternative circle is presided over in the novel by the influential Duchess of Heaviland, identified in the Key as the Duchess of Northumberland.

The extended description of Lady Oriel's exclusion and embarrassment echoes Blessington's own ambiguous social position. Samuel Carter Hall, who was quite willing to have Lady Blessington as a contributor for his magazines, nonetheless records that

> her visitors were all, or nearly all, men. Ladies were rarely seen at her receptions. Mrs. Hall never accompanied me to her evenings, although she was a frequent day-caller. We were not of rank high enough to be indifferent to public opinion; for putting aside the knowledge that slander was busy with her fame, there was no doubting the fact that she had been the mistress, before she had been the wife, of the Earl of Blessington.⁴⁴

Lady Morgan, who had moved to London with her husband in 1837, disliked the deceased Earl of Blessington since earlier encounters in Ireland and had caricatured him as 'Lord Rosbrin' in *Florence Macarthy*.⁴⁵ Morgan perceived Lady Blessington's literary salon as a rival to her own and spoke venomously of her at every opportunity, as her opponent likewise did of her. One observer pointed out:

> Lady Blessington has the worst of it, having a weak point, whereas Lady Morgan, besides being undoubtedly the cleverest of the two, is wholly impeccable. The one cannot deny the beauty of her rival, but takes care to record the frailties which have been its consequences. The other does not dispute the virtue of her antagonist, but ascribes its existence to the absence of temptation, from the fact of her always having been 'too ugly to have a lover.'⁴⁶

Within *Grace Cassidy* the social dilemmas are resolved for the central characters by the end of the second volume, through the patronage of the Duchess of Heaviland, following which

> the select and distinguished guests whom the Oriels frequently met at Heaviland House, all sought the acquaintance of Lady Oriel. [. . .] Those who had formerly dropped off from her, now

> as eagerly sought a renewal of her acquaintance, and she
> conducted herself so mildly and decorously towards them, that
> they accused themselves of injustice, in ever having doubted her
> purity. (vol. 2, 217)

This social rehabilitation did not come true for Lady Blessington herself, who remained a subject of gossip and exclusion until her spectacular bankruptcy and flight more than ten years later.

Towards the middle of the final volume of *Grace Cassidy*, the focus of the narrative returns to Ireland when the fashionable London characters undertake a tour there. In this final section Lady Blessington attempts, as Maria Edgeworth and Lady Morgan had done before her, to instruct her English readers in the positive, as well as negative, aspects of the Irish. One element that receives high praise, perhaps surprisingly, is the food:

> The excellence of the provisions at the inns at which they stopped
> surprised them; and Lady Oriel declared that the butter was more
> delicate, and finely flavoured than any she had ever before eaten;
> it looked and tasted as if the cows had fed only on buttercups and
> primroses. The slim-cake and hot griddle-bread, luxuries to be
> had only in Ireland, met with great success; and the newly laid
> eggs were pronounced to be so good, as to verify the Irishman's
> boast that 'sure it was only Irish hens that ever laid fresh eggs.'
> The crimped salmon [. . .] was allowed to be far superior to any
> English salmon they had ever tasted; and the speckled trout, fresh
> from the water, was pronounced matchless. (vol. 3, 181)

The Irish breakfast receives similar praise:

> They entered the breakfast room as the bell summoned them to
> that repast, and found a table plentifully piled high with all the
> luxuries that Ireland can furnish. Honey, bright and sparkling as
> topaz, raspberry jam that might vie in tint with the ruby, fruit of
> every description, and cream and butter such as Erin alone can
> produce, graced the board. (vol. 3, 193)

Such detailed descriptions of the food available in rural Ireland, admittedly provisions for distinguished visitors, is rare in the fiction of the period, and may reflect the fare prepared for Marguerite and the Earl of Blessington when they visited his estate after their marriage in 1818, if not the meals available in her father's house in Clonmel during her girlhood.

There are several discussions of political issues relevant to Ireland in the novel. Mr Desmond visits Westminster during a debate in the House of Commons on the Peace Preservation Act of 1833, the year of *Grace Cassidy*'s publication. Among the thinly disguised personalities whom he sees there are Sir Robert Peel (Sir Robert Neil) and Daniel O'Connell (The Agitator):

> 'The Agitator, of course, you know by sight–there he is; his countenance is good, and peculiarly Irish; his voice well-suited to the powerful bursts of eloquence with which he inundates his auditors; and it must be admitted, he is one of the most effective speakers in the world, as he dazzles where he cannot convince; and though he often leaves Reason free, he makes captive the passions, which but too generally prevent her using her freedom.' (vol. 2, 277–8)

In spite of her late husband's support of Catholic Emancipation, and her own reasons to be interested in the removal of penalties for Catholics, Lady Blessington transformed The Liberator into The Agitator, and held him and other political activists to blame for the rural unrest still evident in the Irish countryside, and which her novel discusses. Mr Desmond is the spokesman for the political position of Lady Blessington in the novel, saying for example that 'emancipation had been considered as the panacea that was to heal every disease, and all parties concluded that tranquillity would be established', but that instead turbulence has resulted (vol. 1, 178–9). Earlier he had visited Dublin Castle, and met the Secretary for Ireland Mr Manley, a thin disguise for Mr Stanley, advocate of the Peace Preservation Act of 1833, in opposition to Daniel O'Connell and his supporters (vol. 1, 160–9).[47] Desmond supports this restrictive measure:

> The question is, are the well-conducted and orderly to be left to the tender mercies of the infuriated miscreants who have taken the law into their own hands, or are measures, strong and illegal as they may be considered, to be taken to protect the good, and check the bad? (vol. 3, 172–3)

Clearly Lady Blessington was aware of the implications of the legislation proposed for Ireland, but she did not lose sight of the interests of the landlords either, on whose security her income depended.

However, Lady Blessington's support for the system was not unconditional, and while it is evident that she had no sympathy with repeal politics, she also indicated that part of Ireland's problem was the lack of understanding in England of Irish conditions. She principally conveyed this through the contrast between Mr Desmond and Lord Abberville. Desmond is portrayed as a resident landlord, concerned to improve the conditions of his tenants, while Abberville, identified by Sadleir as Lord Charleville,[48] is an absentee and an opportunist, abusing his position to increase his own wealth:

> Lord Abberville owed his title to the Union, and a certain, or rather uncertain, portion of his income to a judicious and persevering system of jobbing, known only in Ireland. The rents of his overlet property were paid by presentments, which he had influence with the Grand Jury of the County to get passed, and which allowed large sums to be expended in making roads over his estates; the work to be done by his tenants, and the money to find its way into his coffers. Presentments for roads never required [were] passed at every assizes, until his property was intersected by as many lines as a miniature map of Europe; while the roads really necessary for establishing communications for agricultural or commercial purposes were totally neglected. (vol. 1, 279)

It is indicated, however, that even the efforts of resident landlords may not guarantee peace and harmony. Mr Desmond realizes that 'few reflect on the misery of residing in a country where laws are trampled on, and murder and rapine stalk abroad in open day' (vol. 3, 170). The landholding system itself was the problem, not whether it was well or badly administered.

Since her husband had been an extravagant absentee for years, and Lady Blessington had resisted, rather than encouraged, plans to return to Ireland, she could hardly take the high moral ground on this issue. Clearly she was not a nationalist; furthermore, her income after her husband's death derived from his estates in Ireland. Her own personal extravagance provoked a rare rebuke in Madden's biography. Referring to the refurbishment of her rented house in Paris he says:

> The gilt frame-work of the bed, resting on the back of the large silver swans, it does not do to think of, when visiting the Mountjoy Forest Estate, in Tyrone, that did belong to the late Earl of Blessington, when one enters the cabin of one of the now indigent peasantry, from the sweat of whose brow the means were derived, that were squandered in luxury in foreign lands.[49]

She was a beneficiary of the landlord system, and thus never questioned it. As a result, she was opposed to political agitation in general and land agitation in particular, although she did argue in *Grace Cassidy* in favour of responsible land-management and against political corruption.

Lady Blessington depicts Grace Cassidy as an alternative if rather fanciful representation of how to reconcile the two opposing worlds. Grace embodies domestic order in her appearance and her home, and she opposes any involvement of her husband with the repealers, and urges him to give up drinking, and to vote as his landlord wishes. She and her neighbours, like the tenants in Maria Edgeworth's novel *The Absentee*, are grateful when their landlord and his wife return at the end of the novel. Finally, she uses her ingenuity to persuade the activists not to burn Springmount House. That, however, is as far as the novel takes it. Grace saves the Big House and is suitably rewarded. The social difficulties of the fashionable families are resolved and all the marriages are confirmed by the birth of children so that succession is secured, both in high society and in Grace's cottage. The fundamental issues are left untouched; the closure is tentative and unconvincing.

In conclusion, the unwieldy narrative reveals the existence of a number of festering sores in the political and social relationships of the two countries, and in the gender expectations enforced by society. Lady Blessington was perhaps more sensitive to the inequalities suffered both by Ireland and by women than she herself was actually aware, but neither her fiction nor her life were able to vanquish them. In her lifetime, the public interest in her as a subject for gossip overshadowed her activity as a writer, and in today's terms she might better be considered as a celebrity media figure than as a serious novelist or travel writer. However, her publications provide a barometer of the cultural pressures in London in the 1830s, bearing especially upon the issues of social standing, and the emerging complexities of the relationship between England and Ireland as the Union bedded down. In order to account for her impact at the time, it is necessary to consider more complex models of colonialism, as Tom Dunne has advised in another context, 'replacing black and white polarities of "difference" with an acknowledgement of the hybrid cultures that always evolve from colonial encounters'.[50] From this perspective, the writings of Marguerite Power, later Countess of Blessington, become emblematic of the flux of identity between the two countries, representing in one career the cultural consequences of the political union: a hybrid commentator on London society. Her many and varied writings, especially her novel *Grace Cassidy*, convey a sense of the personal and political tensions at work in Ireland in the early years of the nineteenth century, in a manner more intimate and at least as evocative as the more formal pamphlets of the day. Her writings and her life navigated the space between Ireland and England, between the interests of emerging nationalism and the landlords, between the middle and upper classes and between the roles expected of women and of men, indicating the chasms and the bridges between them, and also challenging their boundaries.

The Art of Bookmaking:
Selina Bunbury's Northern Journeys

Maria Lindgren Leavenworth

Despite Selina Bunbury's prolific production of tracts, novels, essays and travelogues, there are only sketchy pieces of information about her life.[1] What can be determined is that she was born in 1802 at Kilsaran House in County Louth as one of fifteen children. Her first book, *A Visit to my Birthplace* was published in 1821, according to some of her own statements, although there is no surviving copy to corroborate this. In 1843 she had this to say about the publication of the book, according to *The Irish Book Lover*:

> Although in every sense the little book may be deemed a childish effort, its publication at the period was considered an enterprise for a Dublin publisher. I know not whether I can be controverted in the idea I have, that almost the first copyright work published in Dublin after the Union was published by Messrs. Curry, and that work was my first.

Again, in 1852, she writes: 'Its immediate success was admitted to have been the first cause of reviving the publishing business from the decline consequent on the change in the copyright law by the Act of Union.'[2]

In addition to reviving the Irish publishing business, a statement a tad exaggerated it seems, the book provided Bunbury with a promising start to her career. She travelled quite extensively 'visiting every country in Europe except Greece and Portugal'.[3] Although, as it is put in *The Irish*

Book Lover: '[i]t cannot be said that Miss Bunbury was a great writer [. . .] she possessed the seeing eye and brought to her observation of foreign places and people a freshness of outlook and a sense of humour then conspicuously absent from travel books.'[4] Bunbury died in 1882, still busy writing.

What I will discuss here are three of Bunbury's travel texts, *Evelyn; or a Journey from Stockholm to Rome in 1847–48* (1849), *Life in Sweden; with Excursions in Norway and Denmark* (1853) and *A Summer in Northern Europe, Including Sketches in Sweden, Norway, Finland, the Aland Islands, Gothland, &c.* (1856), all texts published in two volumes.[5] Of interest are the descriptions of the encountered places, people and customs and how these are presented in contrast to conditions and behaviour in England, her most frequent point of reference. Her native Ireland usually becomes a lowly relative to the England she wishes to identify with. Further, I will analyse issues connected to truth-claims, originality and the writing process and I will also look at references to guidebooks and to travel in general. Finally, I will discuss how Bunbury in various ways criticizes what she encounters, or how she uses her new experiences to criticize conditions, practices and behaviour elsewhere.

First, however, we might again note the quotation from *The Irish Book Lover*, where the commentator sees 'freshness' and 'humour' rather than any literary merit as characteristic of Bunbury's travel writing, and see these comments as part of a larger context. Similar statements can be found in a review from *Littell's Living Age*, where it says that in the age of 'odd, female travellers' Bunbury's texts do not convince the author 'to withdraw the epithet'.[6] She is said to write 'in a manner to suggest whimsical thoughts'[7] and it is concluded that Bunbury 'is not so much wanting in good nature as wanting in taste'.[8] Bunbury is not alone among her female contemporaries to have her writing described in this manner. Travelling women in the nineteenth century, like women both before and after this period, were often seen as eccentric, curious and entertaining rather than, as their male counterparts, bold, adventurous, serious and determined. Shirley Foster has pointed out that '[t]he eccentric lady traveller, like the old maid and the scribbling bluestocking, took her place in society's collection of caricatures.' It was difficult enough, Foster argues, to be recognized in professional capacities, as teachers, authors and doctors; 'as travellers they encountered if not outright hostility at least patronizing ridicule.' The result becomes 'a continuing reluctance to consider female travellers on the same terms as their more "serious" counterparts'.[9] In contemporary theory and criticism, women travellers are increasingly being discussed alongside their male counterparts, but the verdicts in the *Irish Book Lover* and the *Living Age* are indicative of the traditional 'genderbased dismissal [. . .] masked as patronising admiration'.[10] This should be remembered in the subsequent discussion as it can, in part, account for some of the strategies Bunbury employs in her writing to lend credibility, authenticity and originality to her observations. By situating Bunbury within the context of travel writing rather than as marginal to the genre, I wish to illuminate issues not only applicable to her texts but to travel writing in general.

As Bunbury's titles make clear, all the journeys in focus here are through parts of Scandinavia (in addition, there is a brief excursion to Helsinki), with emphasis on Sweden. In *Evelyn*, the narrator, Bunbury herself, meets young Evelyn in Stockholm and after several complicated twists and turns they travel together from the Swedish capital, through the mid-south of Sweden via Göta Kanal, through parts of Denmark, Germany and Italy until they reach Rome. The romantic interludes, the continuing story of Evelyn, shape their itinerary. Because of the focus on Evelyn's story, the instances of pure travelogue are interspersed, interrupted and disjointed. To make matters worse, Evelyn is described as extremely secretive and her story is only revealed a bit at a time. Bunbury therefore presents herself as sometimes left with nothing but time to spare, while at other times she is forced to chronicle only briefly what she experiences and sees. As a result, *Evelyn* is a precarious balance between travelogue and romance.

The second volume of *Evelyn* ends with Bunbury lamenting the way the narrative has ended. She proposes to 'go to Sweden, and compose there a second edition of our journey from Stockholm to Rome, for I fear this one ends like a mere novel' (*E* II 396). This, however, is not what will happen. The two following texts do not deal with the European continent to any great extent, nor with Evelyn, despite the fact that she has allegedly relocated to Sweden. Rather, they deal with the year and a half the author spends in Scandinavia. Gone are the romantic events and the novel-like intrigues, and we are left with more straightforward travelogues.

Life in Sweden starts in London. From that point of departure Bunbury moves on to Ghent and Hamburg and, although her narrative is interspersed with other travellers' stories, she seems to be journeying alone. This trip enables her to visit and describe Copenhagen and other places in Denmark more closely. She also visits Norway for the first time, and a comparatively large part of the text is devoted to descriptions of Christiania (modern day Oslo) and a period of waiting for a solar eclipse. She travels by boat to Strömstad and Göteborg and then retraces her previous journey through Göta Kanal. She spends the rest of the year in Stockholm and its surroundings, giving quite detailed descriptions of customs, traditions and people. She intends to leave Stockholm for a summer tour of Sweden and finally departs in May.

In contrast to *Evelyn*, this text includes a departure from home, although it should be noted that this home is England rather than Ireland. As *Evelyn* is more of a romance, the stages denoting the journey (departure, passage, return) are largely absent. We are *in medias res*, already present in the original setting of the love story, whereas in *Life* the first phases of the journey are delineated.

The first chapter of the third text to be discussed here, *A Summer in Northern Europe*, repeats the farewells taken in the previous book. It actually starts in Stockholm at the end of winter. After this, Bunbury travels on to Åland, Åbo and Helsinki before returning to Sweden. By boat she goes to Gotland and then on to Småland, via Kalmar and Karlskrona. For the third time she includes descriptions of Lake Vättern. Volume one leaves off at the ironworks in Motala and in volume two we are abruptly back in Stockholm. Many of the characterizations and descriptions are repeated from the previous texts. After a visit to Falun, Bunbury celebrates midsummer in Leksand and then spends some time travelling around Dalarna. This is followed by a brief account of a journey north along the coast of the Gulf of Bothnia and the return journey by steamer. From Stockholm she traverses Uppland, Närke and Värmland on the way back to the west coast and the text comes to a close with her return to England.

*

Evelyn is markedly different from the other two texts and illustrates how the journey can be used as a narrative device, as a vehicle for the romance rather than a travelogue *per se*. This is not especially unusual; as early as the eighteenth century, journeys were used in a similar manner. This was also the time during which travel books gained popularity among the reading public. One result of the increased prevalence of travel texts was a feeling of anxiety in the travelling subject. Karen Lawrence has noted that '[e]ven voyages of discovery betray anxiety that someone else's marker has preceded the explorer both geographically and textually.'[11] That is, the pressure felt by the traveller to contribute something new and interesting to the reading experience is coupled with a feeling of having already been beaten to it. Although the feeling of belatedness is not particular to the eighteenth century, the problem was formulated and continuously discussed in this period.

Lawrence continues to observe that '[t]he almost desperate attempt in eighteenth century travel writing to make it new, to find a new angle from which to cast a travel book recognizes that it was getting harder and harder to be the first'.[12] One result of the quest for originality is that subjectivity and self-discovery are more strongly emphasized, that is, straightforward descriptions of people, places and customs at times give way to accounts of how the traveller him/herself is influenced and affected by the encounters.[13] In the case of *Evelyn* the subjective coming-of-age romance often supersedes the travel account.

The European Grand Tour and the beginnings of mass tourism also influenced the problem of originality with regard to nineteenth-century travel and travel writing. Travelling and reading went hand in hand. As James Buzard has noted, these two practices

> were seen to complement each other, constituting a cyclic ritual in which readers both shaped their expectations and relived their past travels through texts. It had long been true that preparatory readings–not only of travel books but of histories, poems, plays, novels–could help to establish future travellers' expectations; that travel could test those expectations; and that further reading could strengthen remembered expectations and experiences, recharging the reader's sense of having accomplished something meaningful by travelling.[14]

Although no evidence suggests that Bunbury undertook a Grand Tour in the traditional sense, she undoubtedly read much about the places she visited. She quotes Byron at length; she refers to Shakespeare, Marmier, Goethe and Hans Christian Andersen. The problem here, again, becomes one of originality. Knowledge of all the previous texts enables her to recognize and appreciate sights and experiences. However, as she intends to publish travelogues of her own, she also has to supply her own original descriptions. A multitude of references to originality, as well as her repeated truth-claims, are results of the need to claim new territory within the field of travel writing.[15] Nevertheless, it is easier for Bunbury to achieve originality when travelling through the comparatively lesser known Scandinavian countries than when confronted with the more often described, and (albeit only theoretically) well-known Rome.

Thus, *Evelyn* differs from the other texts not only in destination, but also in content. The work can be described as a romance, a tale of star-crossed lovers. Whether or not there is any truth to the events may be left to the reader's own discretion, but Bunbury repeatedly states that the events she recounts are true. 'I do not *invent* any part of my story,' she says, 'and this may be received as well as any declaration before a magistrate, for I put that great bug-bear, called the public, in his place' (*E* I 161, original emphasis).

Evelyn, however, starts with Bunbury's announcement that: 'The style is that of a record of passing occurrences; the light character of a work designed more for amusement than instruction was best preserved by maintaining that style' (*E* I iiv). This comment obviously signals the romantic nature of the text, but it is also an apology for not incorporating certain events. It is easy to see that Bunbury is aware of the potential reader's knowledge of political affairs at the time, the revolution year of 1848, and later in the text she makes only very heavily disguised remarks about current events, often expressed in footnotes. The disclaimer may further be seen as an attempt to remove claims to a certain kind of veracity. Bunbury is very careful not to include non-empirical information; all the descriptions and discussions, she claims, are based on her own observations. When she is forced to leave Copenhagen prematurely, for example, she says that: 'I have seen and known enough to make me long to see and know more: and there is no use talking about what I have neither seen nor known' (*E* I 237). She is also weary of other peoples' truth-claims. A young captain tells her a story of the Danish artist Thorvaldsen, but as she cannot find any proof of the tale's truthfulness she states that: 'I have some doubts that the naughty young captain meant me to record the tale as true, which I am careful not to do' (*L* I 71). Her own experiences provide grounds for descriptions, conclusions and opinions, and nothing less will suffice.

At times Bunbury worries about fantastic events, episodes too good to be true, and how the reader will receive them. At one point she states:

> I must leave a short blank. There are scenes and circumstances in life not sufficiently like those of a novel to be written or printed, yet which, in what is termed romance, so far surpass the incidents of a book, that the writer of them would be accused of exaggeration. (*E* II 302)

She thus consciously leaves out certain occurrences for fear of the reader's disbelief. In *Summer*, we find a similar strategy, for instance when she describes an unlikely chain of events connected to a chance meeting, and comments: '[A] circumstance occurred which I am sure will subject me to the critical charge–always to me unintelligible–of book-making, if I repeat it' (*S* II 133). Although the incident *is* recounted, the 'critical charge [. . .] of book-making' is stressed. Book-making, however, is not always a negative thing, and especially not when it is connected to the sights and experiences of travel. When she is presented with the opportunity to go to the little-known island of Dådran in Svärdsjön she remarks:

> Certainly, in an age when it is so difficult to write a book that shall possess the least claim to originality, or novelty, the discovery of untrodden ground was enough to inspire one with the idea of an attempt at the art of book-making. (*S* II 147)

The emphasis on the 'untrodden ground' is important. Bunbury repeatedly makes comparisons between the sights she sees and other renowned cities and places. The feeling communicated is that the cities and sights of Scandinavia are lesser known to the reading public than, say, Venice or Rome. When presented with an opportunity to 'claim [. . .] originality' the 'critical charge [. . .] of bookmaking' is transformed to 'an attempt at the art of bookmaking.'

Bunbury repeatedly comes back to the idea that an experience is especially worth recounting if it is original, that is, if no other traveller has attempted it or, at any rate, described it. This also applies to stories she hears, or versions of past events. For example, she says that

> There is a story, or legend, of Waldemar and his war with Wisby,
> which, although not given much to story-telling, I must relate,
> and the more willingly because I do not know that any traveller
> has yet related any legends of the Island of Gottland. (*S* I 171)

What she is saying is that she cannot make any truth-claims about the
'story, or legend'. Since she has previously stated that she is uninterested
in anything but facts, she stresses again that she is 'not given much to
story-telling', but that since this is a story unknown to the majority of her
reading public, there is a point in retelling it. The insistence on truth and
personally experienced events is ignored in favour of a hitherto unknown
(and therefore in a sense original) narrative.

The reading experiences and the theoretical preparation for the
journeys sometimes take unexpected turns. When Bunbury recounts her
experiences from Falun in *Summer*, she is clearly aware of previous texts
describing the local mines, but she is able to prove them wrong, and to
give her own original account of the events. She states that

> Any writers who have mentioned the mode of descent to this
> mine has stated it to be particularly easy; yet I have read in some
> English book the remark that Dr Clarke made it appear far more
> terrific and picturesque than it really is. The writer probably
> confused the famous traveller's account of the mine of Persberg
> with that of Falun, for Clarke says there are few sights of the kind
> that better repay the traveller [. . .] at the same time I have
> remarked that it was Dr Clarke's description of the particularly
> easy descent of the mine called Stora Kopparbergen that led me
> to attempt it. (*S* II 71–5, original emphasis.)

Bunbury's own difficult descent differs considerably from the one she has
been led to expect from the previous texts, and she concludes that there
must have been a confusion between different mines:

> The descent of this latter mine *was* easy when Clarke visited it
> fifty years ago, and continued to be easy until about two years
> previous to our visit, when an extensive run took place which
> destroyed the winding, easy flight of steps, which I had
> understood led all the way, for two hundred fathoms, down to

the bottom. My descent, therefore, was, after all, to be made almost exactly as Dr Clarke describes the terrible descent into the iron mine of Persberg. (*S* II 75)

She equates her descent into the mine Stora Kopparbergen with Clarke's account of the mine of Persberg and, although the mines differ, the experiences of fear and danger are the same. At the same time, Bunbury gets the opportunity to rectify and update information for the benefit of future travellers. Truth-claims abound in travel literature, a genre notoriously fraught with the possibilities of exaggerations and outright lies. Since potential readers of the work once it is published seldom have or will have first hand experience of the place described, assertions of this kind are continuously emphasized.[16]

The insistence on proper place names is connected to the idea of veracity, and the importance of correct spelling surfaces repeatedly. Bunbury asks: 'When will our world become sufficiently enlightened to allow countries, capitals, towns and rivers to be called everywhere as their own respective geographies name them?' (*E* I 200). A tale of warning follows, in which a party of travellers want to visit a place but are unable to find it since they do not recognize the Danish name. In this context, however, it is important to note that Bunbury herself sometimes misspells names or gets them confused.[17] The insistence on correctness, however, reveals a claim to veracity and authenticity. The Anglicized spellings belong, it is felt, in a colonial setting in which people and places are appropriated and 'used'. The use of authentic place-names marks a difference between the traveller and the tourist.[18]

The description of the boat ride to the island of Dådran, ending with Bunbury's assertion that 'the discovery of untrodden ground was enough to inspire one with the idea of an attempt at the art of book-making' (*S* II 147) can also be analysed from the perspective of originality.

> 'Should you not like,' said Friherrinan [the Baroness], with a slight look of mystery upon her countenance, 'to go to a place where no English person has ever set a foot?' I remained in thought, considering what place between sky and earth there might be found untrodden by an English foot. 'It would be something for you to have to tell that in England, and would be a great advantage if you should write a book,' she added

suggestively, 'and if you like to go I can manage it for you.' (*S* II 146)

The trip to the island turns out to be anything but comfortable, but Bunbury remarks that: 'Travelling recollections ought not, I suppose, to be all rose-coloured . . .' (*S* II, pp. 149–50). She continues:

> Finally, we arrived at the wonderful island, and I set an English foot upon it, so heavy with wet and weariness as to be insensible to the triumph over every roving Englishman–over all Englishwomen that ever had travelled. (*S* II 150)

The 'hitherto English-undiscovered island' (*S* II 150) evidently does not make a favourable impression on her but, more importantly perhaps, she remains aware of the fact that she *ought* to be triumphant. There may also be a point to the understated manner of retelling the incident: by underplaying her own achievements, the sense of originality may actually be strengthened. To be wet and weary and 'insensible to the triumph' adds to the authentic tone of the passage.

There are several similar references throughout the texts. Of Sorö, an island off the coast of Denmark, Bunbury says that: 'I had long had a fancy to go there, and why I know not; for, at the place I went to, I was told only one English lady had been seen before me' (*L* I 74). The same reason that made her eager to attempt the trip to Dådran is now seen as a reason to hesitate. She does not know why she wants to go to Sorö, since 'only one' of her countrywomen has been there before her. Perhaps that, in the end, is a major difference, although it is not explicitly stated. In the case of Dådran the island is completely 'unknown' and she can be the first; where the island of Sorö is concerned she may only be the second.

The stress on originality undergoes a curious alteration when the time comes to visit the northern parts of Sweden:

> I am here, however, reminded of one of the fatal consequences which in the present day result from a lengthened course of travel–it is that in the attempt to describe it one produces also such a lengthy MS. as a publisher would fear to make into a book in these days of light literature. For this reason I now abandon the narration of our own proceedings, and no longer taking pains

duly to record where we changed horses, or where Friherrinan [the Baroness] and myself ate, slept, enjoyed, or suffered, I shall fill my narrowing limits with general descriptions of the country we travelled, or those provinces of Northern Sweden which are yet very little known either to English travellers or English readers, and were quite as unknown to myself until my residence at Stockholm led me to visit them. (*S* II 184)

Suddenly, the length of the narrative becomes an issue, the importance of being brief overshadowing the opportunity to give original accounts. What could potentially be of the most interest, because of scant previous writings and little general knowledge of the region, is reduced to generalizations about customs, traditions, practices, history and anecdotes. The recent experiences of northern Sweden is one area where she could achieve originality and it is rather curious that she does not take the opportunity. Focus remains on Stockholm, so well known already, and the sights of Dalarna and the south.

A more familiar place to the reader is perhaps Naples, and Mount Vesuvius. The volcano presents a new challenge to Bunbury. How can she possibly make the description original and thus worthwhile for the reader? She begins by acknowledging the many stories and descriptions of the area:

They had told me Vesuvius was there, and I had heard of Vesuvius so long as a familiar thing, which millions of travellers had gone up and down in one manner or another, been pulled up, or carried up, or even walked up; and had looked into its crater, or gone down into it, and eaten eggs roasted in its ashes, and burned their sticks in its crust, and done all sorts of tricks that showed that they were on intimate terms with the monster, that Vesuvius was, in my imagination, a very common-place and hacknied thing.(*E* II 180)

Other travellers' 'intimate' knowledge is mockingly stressed. Bunbury, however, discovers something that suddenly brings originality to her description, a 'deep red spot: and while I looked, I saw it grow larger and larger, and brighter and brighter: it did not come from the crater, but from an orifice on the side of the mountain below it'(*E* II 180). She continues:

Wonderful, glorious sight! And I was permitted to enjoy it! to sit there during the soft, warm hours of an Italian night, while the flames or red light of Vesuvius was all the light I had [. . .] It is one of the happiest of my numerous accidents of travel, that I should, quite unpremeditatedly, have caught Vesuvius in a state of activity. (*E* II 181)

The Vesuvius which has been climbed by millions, the 'commonplace and hacknied thing,' is altered by this activity. It transforms the good-tempered monster into a partly inaccessible and uncontrollable beast. Bunbury goes to see the volcanic activity up close, and goes as far as to call it 'my own lava-stream, which I had nightly watched from my window' (*E* II 90–1).

In *Life* she returns to her experiences on Mount Vesuvius. The return is prompted by a visit to a waterfall in Norway. She muses:

and to think how often I had watched the burning, roaring, blazing Vesuvius,–gazing upon it through the hours of night. The cool contrast pleased my fancy. I placed the pictures side by side–the burning mountain of Italy, the foamy waterfall of Norway, and then–I went to sleep. (*L* I 136)

The comparison between the lava stream and the waterfall may seem far-fetched, and there are no further comments pertaining to her previous journey. Nevertheless, the impression left is that the instances *are* comparable. If anything, the falls seem to impress her more because they, and the spectacular view they offer, are unexpected, far from 'a commonplace and hacknied thing'.

The awareness of previous texts and descriptions that influences Bunbury's impression of Naples and Mount Vesuvius finds a counterpart in *Evelyn* when she reaches Rome. She wonders: 'What relation has the modern supplement to the original? I see it not. But in that hour to sit among the ruins of the palace of the Caesars! Yes; there the heart may muse, the brain may think; but woe be the pen that writes.' (*E* II 278–9) She seems acutely aware of the fact that there are restraints on what can be recounted. Others have already written about this place, and even though she herself has a sublime experience, it is difficult to find a new way of writing about it. '[W]oe be the pen that writes'–the acknowledgement of the danger inherent in repetition closes the chapter.

A feeling of disappointment, similar to the one she experiences in Venice is also articulated when Bunbury sees Rome for the first time:

> [W]hy is it that I ask, without the least emotion or feeling in my heart–'Is that Rome?'–I do not know, and perhaps thousands of other eager visitants, who had just attained the ultimatum of their wishes, have been as unable to account for their sensations on first seeing Rome from the Campagna. There is so little imposing in its aspect at a little distance; and our minds are in the past while our eyes at first behold only the present. (*E* II 210–1)

Past descriptions seem to take precedence and Bunbury's expectations are tempered by reality. In the case of Rome, however, the past re-enters her mind. 'Diverted from the littleness of its present, the memory of its past was stealing back upon us: even then, its ruined monuments awoke once more our banished sympathies for her, 'Lone mother of dead empires!''' (*E* II 213). The past, as it is visible or felt within the present, salvages the moment and lessens the disappointment.[19]

It is safe to assume that Bunbury's readers would be more acquainted with the Italian cities she describes than with Stockholm; more familiar, in theory at least, with Naples than with Motala. This is not to say that there are no texts preceding Bunbury's. The best-known example is probably Mary Wollstonecraft's *Letters Written During a Short Residence in Sweden, Norway and Denmark* (1796), but Sweden and the other Scandinavian countries were not part of the Grand European Tour like Venice and Rome, and the North represented the periphery in relation to the European cities.[20]

The less knowledge there is about a place, the more freedom the writer/traveller has to describe it. Rome is difficult to describe in an original way since many of the readers are already familiar with it, whereas the lesser known church in Solna, the stretch of the Göta Kanal outside Söderköping or the ruins of Vreta Kloster may be more freely described. Bunbury approaches Stockholm and Venice in very similar manners but describes her impressions in quite different ways. Her first view of Venice is slightly disappointing:

> And now, up springing with the new-born rays, up from the same ocean-bed, rise the towers, and domes, and spires of wonderful

> Venice! I saw them thus in the fresh, glittering, half-risen sun, growing up out of the sea, and seeming to grow higher and higher; and, strange effect of a sight I had longed for but never before beheld, I laughed. Cowper says he danced with joy on reading Milton when a boy; but it was not joy that made me laugh. I do not know what it was. The vision of that morning was unlike anything my fancy had ever imagined. The result was caused by the strangeness of the sensations it produced; excessive mental agony will sometimes produce a laugh. (*E* II 160–1)

She has longed to behold the sight, she has expectations raised by other accounts and these expectations are not entirely met. What causes the 'mental agony' is not clear, but even though she describes the beauty of Venice, she has reservations. The first description of Stockholm, on the other hand, is free from expectations:

> In summer there is no night here: the invisible sun has left its light when its beams are withdrawn; but when we set out for the Djurgard, those gorgeous beams were not extinguished; and Stockholm, the bright Venice of the North, viewed from the western side, flashing in reflected light from the radiancy of a sinking sun, appears to a dazzled stranger like some enchanted city of palaces, rising from the waters, and illumined by the many-coloured northern lights. (*E* I 2)

It is hard to detect any previous expectations in the description–this is what she sees, and she is content. There is no 'mental agony' here, no agony, perhaps, about producing a text about a place already described in often-read and well-known works.

Comparing Stockholm and Venice, Bunbury seems to prefer the Swedish capital: 'The romantic aspect of the surrounding rocky and woody scenery gives it a charm, which the queen, or rather the mournful widow, of the Adriatic, lacks' (*E* I 3). She returns to the image of Venice as a widow later when she states that:

> if it were not for that beautiful singularity, and for the romance-history which invests the widow of the Adriatic with a character all her own, in beauty or in grandeur, the water-approach to the

capital of the north might well compete the palm with her.(*E* I,
p. 103)

In *Summer*, the comparison between Stockholm and Venice is repeated, in
almost exactly the same words as in *Evelyn*: 'The romantic nature of the
rocky and woody scenery gives it a charm which the Bride, or rather the
mournful Widow of the Adriatic, lacks' (*S* II 6). Bunbury gives no hint
of having used the phrase before, gives no reference to the previous work.
It would be tempting to suggest that as a romance, *Evelyn* is seen as
different enough to make Bunbury expect different readers, but this
cannot be the whole explanation.

Previously, Bunbury has also named Stockholm 'the Paris of the north'
(*E* I 29) and the labels she attaches to the lesser known Scandinavian
places may, perhaps, be seen as an attempt to make the intended reader
form a better understanding of the places described, and be guided to the
correct emotion. Hence, the parallels, equations and labels may work to
communicate the 'feel' of a place.

Although parallels and equations abound, it is important to point out
the differences Bunbury emphasizes. These differences are part of the
project of originality. A preliminary sense of recognition is established
through the comparisons with the more well-known places, but Bunbury
then moves on to describe the Scandinavian location in some detail,
focusing on the differences rather than the similarities. Since the small
towns of the southern parts of Sweden are not known to the reader to the
same extent as Rome, this is where we find the artistic licence, the freedom
to report on *her* experiences, *her* impressions.

Describing her journey back through the Göta Canal in *Life*, Bunbury
displays another kind of awareness of a previous text, this time her own.
She points out that she is travelling in her own footsteps 'retrac[ing] the
curious and interesting water-journey by the canals, lakes, rivers, that lie
between the two chief towns of Sweden' and she remembers doing it
before 'four long years ago, in a sweet midsummer tide'(*L* I 223). The two
journeys, one made in the summer, one made in the autumn, blend
together, but Bunbury is very careful to acknowledge the fact that her
observations stem from two different sources, the recounted journey in
Evelyn, and the one she is undertaking and describing in *Life*.

The fact that the two journeys take place in different seasons naturally
makes the impressions markedly different. Lake Vättern, for instance,

which she remembers fondly from the midsummer journey, is changed during the autumn journey. She recalls the 'poetic, visionary, dreamy, yet most beautiful light' that originally drew her to this 'most interesting water.' She goes on

> Sweet and pleasant Wettern! says the traveller who passes it on a summer's day, or a summer's night. But I, passing over it in the storms of a northern autumn–ah! I have now quite another character to give, another temper to describe. (*L* I 232)

Again, it is possible to connect these sentiments to a notion of originality. A boat ride on Lake Vättern in an autumn storm is a trying and potentially very dangerous and frightening experience. The lake is most certainly at its best, or at least its most navigable in the summer, and this is (as it was in Bunbury's time) when most people choose to cross it. Bunbury's experiences are therefore unusual because of the change in climate and the change in the lake's 'temper.'

The first journey conducted with Evelyn is ever present in this section of the text and Bunbury even, at times, openly quotes herself (see *L* I 235). The journeys stay connected and it seems as if Bunbury wants to give the impression that she, too, is an amalgam of who she was and who she is. 'And so leaving myself asleep in the cabin on stormy Wettern, in the autumn of 1851, I return to myself just at the moment when we are passing Motala, in the bright Midsummer time, when nature was so fair to me, and all else so very dear' (*L* I 237). The arrival in Stockholm is also described with emphasis on the past:

> And thus did I land at Stockholm, so long, so very long ago! Four years ago! Let me return, let me leave the midsummer tide; I am now in the autumn of 1851. Ack! say the Swedes, when anything goes wrong; and so I say when I attempt to show the miserable reverse of my sun-illuminated picture. (*L* I 244)

*

There are opportunities for criticism in these descriptions of Scandinavian locations, to a greater extent than where better known cities are concerned. It should, however, be noted that Bunbury's careful descriptions of customs, political, religious and educational practices also give her ample opportunity to criticize England and, above all, Ireland. The safety she experiences in Sweden, for instance, is given the comment: 'Alas! I said to myself, could this have been so if English feet and English hands were more plenty here?' (*S* II 154). It is not only the lack of safety in England that is being criticized, but also the failure of keeping people employed, not succeeding in keeping the beggars off the streets, etc., (*E* I 211–12).

The subject of religion comes up repeatedly, and Bunbury, a devout Anglican, comments on several practices. In Rome, for instance, she criticizes the worship of idols but she also has opinions about the 'cold, cheerless, neglected' (*L* I 63) look of English churches abroad. This feature of English churches finds its equivalent in some churches in Sweden in which '[t]he deforming spirit of Protestantism is singularly manifest' (*L* I 306).

When visiting Ghent on her way to Sweden for the second time, she discusses and criticizes the religious practices in Ireland. This discussion gives a clearer view of Bunbury's opinions, but also of her way of voicing these:

> Most persons who wish to cut the Gordian knot by which the miseries of a part of the otherwise flourishing British dominions are inexplicably tied, ascribe to the Popery the concatenation of evils that afflict poor Ireland. But how is it, then, that two countries wherein Popery, *i.e.* the Roman faith, is dominant and uncontrolled,–I mean Belgium and Tyrol, are in conditions so very different from that of our poor little step-sister? It would be hard to find two Protestant countries where industry, perseverance and activity are more plainly seen, or better rewarded, than in these; and such qualities are precisely those in which our step-sister of the West is so lamentably deficient. Yet their religion is the same; piety characterises the Tyrolese at least as much as activity, independence, and loyalty. And here, the very aspect of the beautifully and thriftily cultivated land is so contrasted with that of Ireland, that in this country of priests one feels unable to use that master-key of Protestants, which is supposed to have been the only one capable of unlocking the box from which all evils poured forth on Ireland. Popery cannot, in

itself, be the source of these evils. It is in the Irish themselves, high and low, rich and poor, priests, parsons, and people, that the source of evil should be sought. (*L* I 11–2)

What starts as criticism of Catholicism and its institutions moves towards criticism of the country itself and its people. Belgium and Tyrol are presented as successfully industrialized, active areas, despite their Catholicism. Ireland, on the other hand, the 'poor little step-sister' is markedly different. Bunbury's conclusion that the reasons are to be found not in religion but in the people, both 'high and low', is vague but still unsettling, as she hints at unnamed deficiencies in the Irish population. The reference to Ireland as a poor uncouth relative of England can be found in various places and contexts throughout her texts. Bunbury distances herself from her country of birth and becomes, through these recurring references, rather an embodiment of the Englishwoman.

Scandinavia is, of course, also criticized from a number of perspectives. With the seasoned traveller's tone of voice Bunbury remarks that inns in both Sweden and Norway 'seem built purposely to exclude a view.' The result is 'wild, dirty, viewless place[s]' disappointing to the 'tourists in search for the beautiful and picturesque!' (*L* I 127). The landscape clearly makes up a contrast to what she perceives as beautiful.

The very landscape of Sweden is at times criticized, as in her comments about Gotland: 'There is little, if any beauty to be seen, a degree of prettiness being generally the highest epithet that can be applied to the scenery. The coast is low and the interior level, not rising more than a hundred and eighty feet above the sea' (*S* I 210–11). That is, she is denied the opportunity to look at the scenery and control it by the gaze through the very placement and construction of the inns. She goes on:

> The general want of water in rivers, brooks, streams or fountains, together with the level uniformity of the whole surface of the island, scarcely broken by an undulation, and the slovenly aspect of the fields, whose bare defences of loose stones, as is common in Sweden also, of rugged palissades of stick, remind one of parts of Ireland, but are quite unlike the green hedgerows of England–combine in depriving Gottland of much appearance of beauty or interest. (*S* I 215)

The landscape of Gotland is characterized as barren and rugged and linked to the similarly unattractive Irish countryside. Both Gotland and Ireland are then contrasted with the beauty she prefers, the beauty of England. When she mentions Ireland at all, it is often as a 'poor step-sister', as a barren, backward place. There are only a few occasions when she refers to Ireland as 'my island home' (*E* I 14).

Besides aligning herself with England, Bunbury also seems to prefer to align herself with the upper classes, claiming to have little or no understanding of the 'lower class'. '[W]hen the lower class voices are in full play, I could fancy myself listening, with as much intelligibility, to a group of Irish talking their native tongue in a market place' (*L* I 93). Giving the impression that she cannot even understand the words spoken, she clearly distances herself from the 'lower' classes. This alleged lack of understanding does not prevent her from occasionally enjoying the company of these poor uneducated groups of people, however.[21] Where different social classes are concerned she also emphasizes differences between Scandinavia on the one hand and England on the other. Near Fredrikshald she is told by some young boys a local story about Charles XII's attempt to take the fortress. She notes:

> One thing is certain, I came away impressed with the idea, that if Fredriksteen were in England, very few poor little peasant boys would tell me anything of its history, and still fewer would feel so much pride in pointing to the untaken fortress, and saying of the invader, 'he tried to take it, but he could not do it!' How much do our peasants know of our history? (*L* I 207)

Again, it is by comparisons, by seemingly innocent stories, that the lasting impression of difference is attained and through that, the opportunity of criticism. Where the arts and high culture are concerned, Bunbury considers England to be above Sweden, whereas where practical things are concerned, the Scandinavians seem to have the upper hand. The art of building houses, for example, is seen as more highly evolved among the Swedes, and during a Swedish storm Bunbury remembers 'the groaning, creaking, rattling of an English house in a storm'. She contrasts this memory with the well-built room she is in and wishes the English 'could borrow a hint from a nation that is admitted to be a country behind us in the arts, and manufacturers, and conveniences of life' (*L* II 176).

*

The intertextual references in Bunbury's books are by no means obscure; on the contrary, textual representations seem to make a more lasting impression on her than the actual sites. She says, for example:

> After all, perhaps our Shakespeare will cause Venice and her
> Rialto, Verona and her gentlemen, her Montagues and Capulets,
> to be places of note longer than any of their own monuments will
> do. Here, in this old Verona, a history of love casts into the shade
> the memory of all its other histories; so that, look into what
> Englishman's book of travels you will, be assured under the head
> of 'Verona' you will find 'Romeo and Juliet' just as under that of
> 'Venice' you will meet 'Shylock.' (*E* II 169)

The operating idea is the transitory nature of man-made structures, and the emphasis on immortality achieved by written descriptions and textual embodiments. Shakespeare may be the chief inspiration according to this paragraph, but he is by no means the only source of inspiration in Bunbury's text. In Sweden, the Danish author H. C. Andersen's own words are used when she compares the falls in Trollhättan to other exotic 'cascades'. 'None of the cascades of Switzerland, none in Italy, not even that of Terni, have in them anything so imposing as that of Trollhättan,' she says (*E* I 138). Bunbury aligns herself with the description from Andersen's *Story of a Life* and the quotation implies that she, too, is aware of the other sights mentioned.

Dickens' *Pictures from Italy* is mentioned as a source of inspiration in connection with Genoa (*E* II 173), Goethe's *Faust* is traced when she travels through Germany (*E* I 275) and Gustave de Marmier's *Lettres du Nord* is deemed untrustworthy by a fellow traveller (*E* I 191–2). The most profound inspiration, however, comes from Lord Byron, and in particular from *Childe Harold*, to which she refers repeatedly and at length. For example, she states that: 'Childe Harold is the best Cicerone in Rome; many others have said the same; but I have found him better even than my old Jacobo. I never knew his excellence until I read him *here*' (*E* II 280, emphasis added).

Seen in a more general perspective, Lord Byron's texts, especially when considering tourism in Europe during the nineteenth century, are used strikingly often as guidebooks of sorts. Buzard has noted that '[o]n the Continent, Byron's celebrated capacity to revivify the well-known tourist haunts contributed to the shaping of new social aims for leisure travel and new means of distinguishing genuine from spurious ('touristic') cultural experience'.[22] That is; the reading of Byron *in situ* was thought to deepen the experience, to result in a more profound experience. It functioned as a means to authorize the traveller and, in a sense, make clear a distinction between traveller and tourist. Being surrounded by what Byron describes also explains 'his excellence', as Bunbury's statement makes clear.

The reading of Byron was most often accompanied by more traditional guidebooks such as Murray's or Baedeker's, but the two types of texts, the literary and the information-based, fulfilled different functions. Where Baedeker's or Murray's guided the reader to the appropriate place, Byron guided her or him to the appropriate emotion.[23]

In Bunbury's texts, descriptions of places by renowned novelists and poets are indeed accompanied by quotations from more traditional guidebooks; and her knowledge of the Scandinavian countries has, on the whole, been clearly influenced by the descriptions found in texts of this kind. In *Life*, Murray's guide is quite extensively discussed and quoted, for instance in connection with a proposed visit to the Danish island of Möen, which the people of Denmark consider unusually beautiful. Bunbury continues:

> but it was not their description that made me think a trip to Möen ought not to be neglected; it was that given in a famous work called Murray's Hand-Book–a work, the descriptions of which are seldom quoted verbatim by writers of travels; so I will give you his description in his own words, to save myself trouble. (*L* I 42)

She proceeds to do so, in quite some detail. Murray's handbook is described as an object of study that all travellers should devote some time to, and she concludes that she 'always [tries] to do what Mr. Murray tells [her]' (*L* I 46). At times, of course, the expectations raised by 'Mr Murray' are not met, and then she is quick to say so. At one point she is led to believe that 'foamy billows' will 'roll at the feet' of some cliffs. Disappointed and slightly sarcastic, she notes that: 'Not a foamy billow was there. That was a decided error in the Hand-Book' (*L* I 53–4). There is a certain space in which to exert some criticism, however mild, where guidebooks are concerned. When she makes use of Lord Byron, this is not the case.

Paradoxically, Bunbury also cautions against excessive use of a guidebook. She retells an incident in the Vatican where she is admiring the Apollo Belvedere. A friend with whom she has corresponded comes to greet her, looking for 'something to see' and positions himself between her and the statue 'intently to read the whole of the lengthy description, &c. in Mr. Murray's Hand-Book, which, having finished, he raised his eyes with half-a-second's glance to the statue, and walked off with the red book "to see" something else' (*E* I 31–2). In this context, the use of a guidebook stands in the way of the real experience.

Heather Henderson has remarked that

> the value of a scene, landscape, or monument lies not so much in its own intrinsic qualities as in the pleasure of seeing for ourselves what someone else has already seen or described before us. The observer's relationship to the scene is indirect, filtered through the literary representations by which he [*sic*] first came to know it.[24]

It is evident that the travel writer making use of quotations and references may encounter several problems. A certain 'obligation to think, feel and see in a particular way'[25] may result in disappointment when the reality of the encountered scene falls short of the expectations, but it also has implications for the writing process, and for the familiar issue of originality. How is one to achieve originality while being aware of scores of previous texts? Bunbury effortlessly incorporates quotations and references into her narrative, and by doing so appears to master the previous texts. Even though she, at times, quotes quite extensively, she assumes that the reader recognizes the quotations, which implies that the reading of these texts is something normal, and that everyone, travellers as well as readers, should be aware of the European literary heritage.

The intertextuality discussed here can also be seen to apply to Bunbury's three works related to Scandinavia. There are connections, almost dialogues, between the different texts. In one text, Bunbury promises to return, and when she does, in another text, she comments on the fact that she is coming back. Two journeys made in different seasons are blended, and cause the author herself to merge with a previous persona. Phrases, descriptions and discussions are to an extent 'recycled', at times obliquely, at times openly.

*

The view of women travellers (especially during previous centuries, but to a certain extent to this day) as humorous, eccentric and impulsive rather than bold and determined needs always to be critically addressed. If this is not done, we run the risk of either trivializing or overly romanticizing texts by female travellers. Without neglecting the fact that they are encroaching on what traditionally has been seen as a male territory, women travellers need to be situated in their theoretical context and their texts discussed with emphasis on the genre rather than gender traits.

Whether or not Selina Bunbury can be said to be a great travel writer may be yet to be decided. It may even be beside the point. She is a woman travelling through and writing within a predominantly male domain and her own hesitancy towards the projects is at times considerable. The characterization of her travel writing as only 'fresh' and 'humorous' is, and has been, far too limiting and confining, suggesting as it does an unwillingness to see her travel books alongside those by her contemporary male counterparts. However, her texts negotiate issues prevalent in travel literature in general. Truth-claims, originality, intertextuality and both the factual and theoretical distance from the site of departure are all issues that illuminate both travel and travel writing in the nineteenth century.

'Factual Fictions':

Representations of the Land Agitation in Nineteenth-Century Women's Fiction

Margaret Kelleher

Writing in 1997, the critic Siobhán Kilfeather observed: 'Although the narrative of nineteenth-century fiction is often traced from Edgeworth to Somerville and Ross, I would argue that in this debate there is an exclusion of a certain kind of women's writing and a demotion of the melodramatic and sensationalist aspects of nineteenth-century fiction that in Britain were associated with an appeal to woman readers.'[1] In spite of the best efforts of the editors of the *Field Day Anthology of Irish Writing*, volumes IV and V, few signs yet exist of any significant change in this condition of exclusion.[2] In this essay, I wish to highlight another demotion, that of domestic or sentimental fiction, with specific reference to Irish women's fiction from the late nineteenth century. This body of writing is especially interesting since it sought the incorporation of contemporaneous and often highly charged political subject matter into the existing modes of sentimental fiction, a notable example being the representation of contemporary land agitation by female novelists.

Between 1881 and 1890, at least nine novels by female authors were published on the subject of the Irish 'land question', and at least six by male authors.[3] Today, the most famous of these novels is the work of an Englishman, Anthony Trollope's *The Landleaguers*, while a few other novels, chiefly George Moore's *A Drama in Muslin* and Emily Lawless's *Hurrish*, have returned to critical attention in recent years.[4] The first section of this essay deals with three much less well-known texts: Letitia McClintock's *A Boycotted Household* (1881), Elizabeth Owens Blackburne's *The Heart of Erin* (1882) and Fannie Gallaher's *Thy Name is Truth* (1884), all three of which deal with the activities of the Irish Land League, founded in 1879. Like many other novels of the period, they employ standard plots from sentimental fiction–social and economic obstacles to lovers' relationships, love triangles, etc.–but in their depiction of contemporary politics they also take on a substantial burden of representation involving political tensions, contemporary class antagon-isms and debates regarding gender roles. Yet the significance of these novels is not confined to their historical content, or documentation of contemporary events, wherein their value *is* considerable; to read them only in this manner is to ignore their literary form, their status as novels. A fuller evaluation of their importance, the subject of the second section of this essay, will therefore involve a return to long-standing debates about literature as historical source, along with a re-examination of the theoretical models offered by more recent studies of the Irish nineteenth-century novel.

*

The novel, according to Lennard Davis, is 'a factual fiction which is both factual and factitious. It is a report on the world and an invention that parodies that report.'[5] Thus it possesses both a reportorial and inventive function, roles which may be difficult to disentangle when contemporary subject-matter is deployed. Letitia McClintock's strongly anti-League novel is a good example of this: it was available to readers in England by September of 1881, exactly twelve months after the Boycott incident occurred in Lord Erne's estate, County Mayo. Set in King's County (Offaly) and County Donegal, *A Boycotted Household* details the experiences of a landlord's family from Christmas 1879 to early 1881, together with the boycotting of one of their tenants. Overall, the general argument of the novel is that 'the cry of poverty has been got up by the Home Rulers for their own ends'; the Land League, having ordered non-payment of rent, is blamed for creating 'a perfect reign of terror' and for ending the good understanding between landlord and tenants.[6] Hamilton, the central character, is, as the novel emphasizes repeatedly, an 'indulgent landlord', whose land is set below Griffith's valuation[7] and who has evicted only one tenant; the boycotted man, McPherson, is characterized as having 'the dogged resolution of his Scottish ancestors.'[8] Of particular interest is the shifting political terminology employed by McClintock, for example in the following description of conditions in County Donegal in 1880:

> The Roman Catholics, or Irish, and the Protestants, or Scotch and English, lived side by side and, when the agitators let them alone, amalgamated pretty well but by the time of the story in fermentation, the Irish read of the doings of the Land League, and rejoiced, and the settlers read and trembled.[9]

In later chapters, landlords discuss their 'grave mistake in deserting the Orange cause fifty years ago', and the novel gives much prominence to the work of the Orange Emergency Committee in aiding beleaguered landlords.

Midway through the novel, in autumn 1880, is a scene of reading in which the members of the Hamilton household read newspapers 'filled with accounts of atrocities that were making Ireland a scandal to the whole civilized world', accounts which, the narrator continues, 'brought daily consternation to the breakfast tables of Irish landlords':

> The so-called 'English garrison,' felt themselves helpless to break the meshes that were being cast round them, while unaided by England; [. . .] just rights unrecognised, they began to think themselves utterly abandoned to the enemies of their race.[10]

The novel's own role in this 'fermentation' comes to mind here, as read by 'the so-called "English garrison"' and by a contemporary reading-public in England.[11] For example, in a review published on 17 September 1881 in the influential *Athenaeum* periodical, the novel was highly praised and its author complimented as one 'who knows her subject thoroughly and is well able to communicate her knowledge.'[12] 'Her book', the review concluded, 'which–be it said in passing, is written in the landowning interest–is one of more than common merits. It is spirited, vigorous, and able from beginning to end, and should find many readers.' However 'passing', and implicitly approving, this observation on McClintock's political perspective, the *Athenaeum* reviewer was made distinctively uneasy by the combination of politics and sentimental fiction. 'There is perhaps a little too much lovemaking in *A Boycotted Household*', is the opening comment, and this is expanded later in the review: 'Certain it is that, while dealing liberally in siege and arson and murder, Mrs McClintock has not refrained from mere flirtation, and that two of her girls are mated and married ere the Land Bill passes, and the curtain falls.'

The ending of McClintock's novel offers a carefully contained agency to some lower-class female characters since the boycott ends when a number of tenants' wives come to the Hamilton house to pay their rent. Significantly, in the light of later studies of the social consequences of the land movement, these are 'the wives of small farmers in comfortable circumstances', though the narrator refers bitingly to their efforts to differentiate themselves from the wives of servants and labourers.[13] Such narrative comment is frequently unpleasant, yet, in terms of narrative focus and argument, the novel is well sustained. McClintock's cultural affiliations are more complex: she contributed a number of articles on the folklore of County Donegal to *Cornhill's Magazine*, the *Dublin University Magazine* and *University Magazine*.[14] One Donegal tale, entitled 'Jamie Freel and the Young Lady', was anthologized in the influential 1904 ten-volume anthology, *Irish Literature*, edited by Charles Welsh, Justin McCarthy and others; the biographical note records that 'the MacLintock [sic] family, of which this clever authoress is a member, is principally connected with Dundalk and other places in the County Louth.'[15] The editors were obviously unaware of the existence and tenor of *A Boycotted Household*, noting that 'Miss McClintock has so far we believe published no volume but she has written some delightful folklore.'[16]

McClintock's is not the only anti-Land League novel of the period but it is one of the most interesting, in particular because of the nearness in time of the events described.[17] Gallaher and Blackburne's novels, in contrast, are broadly sympathetic to the cause of land reform, though with frequent equivocations regarding the methods used and sometimes explicit condemnations of violent action. At the time of writing her Land League novel, Elizabeth Owens Blackburne (Casey) lived in London, where she supported herself as a journalist and novelist.[18] *The Heart of Erin*, her seventh novel, published in 1882, begins with high praise for

the few adventurous spirits, more daring than the rest, who ventured to call together the poor down-trodden, rack-rented

peasantry and to ask them calmly and dispassionately to review
their appalling condition, and to consult together and to try what
could be done for the amelioration of their lot.[19]

The programme of 'calm and dispassion', thus constructed as the frame
of interpretation for the novel, proves impossible to sustain as the story
unfolds and a direct authorial comment ultimately concedes the existence
of 'abominable practices' and 'disagreeable accompaniments' to the
campaign of reform: 'horrible murders and shocking practices such as the
mutilation of cattle which justly brought discredit upon Irish peasantry
and were sternly reprobated by the leaders of the movement.'[20]

The plot of *The Heart of Erin* involves the common 'twist' of
sentimental fiction, whereby the hero Standish Clinton, leader of his
local land reform movement and believed to be of illegitimate birth,
emerges as the legitimate heir of the anti-reform landlord. Yet
interspersed throughout the narrative are quite intricate negotiations by
Blackburne for her English audience—not unusual among Irish writings
of the period but more rare in the explicitness of their phrasing.
Violence, the novel is at pains to emphasize, is neither necessary nor
fundamental to the reform movement; the author is especially nervous
about the no-rent manifesto proclaimed in late 1881, conceding its
damage to 'good and lenient landlords' but also stressing its support by
'honest farmers' who 'in all sincerity believed by so doing they were
helping towards a state of things which would tend to reform the present
system of land tenure in Ireland.'[21] Such equivocation, however, was not
sufficient for the *Athenaeum* reviewer in May 1882 who strongly
criticized the novel. Blackburne's novels were regularly reviewed in this
periodical—an important marker of her status in the late 1870s and early
1880s—though not uncritically. The most frequent criticism was
Blackburne's use of improbable plots; in the case of *The Heart of Erin*,
however, the grounds for complaint were much more immediate: 'Miss
Blackburne in her latest book writes as a thoroughgoing partisan of the
Land League; and it is impossible to help thinking that her zeal for the
cause and obvious haste in the production of her story have to some
extent spoilt it as a work of art.'[22] Political material with a strong
contemporaneous relevance is thus opposed to aesthetic success and
Blackburne's transcription of recent public addresses by Irish
politicians—in the reviewer's words, 'pages taken up with all the common

forms of stump oratory'–is deemed particularly objectionable. Most damaging of all is the faint 'praise' delivered in conclusion: 'It is, perhaps, being thankful for small mercies, but we note with some pleasure that our author regards the murder of bailiffs as "foolish" and the incitement thereto by agitators as "unwise".'[23]

In grossly simplifying her political views, the *Athenaeum* review itself exemplified a trend judged by Blackburne as especially contributory to the current crisis, namely the blindness of the English press to Irish affairs. In chapter 10, one of the liveliest chapters in the novel, she castigates English newspapers for their misunderstanding and ignoring of Irish news, and English people for their failure to read Irish newspapers.[24] Her own three-volume novel, subtitled 'An Irish Story of Today', offers itself, in this context, as a vehicle for better understanding between England and Ireland, complete with lengthy political addresses and requests for solidarity from the English working man. In one such speech, Blackburne quotes extensively from Bishop Nulty's famous 'Essay on the Land Question' distributed in April 1880 and 'dedicated to the clergy and laity of the diocese of Meath', in which Nulty argued that 'no institution, whatever may have been its standing or its popularity, is entitled to exceptional tenderness or forbearance if it can be shown that it is intrinsically unjust or cruel'.[25] The power of rhetoric is itself a central concern in the novel: Blackburne provides some insightful analysis into the rhetorical strategies employed by Land League speakers and their appeal; she also depicts the burial of a child-victim of evictions in which the conscious politicization of this event by the League leaders is emphasized and implicitly questioned.[26]

The *Athenaeum* review was published just two weeks after the Phoenix Park murders of 6 May and thus its charge of partisanship was especially damning. *The Heart of Erin* proved to be the last new work published by Blackburne. The archives of the Royal Literary Fund, a charitable fund for the relief of impoverished authors, give some glimpses into the hardship she encountered in later years. She applied for assistance in 1887, recommended by Samuel Carter Hall, and received £40.[27] She reapplied in 1892, unsuccessfully, and the last pieces of correspondence include an enquiry on her behalf from a union infirmary in London. She died in poverty in Dublin in 1894, at the age of forty-six. The Athenaeum of 14 April 1894 provided a brief notice: 'The decease is announced of Miss Owens Blackburne, the writer of several clever novels.'[28]

The interconnection of novel writing and journalism in mid to late nineteenth-century Ireland, and among Irish writers in London, is a significant though unexplored topic, with particular relevance for female authors of the period. Many connections existed within women's professional careers, Blackburne being one example of journalist and author; also, as argued earlier, their novels frequently performed a quasi-journalistic function, drawing their content liberally from newspaper and periodical articles. In *Thy Name is Truth*, written by Fannie Gallaher and published anonymously in 1884, the world of contemporary journalism is made central to the novel, with many scenes located in the newsroom of a Dublin newspaper.[29] Gallaher's father, John Blake Gallaher, was, according to Stephen Brown, editor of the *Freeman's Journal* for twenty-six years[30] and the influence of the *Journal* appears not only in the novel's accounts of political speeches and political rallies (many of which read like journalistic treatments) but also in the author's ambivalence towards the methods employed by the Land League. Set in the period immediately preceding the passing of the 1881 Land Act, the novel abounds in contemporary detail and is a fascinating, and sometimes perplexing, document of the time. Many of Gallaher's characters are thinly disguised portraits of contemporary politicians, with brief references to O'Malley (Parnell) and Roche (Davitt); one of the novel's central characters is Tim Maguire, the MP for Bluster, clearly recognisable as Tim Healy, then MP for Wexford. In her rendering of Maguire's orations, Gallaher quotes extensively from contemporary accounts, frequently conflating details from speeches by Healy with those of Parnell; for example, Parnell's speech on the motion for the second reading of the Land Bill, May 1881, or his address to the people of Wexford, 9 October 1881.[31]

Subtitled 'A Social Novel', Gallaher's novel is a rich, and unjustly neglected, source of information regarding upper middle-class Catholic life in late nineteenth-century Dublin. It includes, for example, a fascinating chapter on Alexandra College (called Pallas in the novel) where the heroine is educated,[32] and also extensive dialogue treating of the difficulty of women's access to the writing profession. Politically, Gallaher is generally sympathetic with the motives for land reform and her novel contains a number of extended denunciations of the existing land system. The novel also, however, includes some sharp critique of the methods employed not only by the League but also by the parliamentary members. At such moments, Gallaher resorts to direct authorial comment to underline her point; conversely, the novel is at its most successful when the authorial point of view is ambiguous and the disputes between characters are allowed to stand unresolved.

Memorably unambiguous is the depiction of the Ladies Land League in Gallaher's novel–a topic which appears surprisingly rarely in women's fiction of the period. Given the detailed commentary on the topic of women's education in *Thy Name is Truth*, one might expect a favourable treatment of the women's organization; instead the characterization is sharply satirical. In an early chapter, a young journalist describes the proceedings of a Ladies Land League protest as 'consummate twaddle' and Gallaher's naming of these characters speaks volumes: the meeting is presided over by Miss 'Peckant', the company included 'Miss Whitless', treasurers 'Miss Versatile and Miss Looney' and honorary secretaries 'Miss Blab and Miss Booley.'[33] The activities of 'the ladies'–and care is taken to emphasize their 'unmarried' status–are presented on the one hand as frivolous 'palaver' but, on the other hand, as potentially dangerous in their challenging of the doctrine of separate spheres which the narrative quite explicitly seeks to reinforce.

The combination of contemporary political subjects with the standard plots of domestic fiction–which, for the *Athenaeum* reviewer, was a fault in both McClintock's and Blackburne's novels–is particularly uneasy in Gallaher's novel. As in all of these works, the burden of resolution is most to be felt in the novel's closing chapters, and is evidenced by plot developments that increasingly strain, and ultimately defy, credulity. Gallaher's plot is one of the most sensationalist of all of these 'land novels', markedly so given the attention to realistic detail earlier in the novel. The landlord's assassination, which ends the first volume of the novel, leads to the wrongful accusation of a tenant and also to the revelation of the heroine's illegitimacy, as the daughter of a peasant woman seduced by that landlord's father; to complicate the plot further, her mother's father is the assassin of the son of the seducer, i.e. her grandfather is responsible for the death of her half-brother. The conclusion of the narrative brings the familiar revelation that she is the legitimate heir of the estate; and the novel ends with her plans as landowner, under the tutelage of her adopted father, 'to make all of her tenants so happy and comfortable by means of peasant proprietorship, or of fixity of tenure, fair rents and free sale, that it would never enter into their heads to look on the land question as unsettled.'[34] This 'happy ending' is partly undercut, however, by the character's inability to distinguish between these two very different options, of peasant ownership or the more limited option of reform,[35] and perhaps also by the author's own equivocation on the preferred outcome to the 'land question'.

Gallaher's fiction shares a number of similarities in plot with Mulholland's better known *Marcella Grace*.[36] Evident in these novels and others is a recurring female character, heroine-turned-landowner, who possesses both peasant and upper-class ancestry and through whose fate contemporary class and gender anxieties gain an imagined reconciliation.[37] As James Murphy has shown, the narrative of *Marcella Grace* is saturated with class and religious issues: Marcella, the daughter of a weaver and of an upper-class woman, feels the instincts of her upper-class mother when poor, but when she emerges as the heiress of a landed estate, her common blood with the poor renders her the ideal landlord.[38] *Marcella Grace* thus operates very much as fantasy–the fantasy of an ideal union; unlike earlier nineteenth-century narratives, however, where the imagined union is of Englishman and Irishwoman, Mulholland's reconciliation occurs largely within the female character and in the disparate classes which she embodies. In both novels, this union within the individual character is then reinforced by marriage, a marriage that also serves to restrain some of the more radical implications of the heroine's identity: in *Marcella Grace* marriage to a reformed Fenian member, now reformist landlord; in Gallaher's novel to 'Boy', a journalist, who is opposed to Maguire (Healy) throughout the novel and who voices the novel's strongest denunciations of the 'agitators [. . .] ruining our country'.[39] Lower-class tenants' ambitions for land ownership are slyly derided by Gallaher and Mulholland: that the tenants of Marcella Grace should misname the contemporary campaign as one for 'pisant propriety' is a particularly revealing example.

If the ideal of the realist novel is a resolution in which 'individual and society are reconciled', the particular conditions of nineteenth-century Ireland, as the critic David Lloyd has argued, 'preclude the projections of such reconciliations [in nineteenth-century Irish fiction] from carrying any sense of verisimilitude, of "probability".'[40] The strained and improbable novel endings discussed above are clear examples of this, from a rarely discussed category of nineteenth-century Irish fiction, that of Irish domestic fiction. Similarly the negative views accorded to McClintock and Blackburne by contemporary English reviewers may be seen as part of a more general trend in the reception of nineteenth-century Irish fiction, one which Lloyd extends to the role played by culture in a 'colonial sphere':

> Hence the frequent appearance of vulgarity, of non-aesthetic concerns and heterogeneity of form and matter, that aesthetic judgement traces in colonial artworks. Their contents are too explicitly charged with social designs and their narratives too directed at the stimulation of immediate and powerful sensation to achieve the equilibrium and 'disinterest' of the aesthetic work.[41]

And yet in studies of the nineteenth-century Irish novel and its deviations from realist norms, domestic or sentimental fiction remains largely ignored, for reasons to be explored below.

*

The significance of novels with political and social content has been recognized by some Irish historians in recent years, as part of a fuller consideration of literary source-material from the nineteenth century. The specific value of literature as historical source has, however, not yet received the theoretical consideration it deserves, and questions concerning the distinctive character and function of literary genres are generally elided by historians. A notable exception is the collection of essays *Writer as Witness*, edited by Tom Dunne and published in 1987, which continues to be one of the most useful discussions of the topic.[42] In this collection, however, and as early as its title, an emphasis on literature's mimetic function dominates: the writer as witness, or literature as testimony, holding 'a mirror up' to its times. One of its most suggestive analyses of the interrelationship of literature and history is Oliver MacDonagh's contribution to the collection, a reading of Jane Austen's 'Regency novel', *Sanditon*.[43] MacDonagh outlines three elements to the novel's significance for historians of the Regency period: firstly, the novel 'vivifies, personalizes and renders concrete what the historian already holds'; secondly, 'this very particularization suggests fresh ranges of historical investigation, *precisely* because it is so firmly located in the very day of its composition'; and thirdly, the novel may 'refine' such periodization–'our piece of historical shorthand, the phrase, Regency period, is enriched and sensibly enlarged.'[44] All three of these elements may be applied to the Land League fiction discussed above, novels which were composed contemporaneously with the events narrated and whose social detail gives considerable life to the historical record. It is worth emphasizing, however, that even within MacDonagh's model, the dynamism that is envisaged–the process of change and of refinement–operates much more within the historian's activity and much less within the literary text.

Most Irish historians have yet to absorb some of the more productive models of the literary text that have been provided in recent years by cultural critics; in the case of the novel, for example, to return to Lennard Davis's terms, its 'inventive' as well as its 'reportorial' function. Between 1993 and 1995, studies of the Irish nineteenth-century novel by David Lloyd and Terry Eagleton appeared and quickly became landmark works in the field; contributions by others since then have tended to locate themselves as extensions of or in opposition to Lloyd and Eagleton's work. Eagleton's discussion of 'form and ideology in the Anglo-Irish novel', chapter 5 of his 1995 work *Heathcliff and the Great Hunger*, is well on its way to becoming itself canonical; here he argues that the realistic novel is the form '*par excellence* of settlement and stability, gathering individual lives into an integrated whole' and, since 'social conditions in Ireland hardly lent themselves to any such sanguine reconciliation', we may understand why the '*realist* novel thrived less robustly in Ireland than in Britain.'[45] As Eagleton emphasizes in a recent riposte to his critics, the difference of the Irish novel is not to be viewed as a failure on its part and he reiterates his argument that '[o]n the contrary, it is in its refusal to conform to that paradigm, or its apparent unconsciousness of it, that much of its fascination lies'.[46] But the sense lingers of Irish nineteenth-century literature being defined chiefly by 'inadequacy', and, at its best, offering a proto-modernist potential fully realized only at the century's end. Eagleton's definition of the realistic novel is also curiously Arnoldian in its criteria and sets up an ideal of 'disinterested representation' against which all examples, even English ones, must inevitably fall short.[47] More persuasive is Lloyd's model, constructed two years before: since the novel arises 'most frequently as the chosen mode of precisely those social groups who are registering those transformations most articulately', it is possible to argue that 'social instability is itself a *condition* of the novel in demanding access for those voices and narratives that had previously been unrepresented'.[48]

In a later work, *Crazy John and the Bishop*, Eagleton commendably locates himself against 'two kinds of narrowness in contemporary Irish cultural studies': the first, a question of subject, or 'Great Man bias'; the second kind of narrowness 'one of approach.'[49] Yet while he has made some very important recoveries of unfamiliar texts, the touchstones that he continues to employ from the history of the Irish novel are very much 'the usual suspects'. The existence of a large genre of domestic fiction within the Irish tradition, for example, is totally ignored by both Lloyd and Eagleton. In *Anomalous States*, Lloyd rightly criticizes earlier narrative theorists for overemphasizing the subversive character of the novel; yet this is a tendency from which his own work is not exempt.[50] His work on minor literature, while invaluable for many reasons, also privileges texts which may be seen as 'oppositional', in readily recognizable political and aesthetic terms.[51] Works of domestic and sentimental fiction do not easily fit such categories, and appear to embarrass some critics. A consideration of their function and significance within the tradition of the Irish novel is long overdue.

Studies of English domestic fiction, taking their cue from Nancy Armstrong's influential *Desire and Domestic Fiction*, tend to emphasize the genre's downplaying of political and social identity in favour of individualized and gendered desire. As Armstrong states, '[f]rom the beginning, domestic fiction sought to disentangle sexual relations from the language of politics and, in so doing, to introduce a new form of political power'.[52] In contrast to 'fiction which represented identity in terms of region, sect or faction', domestic fiction 'unfolded the operations of human desire as if they were independent of political history,'[53] thus seeking to subordinate political and social differences to those rooted in gender. The privatizing tendency of sentimental fiction has also been investigated in American studies as a particular form of 'liberal political *subjection*'. In Lori Merish's words,

> Sentimental sympathy prescribed forms of paternalism–specifically of 'benevolent' caretaking and 'willing' dependency–suited to a liberal-capitalist social order that privileged individual autonomy and especially private property ownership [. . .] thus reinventing political hierarchy as psychological norms reproduced within the intimate recesses of the desiring subject.[54]

The Irish novels discussed above, most obviously in their endings, ultimately support a social order where individual autonomy is expressed as private property ownership: the hero or heroine's marriage thus serves to resolve anxieties concerning legal inheritance and also to facilitate a transfer of power. The belated legitimation of heirs is the most frequent device used, ostensibly in order to settle class tensions, but these resolutions come after quite lengthy flirtations on the novelists' part with characters 'tainted' by illegitimacy and violence. In her insightful study of the fiction of Irish-American novelist Mary Ann Sadlier, Marjorie Howes has shown how Sadlier employed the genre of didactic sentimental fiction that was 'most popular in her day [. . .] and found herself rejecting or revising some of its most distinctive literary and ideological features.'[55] The novels in question here have much less right to the title of 'revisions' but they do illustrate the instabilities of Irish domestic fiction whereby the inclusion of contemporary social and political content renders the genre's typical privatizing and depoliticizing impulses difficult to accomplish. It cannot have been lost on the readers of these novels that the transfer of land ownership, once countenanced, could occur again and, in class terms, elsewhere.

A more comprehensive analysis of the significance of Irish domestic fiction–what Gallaher suggestively terms 'the social novel'–together with a less defensive evaluation of the Irish nineteenth-century novel more generally, will require greater attention to the audiences of these texts. The notion of 'the audience' remains undeveloped within Irish studies generally, not only because of the scarce attention paid to the reception-history of literary texts but also because of the inadequacy of the conceptual models currently employed.[56] Much more productive work has emerged from American cultural studies. Richard Brodhead, in his study of nineteenth-century American fiction, has for example illustrated the extent to which 'literary production is bound up with a distinct social audience'; '*in* its production', he argues, a text 'addresses and helps call together some particular social grouping'.[57] Thus the literary text, or group of texts, not only reflects the interests and preoccupations of an existing audience but, through its articulation of such interests, produces and determines this audience. Such a process might be traced in the reception of the domestic or sentimental fiction written by Blackburne and her contemporaries, and the part played by these novels in shaping an English middle-class readership with interest and interests in the fate of the Irish 'land question'. The issue of what constitutes an 'Irish novel' thus becomes a much more open and interesting question. To what extent were authors and audiences, familiar with the conventions of sentimental fiction, aware of a difference between Irish novels and their English counterparts? More generally, do the conventions of the domestic fiction genre cross 'Irish' and 'English' divides, as employed by authors and as deciphered by readers?

Such work will involve a considerable refocusing of current critical 'taste' and priorities. In a recent essay, David Lloyd has commented on the 'gravitational force of realism as the generic centre of canonical judgements about the novel as form' and concludes: 'For all that we can argue theoretically the generic interest of the sentimental novel and its sexual and political potentialities, the suspicion remains that we want an Irish *Middlemarch*, not an Irish *Uncle Tom's Cabin*, and that this realist desire continues to organize critical reflection.'[58] Existing critical reflection will continue unchallenged and unchallengeable, however, as long as it continues to organize itself around the predictable selection of texts and justifies this partiality on the grounds of a putatively shared 'desire'. As for Irish domestic and sentimental fiction, the theoretical argument is only beginning.[59]

Hybridization as a Literary and Social Strategy:

Mrs Hungerford's Molly Bawn

Elisabeth Wennö

Although the name 'Molly Bawn' might ring a bell for many people as the title and subject of different versions of an Irish folk song, there is reason to believe that few, in recent years at least, have come across the novel *Molly Bawn* by Mrs Hungerford (1855–97), published in 1878. Mrs Hungerford (Margaret Wolfe Hungerford, or Margaret Argles) wrote more than forty novels, most of them published anonymously, or under the pseudonym 'The Duchess'.[1] Since neither the category of women's romantic fiction nor the quantity produced has been noticeably favoured in literary criticism, it is not surprising that there are few signs of her works in the literature, despite the fact that they seem to have been noted at the time. Several of her novels were translated and published in other countries, for instance, and *Molly Bawn* was filmed in 1916. Stephen J. Brown reports in 1919 that her novels 'had a great vogue in their day'.[2] The two male signatures in this writer's copy of the book, dated in April and June 1923,[3] also suggest that it was read *beyond* its 'day', and so does the number of reissues in, for instance, Sweden (1879, 1906, 1913, 1919). In the US it was reissued no less than sixteen times between 1878 and 1920.

A contemporary assessment of *Molly Bawn* in the *Spectator* goes a long way towards explaining the critical marginalization:

> There is no guile in the novels of the author of *Molly Bawn*, nor any consistency, nor any analysis of character; but they exhibit a

faculty truly remarkable for reproducing the vapid small-talk, the shallow but harmless 'chaff' of certain *strata* of modern fashionable society.[4]

Accused of being devoid of narrative surprise, sustained vision, and psychological depth, Mrs Hungerford's novels are thus effectually rendered as 'harmless' and 'shallow' as the 'vapid small-talk' and 'chaff' that they are said to reproduce so remarkably well. It is this kind of critical discourse, of course, that adds fuel to the persistent feminist claim that books by women are treated like women. In Ernest Baker's *A Guide to the Best Fiction in English* (1913), there is a short description of the story-line of *Molly Bawn* along with an evaluative summing-up, which strikes an equally trivializing note, making us wonder why it was thought to deserve inclusion in a book on 'the Best Fiction in English':

> A love-tale of a tender, frivolous, and petulant Irish girl, who flirts and arouses her lover's jealousy, and offends against the conventions in all innocence. A gay and witty story, spiced with slang and touched with pathos.[5]

Although included in the *Guide*, this description does not do justice to the novel's comic and social vision. The effect is rather that *Molly Bawn* suffers the same fate 'of being dismissed as shallow, unconvincing and laden with stereotypes, or at best, tolerated as harmless gas' that Ferdia Mac Anna suggests is the result when 'a writer's particular brand of comedy fails to impress a reviewer'.[6]

It is not my intention, however, to argue that *Molly Bawn* deserves a place in the English-speaking canon because it rates among the 'best' for some reason. What I will show is that it deserves attention and a place in history because the alleged lack of guile, consistency and character analysis is not a literary flaw, but a significant literary strategy, necessitated by the juxtaposition of comic emplotment and romantic discourse for humorous, ironic and, ultimately, ethical effects, which are designed to reinstate the precedence of social bonds over individual needs.

In the introduction to *The Comic Tradition in Irish Women Writers* (1996), Theresa O'Connor deplores the fact that Vivien Mercier's 'groundbreaking' work, *The Irish Comic Tradition* (1962), more or less excludes women writers.[7] She claims that at least nine women writers have played a role in the shaping of the Irish comic tradition, arguing that these writers, although different, share a double-voiced and bifocal interpretative impulse with 'a focus on boundaries and a hybridizing vision that engages in witty negotiations with established patriarchal, colonial and nationalist orthodoxies'.[8] The double-generic character of *Molly Bawn* suggests that, to this list of nine writers, a tenth, Mrs Hungerford, could be added, because *Molly Bawn* is a novel engaged in the kind of 'ethical dialogue' that O'Connor claims is the result of the hybridizing vision, or the vision of double perspective, common to Irish women writers.[9]

As if to signal a bifocal and double-voiced vision, the concept of hybridization is employed as a witticism in the text itself. A lawyer, Mr Buscarlet, who has 'a passion for the aristocracy' is virtually reduced to tears when his comment about Lady Elizabeth as 'decidedly high-bred' is intentionally misread as a joke:

> 'Hybrid!' exclaims Sir Penthony, purposely misunderstanding the word. 'Oh! By Jove I didn't think you so severe. You allude, of course, to her ladyship's mother, who, if report speaks truly, was a good cook spoiled by matrimony. 'Hybrid!' Give you my word, Buscarlet, I didn't believe you capable of anything half so clever . . . .' (p. 218)

Attention is not only drawn to the ironic potential of the concept of hybrid, which, as Monika Fludernik points out has negative connotations applying to 'all types of interracial subjects' in standard nineteenth-century usage,[10] but also to a particular comic tradition. Sir Penthony is here revealed as one of several Restoration comedy-inspired 'Truewits' in this novel. The ironic direction is clear in the underlying analogy between the impurity of interracial subjects and intersocial subjects: social climbing through marriage is ridiculed by the allusion to the neither/nor status of a hybrid–no longer a good cook, nor quite a lady–and so is anybody who sees only one aspect of the hybrid, that is, title, but not the aspect of loss implied, nor the relativity and social constructedness of the term high-bred. (Incidentally, on a similar note of intersocial impurity, one of Mrs Hungerford's novels is entitled *Nor Wife Nor Maid* [1892].) The many literary quotations and allusions in *Molly Bawn* also suggest a playful awareness of the neither/nor situation of its own generic status: it seems to suggest that it is as impossible to have complete faith in the illusion of romance as it is to write social comedy without it. As we shall see, however, the novel attempts to transcend generic, social and national oppositions by erasing the hybrid hyphenations that Bhabha sees as emphasizing the 'incommensurable elements [. . .] as the basis of cultural identification',[11] thus shifting the balance from the negatively defined neither/nor pole to the positively termed both/and.

Molly, or more properly, Eleanor Massareene, is herself a hybrid: "low-bred Irish"/"high-bred English", a cross between nature and culture in temperament and accomplishments, neither a "nobody", nor a "somebody". The neither/nor status of the heroine is clearly expressed in the different identities that she assumes, or is ascribed. As a country girl she is romantically mythologized as 'Molly Bawn'; as a woman of accomplishment on the stage she is aesthetically mythologized as 'Miss Wynter.' Both personae belong to a world of the ideal, in conflict with social reality. The sublime, public "somebody", yet anonymous, 'Miss Wynter' is opposed to 'Eleanor Massareene', the *un*acknowledged "somebody", socially and privately. Similarly, the divine, and therefore non-human, 'Molly Bawn' is opposed to "the-nobody-socially", yet very human, Molly Massareene. Combined, 'Miss Wynter' and 'Molly Bawn' represent the ideals of male desire which are in conflict with the socially defined identities of 'Molly Massareene' and 'Eleanor Massareene'. The story proper revolves round the negotiation of these conflicting female identities, reaching a resolution in the subjective rejection of the idealized versions ('don't call me Angel'), in favour of an ironically idealized vision of social reality ('call me wife'), which emphasizes a domestic and a functional aspect of female social identity. The opposition between Miss Wynter and Eleanor is resolved in materialist terms as the need to earn money is eliminated through the affirmation of matrilineal succession.

Consistent with her hybrid status, Molly is also a Truewit, capable of double perspective, or metaphorical vision, to use the corresponding rhetorical term. When Molly's non-aristocratic but Truewit step-brother announces that 'this is the day for which we have accepted Lady Barton's invitation to go to the Castle to meet Lord and Lady Rossmere,' the potential grandiosity of the announcement is immediately deflated by Molly, who 'naughtily interrupts saying: "This is the cat that killed the rat, that did something or other in the house that Jack built . . ." ' (p. 19). The reference is to a previous visit when she ('the cat') apparently 'flirted so outrageously with the Lordship' that he ('the rat') was rendered 'imbecile' (p. 20). 'Dethroning the pompous' is, as Mac Anna points out, 'as ingrained in Irish writing as the delight in satire, parody and the grotesque'.[12] Unlike Buscarlet, Molly has no reverence for traditional titled hegemony as such, especially not when it is represented by 'old fogies,' such as Lord Rossmere, who, in particular, she thinks, deserves a place in the British Museum as 'an example of remarkable species of his kind' (p. 20). The target of attack is the triad male–hegemony–British. Rachel Jane Lynch argues that Regina Barreca's theory that the purpose of 'women's often hostile humour is to resist, even dismantle, hegemonic and male-dominated power structures through laughter', goes well with the Irish comic tradition.[13] The power of laughter is strongly felt in the novel, and is not restricted to the dismantling of power structures, but has a constructive function by frequently being employed as a means of resolving conflicts and restructuring relationships.

The novel is not only reminiscent of Restoration comedy in the conception of Truewits and Witwoulds (Mr Buscarlet and Mr Potts, for instance); there are also other typical ingredients, such as hiding behind curtains, secret letters, deceptive behaviour, mercenary motives, adultery and secret identities. In terms of the hybrid character of the novel, these are ingredients borrowed from comedy in the traditional sense of staged domestic comedy, or comedy of manners, or comedy of errors, to which there is also a reference in the text (p. 147). The following description by Pat Gill of the 'typical Restoration comic heroine', taking Millamant in *The Way of the World* as her example, could also serve as an accurate portrayal of Molly:

> [. . .] a heroine who possesses the contrary attributes of being knowledgeable without being in the know. Millamant is lovely, witty, charming, self-confident, cannily playful, and, miraculously, innocent as well. She indulges all her whims and fancies, changes her mind whenever she pleases and without notice, and performs everything in her power to keep herself a mystery, a beguiling uncertainty, to men.[14]

The employment of comic devices or stereotypes is not, however, the main point in my argument but rather, as I will show, the way comedy as a mood and mode of emplotment, in Northrop Frye's definition,[15] interacts with and comments on the elements of romance. For, as Baker described the novel, *Molly Bawn* is not only a 'gay and witty story,' it is also a 'love tale'. As such, it is informed by the prose romance and its cognates romantic fiction, and romantic songs, but only for the strategic purpose of reinforcing the comic vision. As I will show, the result of the cross between the comic and romantic traditions is a dismantling of romantic notions of individual fulfilment in a social universe (transcendence) in favour of a rational view of the processes by which social integration is achieved. The rational view is in turn undercut by the ironic twists of events that make social integration possible.

The story proceeds along the predictable lines of romantic fiction. Molly is an orphaned and penniless country girl of Irish-English extraction, living with her step-brother, John Massareene, and his family. The family is visited by a lieutenant of modest means, Tedcastle George Luttrell ('he is evidently proud of his name' [p. 5]), who instantly falls in love with Molly. The love story moves forward through his infatuation with the reluctant-to-marry Molly, through conflicts due to his jealousy, and complications due to major changes in Molly's life (the deaths of brother and grandfather), to the final union. The composition is cyclical and seasonal in the double sense of being set in different seasons and changing its mode of emplotment in the process. Beginning in early summer with the meeting of the lovers in the harmonious surrounding of the country idyll Brooklyn (Romance), the story progresses through the autumn spent at the ancestral Herst Royal with its intrigues and superficial social life (Tragedy), through the winter in anonymous London and the separation of the lovers (Irony), to spring which brings about the retrieval of Brooklyn, lost through John's sudden death in the autumn, as well as the restoration and rejuvenation of Herst Royal as a family ideal (Comedy).

In terms of character, the novel is structured on a dialectical subject/object relationship, in which Molly, on the one hand, is the object of the yearning lover Tedcastle's subjective romantic desire, and on the other, the subject of the comic emplotment in pursuit of a definable place in society. This double perspective of male desire for transcendence through love, and female desire for social identity based on subjectivity, independence and free will is evoked in the discrepancy between the romantic rhetoric, by which she is objectified and romanticized, and the mode and discourse of comedy, by which she is de-romantized and subjectivized.

Tedcastle, as the romantic hero, is in turn feminized and dethroned. He is as 'strangely passive' as Susan Staves suggests is characteristic of the Restoration hero.[16] He is, as Molly points out, fair-haired instead of dark, which would be more in line with nineteenth-century romantic heroes. Although he is aligned with the masculine world by being a soldier, he has no sword, to the disappointment of the children, and he has never killed anyone. His army life abroad is described in terms of trivial pursuits. In addition, he lacks the fitness to follow Molly's pace up a hill. Uncharacteristically for a male hero, he is loved by all children, and to complete the feminization of the hero we are made to witness his descent, in pursuit of Molly, into the female domain of the kitchen, where he is, to the cook's horror, covered in this novel's absolute feminine colour of 'white,' in the form of the female attribute 'flour.' Like Molly, he is a hybrid: male in gender, but non-masculine in genre. His only masculine attributes are 'a long nose' and a cigar, which is an obvious fetish since he always smokes one in Molly's absence, or resorts to one when feeling rejected. The particular feature of 'nose' is, in fact, a "prominent" feature in the novel (cf. the Anglo-Irish author Sterne's *Tristram Shandy*). A 'long nose' is clearly a sign with sexual and/or phallic connotations. In connection with Tedcastle, they are decidedly sexual, emphasizing biological maleness rather than cultural masculinity, or the phallus as symbolic plenitude and power. When Tedcastle is longing for a cold bath, as we may surmise, to cool his passion, Molly finds amusement in wondering if 'when you were a baby, your nose–in proportion, of course–was as lengthy and solemn as it is now' (p. 36). The phallic, on the other hand, is evoked in the 'singularly long' but extremely 'thin' and 'beak-shaped' nose of Mr Amherst, the 'altogether unlovely' (p. 107) owner of Herst Royal and Molly's grandfather. He lacks the vitality and potency of maleness ('thin' and 'beak-shaped'), but reigns supreme by virtue of his (phallic) patriarchal position and the power of money ('singularly long'). To the description of Mr Amherst's nose is added the parenthetical caution that 'as a rule one should always avoid a person with a long nose' (p. 106), which, in the context and in the tradition of the Irish comic impulse, stands out as a humorous comment on women's double subjection to the penetration of the penis and the oppression of the phallus.

If the de-romanticizing of the romantic hero has an aura of pathos and is designed to make him a fit hero of the comic domestic and matrilineal resolution, the de-romanticizing of the heroine serves humanizing purposes since Molly is certainly *seen* in romantic terms but does not perceive herself in those terms. As early as on the title page, where the first two lines of Samuel Lover's (1797–1868) song 'Molly Bawn,' are quoted, Molly is evoked as the desired and unobtainable object:

> Oh! Molly Bawn, why leave me pining
> All lonely waiting here for you?
> While the stars above are brightly shining,
> Because they've nothing else to do?
> O Molly Bawn! Molly Bawn!
> The flowers late were open keeping,
> To try a rival blush with you;
> But their Mother, Nature set them sleeping,
> With their rosy face washed in dew.
> O Molly Bawn! Molly Bawn!
> The village watchdog here is snarling;
> He takes me for a thief, you see;
> For he knows I'd steal you, Molly darling,
> And then transported I should be!
> O Molly Bawn! Molly Bawn! (p. 25)

Although she claims this song as her own because her beloved step-brother called her Molly Bawn (i.e. 'Fair Molly') when she was a child and despite singing it twice during the novel, she finds it an 'odd old song' (p. 26), as if unable to relate to its meaning. The reader does not suffer the same difficulty since Molly's unparalleled beauty and unique charms are emphasized whenever she appears. The romantic rhetoric defines her in terms of the supernatural, such as Siren, Goddess, Angel, Fairy, and Spirit, or in terms of the ideal, such as a 'perfect creature', 'a thing of beauty' (p. 33), 'fairer than any flower' (p. 33), or simply as Beauty (p. 13) personified. In contrast, her reaction to Tedcastle's mute gaze when they first meet is a firm assertion of the tangible non-ideal, and yet it is double-voiced since it echoes and ironically inverts another scene of fictional romance, that is, the reunion of the blind Rochester and Jane at the end of *Jane Eyre*: '"I'm not a fairy, nor a spirit, nor yet a vision," murmurs Molly, now openly amused. "Have no fear. See," holding out to him a slim cool hand, "touch me, and be convinced. I am only Molly Massereene"'

(p. 12). In the story the 'village watchdog' of the song above comes in the shape of John's children, who ask Tedcastle if he plans to 'steal Molly' from them, while the situation proper is that 'independent Molly' (p. 94), 'at heart a rebel' (p. 74) is not up for either sale or theft. The situation is an ironic reversal of Lord Byron's observation that '[m]an's love is of man's life a thing apart;/'Tis a woman's whole existence'. While Tedcastle proclaims that Molly is his whole life, Molly seems more interested in the *game* of love: '"I can endure a little of it [love] now and again," says Molly, with *intense seriousness* [my emphasis], "but to be made love to always, every day, would *kill* me"' (p. 60). The pursuit of marriage, which is central in romantic fiction, is a male rather than a female concern in this novel, where women, lacking economic control, instead exercise manipulative control over victimized, infatuated and heartbroken men with unmistakable Irish glee and mischief.

Far from being 'transported,' then, Tedcastle suffers constant agony, (the stage of *Inferno* of Romance) thrown between certainty and uncertainty, and accuses Molly of having stolen the best of him, his heart (p. 35). He is enthralled, intoxicated, fervent, 'tempted by her beauty' (p. 57), 'lover and slave' (p. 53) and 'consumed by love' (p. 54). The many references to stereotypical romance elements, such as 'haunted chamber' (p. 18), 'enchanted place' (p. 26), 'witchery' (p. 35) adventure, ghosts, romantic night, 'raven's croaking' (p. 70), Faeries Glen (p. 70) and moonlight, serve parodic functions, thus rejecting the ideology of romance, the Gothic version in particular. The 'visitation,' for instance, which is how Tedcastle interprets a nightly tapping on his window, is quickly revealed by Molly to be a magpie: 'Oh, what a tame ending to your romance! Your beautiful ghost come to visit you from unknown regions, clad in white and rustling garments, has resolved itself into a lame bird, rather poverty-stricken in the matter of feathers' (p. 18). The romantic discourse is always present, but undermined, through comedy and humour, as irrational and illusory discourse. When Tedcastle, for instance, asks how he should 'keep from dreaming' about her, she answers:

'Don't keep from it,' says she sweetly; 'go on dreaming about me as much as ever you like. I don't mind.'
'But I might,' says Luttrell, 'when it was too late.'
'True,' murmurs Molly innocently, 'so you might. John says all dreams arise from indigestion!' (p. 19)

The presence of deflating romantic irony prevents any serious attempt to read the novel as romantic fiction. Another kind of ironic reversal is the reference to a different version of a 'Molly Bawn' song than the one (i.e. Samuel Lover's version above) 'claimed' by Molly in the novel. This song, of which there are eighty-eight variants, tells the tragic story of how Molly, huddling in the rain, wrapped in her white apron, is accidentally shot by her lover, who mistakes her for a swan, which, according to Jennifer Connor, represents a 'rare find' since swans in Ireland are generally grey, not white.[17] There is a subtle point made here about the 'killing' effect of romantic idealization of women. That Mrs Hungerford was familiar with the song is beyond doubt. Not only has Jennifer Connor convincingly shown that the song originates from Ireland in the seventeenth century and that it was printed in a chapbook around 1820 in Galway,[18] but it also occurs as a motif in the novel. As Tedcastle is approaching a lake, shouldering a gun, he hears a voice singing:

> There was a little man,
> and he had a little gun,
> And his bullets they were made of lead, lead, lead;
> He went to a brook,
> And he saw a little———

'Oh, Mr Luttrell, please, please don't shoot *me*,' cries Molly, breaking down in the song with an exaggerated show of feigned terror.

'Do *you* call yourself a 'duck'?' demands Luttrell with much scorn. 'Is there any limit to a woman's conceit? Duck indeed! say rather———'

'Swan? Well, yes, I will, if you wish it: I don't mind,' says Molly amiably. 'And now tell me, are you not surprised to see me here?' (p. 42)

Allusions to the traditional 'Molly Bawn' song also occur later in the novel where Molly is likened to a 'white, white swan' and we are told that her neck and arms are so white that they can be compared to 'the dribbling snow' (p. 260), echoing the line 'like a mountain of snow' in the song. Like the Molly of the song, she also later appears as a 'ghost' with a message of forgiveness. While Molly, then, 'is game' in a double sense, prepared 'to be game' and prepared 'to play the game', letting her lover 'go on dreaming' about her and seeing her as a swan if he so wishes, the intertextual dimension reminds us of the potential threat of confusing appearance with the actual, and of the tragic irony that is the result of desiring the idealized object rather than the human subject. The reader is also implicitly invited to adopt a double perspective in the reading, to take part in the romantic illusion if we so desire, but also to consider the possibility of relevancy in the light-hearted appearance of the novel.

A further step in this direction is provided by Connor, who also draws attention to a folklore motif with its foundation in Irish mythology: the taboo of killing a swan.

> It might be suggested that 'Molly Bawn' reflects this ancient taboo; the ballad might also portray a personal *geis*, or taboo, of the hunter which stipulated he was not to kill swans. His punishment, then, for breaking the general rule, or perhaps his own personal *geis*, was the death of his sweetheart.[19]

It is to be noted that this is a mythological taboo, not a social law. In several versions of the song the lover is told by his father not to flee the country because no one will be condemned 'for the shooting of a swan.' In feminist terms this can be understood as a socially accepted patriarchal refusal to acknowledge the wrongs done to women by excluding them from the human race through objectification, but this novel emphasizes the mythological aspect of the personal act because it has *social* repercussions. It is, in fact, this focus that reveals the key to the conflict of the comic emplotment, to which the romantic entanglements are subsidiary. The taboo-breaking character is not the romantic hero, but the patriarch, Mr Amherst, who is suffering the punishment of having 'killed,' that is, disowned and alienated his children, including his favourite daughter, Molly's mother, for not living up to the demands and expectations of the family name. 'Killing the swan' equals the loss of the loved one. Patriarchal protection of the family as an institution has led to the denial of the purpose and the value of the idea of family, thus corrupting and alienating the actual family.

The central theme of the novel then is not the romantic quest of transcending the social through the passion of romantic love, but of restoring the social through the power of altruistic love. Molly's only displays of "passion" in relationships are in defence of her Irish dead father and her step-brother, who is in place of father and thus significantly linked to filial rather than romantic love. The love that brings about the restoration of the social is the precedence taken by commitment to others over personal happiness. When John dies, leaving his family destitute and Molly without male protection, Molly turns down two proposals of marriage and her grandfather's offer of Herst Royal because his offer does not include John's family. There are many examples in the novel that the breaking of social contracts, for example divorce, is acceptable, and Molly has no qualms about breaking engagements to marry or engagements to dance, but she refuses to break 'contracts' of human commitment.

The paradigms of aestheticism and mythology in which Molly is cast are thus consistently challenged by the paradigms of domesticity and social reality. To be sure, domestic discourse and social reality are notoriously linked to patriarchy, but this novel's rejection of male idealization of women is accompanied by an examination of social values and processes. It is a commonplace in feminist literary criticism to regard a story concluding in a marriage with suspicion, no matter how strong or independent the heroine has proved herself to be. Such female characters are still seen to be the price-paying victims of conservative structures. Like Restoration comedy, the novel criticizes marriages of convenience, but does not challenge marriage as an institution.[20] It is, however, made clear that the upholding of social bonds, as opposed to social structures, has little to do with marriage as such, but with the commitment, interdependence, sharing and loyalty of the extended family. Molly's commitment is not primarily to consanguinity but to those who love her, and it is not until the human social contract is fulfilled that she is prepared to take her place in the social structure by marrying.

As Ian Watts points out, the conventional trend in fiction is to portray female characters who marry upward.[21] As Molly's friend Lady Stafford remarks, 'It is the legitimate thing for us to sell ourselves as dearly as we can' (p. 372); Molly Bawn, however, is an exception. Ironically, her unexpected inheritance of Herst Royal seriously jeopardizes her engagement to marry as Tedcastle does not want to spoil her chances of making a more suitable social match: 'I am no match for you now' (p. 378). It is, of course, vital to the comic resolution of establishing the desirable society that the hero is seen to match the heroine in sacrifice and altruism, and in terms of gendered social structures this is also a 'realistic' motive.

In addition, however, there is an irrational motive revealed in his decision, which stands out not only as a salient factor in the novel's representation of social processes of integration, but also serves to underline its social, and hence comic, centre. This factor is the concept of 'shame.' In sociological theory, shame, unlike other emotions, is a social rather than an individualist emotion. According to Thomas J. Scheff, 'shame' (as opposed to 'guilt' which is individualist and refers to a specific act) is the master emotion in social relationships, arising when our seeing ourselves as others see us constitutes a threat to the social bond.[22] The threat to social bonds in this case is female ownership of property. Tedcastle's honour is at stake as he anticipates the shame of being judged by others as a fortune hunter: 'Think of what the world would say' (p. 378). It is only after Molly's code-breaking proposal that he concedes, to save her from shame: 'I *beg* you to take me. If, after that, you refuse me, I shall die of shame' (p. 379). Male supremacy through economic control is shattered as Tedcastle is her 'property now,' to 'rule with a rod of iron', as Molly humorously puts it. The reversal of gendered social positions is sealed in Tedcastle's words: 'And I–shall hug my chains' (p. 380). In the vein of the double-visioned recognition that 'chains' can be substituted for 'bonds', this mock male subjugation is also an assertion of the value of the 'care and share,' or interdependence, of the socially human contract.

If the effect of Tedcastle's shame is related to a need to re-examine the universal applicability of honour as the male master value, irrespective of its impact on others, Molly's shame is related to an understanding of the relationship between female sexuality and the objectifying male gaze. Singing 'with all her heart for her beloved–for Letitia, and Lovett, and the children, and John in heaven', Molly breaks down and leaves the stage, having by chance discovered her estranged lover in the audience:

> His fascinated, burning gaze compels her to return it. Oh that he should see her here–singing before all these people! For the first time a terrible sense of shame overpowers her: a longing to escape the eyes that from all parts of the hall appear to stare at her and criticise her voice–herself! (p. 336)

In her article 'Elegant Females and Gentlemen Connoisseurs,' Ann Bermingham argues that accomplishments actually suppressed femininity, as a culturally constructed mode of subjectivity in eighteenth- and nineteenth-century culture, instead of challenging it:

> An important role of accomplishments was to mitigate this brazen solicitation and vulgar gazing, and in doing so to mask women's commodity status. [. . .] Accomplishments were intended to arouse masculine desire, yet desire could now be masked and displaced as a detached aesthetic judgement.[23]

Similarly, Richard Leppert, who specifically deals with musical performance, points to the embodied nature of music, the way the ' "musical" gaze was supercharged by the potentiality of sexuality.'[24] Seeing herself as she is seen, Molly is transformed from the state of 'being knowledgeable', that is, aware of the inappropriateness of female public display, into the state of 'being in the know', that is, understanding the reason for this: 'For the first time in my new life it occurred to me to be ashamed. To know that you saw me reminded me that others saw me too, and the knowledge brought a flush to my cheek' (p. 353). According to Scheff, a characteristic feature of shame is that we feel it but seldom know why because its rationale is often hidden. Gratifying the request, 'Miss Massareene, will you sing us something?' (p. 144), in private company and its domestic containment of sexuality is one thing; the public appearance of Miss Wynter for money is another, tantamount to prostitution. As Leppert points out, female performance in public 'challenged the very identity of the category "woman" because it blurred the distinction between the public and the private, the passive and the active'.[25] In this way the novel certainly points to the historical injustice of female limitations, but it also stresses the possibility of asserting the right to move outside them in protection of ungendered categories (i.e. 'those I love') and the determination to continue to 'work for those I love' (p. 355).

The cultural inducement of shame as a means of control is thus ignored because the privileged ideology in this novel is the upholding of social bonds rather than structures of power. The repercussions of shame are instead seen to affect the less valued romantic fulfilment, but for other reasons than internalized female shame. If sexuality is the gendered ground for female shame, then loss of honour related to the provider function is the male equivalent. Honour first forbids Tedcastle to marry a woman who supports herself although he has no moral objections to her singing on stage, and then forbids him to marry a woman of means. Social bonds, not shame, make it as impossible for Molly to marry a man of limited means as it is to accept her grandfather's offer. Her rejection of the latter's offer asserts the necessity of preserving a link between honour and the protection of social bonds, and condemns the intrusion of economic practice and principles in the inter-human sphere:

> 'You strangely forget yourself,' says Molly, with chilling hauteur, drawing herself up to full height. 'Has all your vaunted Amherst blood failed to teach you what honour means? You bribe me with your gold to sell myself, my better feelings, all that is good in me! Oh, shame! Although I am but a Massareene, and poor, I would scorn to offer anyone money to forgo their principles and betray those who loved and trusted in them!' (p. 330)

Although the novel's recognition of the materialist foundation of social reality and its effect on gender relations and social positions is clear, the above passage limits the acceptability of the system of "buying and selling." Buying, for self-serving purposes, which corrupts those who are bought, is the point at which the commodity market turns unethical. In contrast, Molly's selling herself on the stage is not condemned, but is presented as the most logical and expedient option, given her talent, the precarious situation of her dependants, and her determination to 'fall back upon [herself] alone' (p. 304), deciding to make 'my fortune–*our* fortune–out of my voice' (p. 312). In parenthesis, it is worth noting that the typical "honest" alternative of many nineteenth-century novels, that is, being a governess, is rejected by Molly as a 'drudgery' and a 'slavery' that would kill her and prevent her from being her 'own mistress' (p. 312). The contrasting corrupted character in the case of "selling" is Molly's cousin Marcia, who sells herself, her mother and her country to be Mr Amherst's companion and nurse, in the hope of inheriting, thus providing a further example of unethical acting in the human economy and an illustration of its counter-productive effects in terms of love and money.

As we have seen, it is not the sudden reversal of fortune *per se* which brings about the conventional happy resolution of the socially-oriented comedy, but acknowledgement of shame. In the context of a genre that typically centres on social integration and the idea of family as a microcosm of the macro-social, it is interesting to note that this novel makes an unexpected and relevant point in the expected resolution. Scheff suggests that '[a]cknowledged shame [. . .] could be the glue that holds relationships and societies together, and unacknowledged shame the force that blows them apart.'[26] The lovers' union is a result of their mutual bond-strengthening acknowledgement of shame, and Mr Amherst implicitly acknowledges the shame of his previous alienating offer by now bestowing it freely. Not only is matrilineal succession introduced in the process as the expected male heir is thwarted, but the acceptance of Eleanor as a Massareene (i.e. Irish) represents an exercise in double vision where the view of Molly as neither wholly Irish nor wholly British is replaced by a both/and perspective, as is the conflation of Molly (nature) and Eleanor (culture) in Molly's freely chosen request to enter the social role of 'wife,' or in Tedcastle's address 'my *darling*,' the very last words of the novel, which represent the negation of the social order in favour of the personal bond.

The comic focus is thus on the replacement of a flawed and decaying patriarchy by a feminized order, in which the value of social and familial bonds is given a different meaning, inclusive rather than exclusive, and integrated rather than alienated. The "new society" is the result of a bilaterally gendered sacrifice: Tedcastle gives up his public male image, i.e. the male ownership position, and Molly gives up her public female 'voice', i.e. female right of expression. In order for the two to be one, the final hybridizing social vision, then, despite the altogether attractive emphasis on interdependency and free will, ironically involves the double perspective of *female* subjection to the demands of the social order, and *male* courage to transcend them. As Kay Mussell points out, it is virtually impossible for women writers to transcend the culture's imagination about women: 'Over and over again, women write fiction with female protagonists who face traditional and limited female options. [. . .] The subjects differ, but the issues of female identity formation may require that women in fiction confront domestic issues–courtship, nurturing, divorce, marriage, aging, widowhood–even when characters appear to pursue nontraditional lives',[27] or even when the 'heroines are presented as interesting women with courage, spunk, integrity, character and personality'.[28] Despite the reduction of the female to wife and darling, however, there is in *Molly Bawn* a vision of the prerequisites of a changed society, which entails non-gendered distribution of money and property, and the convergence of feminine and masculine ideals in the interest of social bonds rather than social structures. The indictment of patriarchal failure to uphold social bonds is as strong as the insistence that the burden of this task is unfairly placed on the woman. The remedy, it is suggested, lies not primarily in romantic love but in interdependence and sharing.

Patriot's Daughter, Politician's Wife:
Gender and Nation in M. E. Francis's Miss Erin

Heidi Hansson

Feminist investigations into the female tradition in Irish writing have been delayed and complicated by the fact that so many women writers resist political labelling. The critical climate has privileged texts that can be defined in political terms, be it feminist, nationalist or other, and politically ambiguous works have been overlooked or dismissed. But political ambiguity is not synonymous with political ignorance. The ambivalent attitudes expressed in nineteenth-century Irish women's works are frequently an effect of the hybrid identities and divided loyalties the writers had to grapple with. A common manifestation of this ambivalence is a marked tension between surface plot and subtext. Uncovering the subtext does not mean as a consequence that the work's true meaning has been revealed. Rather, the surface story and the submerged plot are in dialogue with each other, negotiating ultimately irreconcilable views.

Rule-governed fiction, like the popular romance or its variant the romantic national tale, is a particularly good vehicle for negotiations, since its conventions are relatively stable and its lessons clear. Familiar messages are transmitted simply because they are inherent in the genre, at the same time as new meanings may be conveyed through authorial comments, topical or historical references, intertexts or other devices that interrupt the flow of the narrative and alert the reader to the presence of a subtext. Because popular fiction was also the literary space accorded to women in nineteenth-century Ireland, the interrelations between gender and genre becomes an interesting area of inquiry. How far do popular romances, for instance, serve to uphold constricting ideals of femininity? How far can their patriarchal messages be subverted? How important is the happy ending in relation to the difficulties that preceded it? Such questions become particularly intriguing when the romance in question is between an Irishwoman and an Englishman, since such stories can also be seen as allegories of the union between Ireland and Britain.

In the nineteenth century, the rhetoric of family and kinship was regularly employed to describe the relationship between England and Ireland. The countries were seen as sisters, brothers, mother and child, father and daughter, and commonly as husband and wife. The plot of, for instance, *Albion and Ierne; A Political Romance* (1886) revolves around the many problems Kathleen, daughter of Lord and Lady Ierne and Albion, son of Lord and Lady Albion, have to overcome before they are finally united. *Albion and Ierne* is an over-explicit political allegory arguing for continued union between England and Ireland, and the romance plot is primarily an excuse for political argument. Nevertheless, the hierarchical implications of the Union are toned down when the relationship between England and Ireland is presented as equivalent to the bond between husband and wife.[1] It is certainly true that family thinking does not exclude aspects of hierarchy, but as Mary Jean Corbett says, 'the family trope may also chart relations of intimacy, yoke the different together, or even call into question the essentialist conceptions of gendered and racial difference that it helps to construct and on which it seems to depend'.[2] In a rather crude manner, *Albion and Ierne* figures the Union as a matter of intimate relations, which masks the colonialist politics involved.

In some measure, M. E. Francis's novel *Miss Erin* (1898) can be read as an allegory of the English–Irish Union, but it is also a work in which the rules of the romance genre clash with the conventions of the national tale. The result of this collision is a much richer but also much more unstable and complex text. As her name indicates, the young girl Erin is identified with Ireland and she dreams of becoming a national hero. Her would-be husband, however, is an English Conservative politician who remains opposed to Home Rule. The tradition of the national tale–as exemplified by Maria Edgeworth's *Ennui* and *The Absentee* and Sydney Owenson's *The Wild Irish Girl*, for instance–requires that the Englishman be made Irish through his love. To a certain extent, this Hibernicization of the man empowers the woman and the values she represents, and, as a result, these national tales imply a reversal of the gender order. The realignment of gender relations typical of the romance, on the other hand, requires rather that the woman should learn to defer to her husband. Because it is informed by both the tradition of the national tale and that of the popular romance, *Miss Erin* becomes an illustration of the conflict between the demands of nation and those of gender. This conflict is enhanced through the novel's two main intertexts, the story of Joan of Arc and Sophocles's tragedy *Antigone*, both of which describe the precedence of a cause over personal happiness. Although the traditional happy ending is delivered in the end, the intertexts problematize the outcome and allow Francis to overcome the limitations of genre as well as avoid the simplifications of national and romantic writing.

M. E. Francis was born as Mary E.[3] Sweetman at Killiney Park, County Dublin in 1859 and died at her home Maes Alyn, Mold, in Wales in 1930.[4] She came from a literary family and both her brother, Walter Sweetman, and two of her sisters, Elinor Mary Sweetman and Agnes Egerton Castle also became writers. Like the heroine of *Miss Erin* she was educated in Brussels, where she met her future husband, the Englishman Francis Nicholl Blundell whose first name provided her with her pen-name. Blundell belonged to a Catholic family from Lancashire, and after their marriage in 1879 the couple settled in Crosby, outside Liverpool where Francis remained for a time after her husband's death in 1884. Many of her fifty-odd works are set in the area, and sometimes, as in the short story collections *Frieze and Fustian* (1895) and *North, South and Over the Seas* (1902), she aims to compare the ways of Irish and English peasantry. She later moved to Dorset where she lived for a long time and finally to Wales where she lived until her death. Both regions figure prominently in her writing. Nevertheless, she thought of herself as an Irish, and, above all, as a Catholic writer, and apart from her novels and plays, she published prayers, meditations and moral tales for children, some appearing under the Catholic Truth Society imprint.

M. E. Francis began her writing career as a contributor to Father Matthew Russell's journal the *Irish Monthly*, the main publishing outlet for serialized novels by Catholic upper middle-class women in the last two or three decades of the nineteenth century.[5] In the preface to her first novel, *Molly's Fortunes* (1887/1905?),[6] Francis describes how she first came to write for the journal and gives a glimpse of her working conditions:

I was almost in despair until on one particular day I happened to enter the lumber-room, and to discover a pile of feather beds heaped in front of a sunny window. An inspiration immediately struck me: here was a safe retreat where no one would think of looking for me and where I might install myself, secure from disturbance. It was rather cold, to be sure, but when one crept well in among the feather beds it was tolerably comfortable. The wintry sun shone gaily in through the bow-window, and a faint odour of old leather and camphor pervaded the room.

So here the main portion of the book was written–in pencil out of regard for the feather beds–with fingers that were blue with cold and adorned with a variety of chilblains, but with a delightful sense of freedom and consequent inspiration.[7]

Although she is almost totally forgotten today, Francis achieved considerable fame in her lifetime, with D. J. O'Donoghue describing her as 'one of the best known women novelists of the day'[8] and W. P. Ryan noting that her novel *Whither?* 'made a stir of no transient kind a couple of years ago'.[9] She was highly prolific and contributed to numerous magazines besides averaging two full-length works a year.[10] At times, the demand for her stories was even greater than this enormous output could satisfy, which further attests to her popularity.[11] Many of her works are dedicated to women, and the preface to *Molly's Fortunes* declares that the story is chiefly intended for 'girl readers'.[12] The expected readership, as well as her identification as a Catholic writer, influenced the tone and content of her works and ensured that her novels never openly challenged conventional taste. As her daughter makes clear, she wanted her novels to be a good influence on young readers: 'Father Matthew Russell and other priests impressed upon her at the outset that she could serve God by using her great literary gift to provide good reading as an antidote to the evil done by harmful books.'[13] Most of her novels are consequently sweet, inoffensive, chastely romantic and moral stories, suitable as school prizes or presents to young girls. As such, they were appreciated by critics disgusted by the open feminism in novels by, for instance, some New Woman writers. Francis's *A Daughter of the Soil* was the first novel to be published serially in the weekly edition of *The Times* and, according to a letter commenting on *The Times* obituary of Francis, she considered this event the real starting point of her literary career.[14] The serial was welcomed by the paper's reviewer as a healthy alternative to the more provocative novels by women that had begun to appear:

> After a course of neurotic novels [. . .] given up to New Women, lawless women, and prodigal daughters, many readers must be inclined to cry: 'Throw open the windows and let in the fresh air.' They will find the tonic they need in a wholesome book. Such a book is Mrs. Francis's *A Daughter of the Soil*. All Mrs. Francis's creations are tinged with a genial glow of optimism which is indeed the characteristic note of a book that leaves one better for the reading of it and more disposed to regard human nature as fundamentally good.[15]

In the *Harper's New Monthly Magazine*, M. E. Francis is said to have 'delicacy of touch, a keen eye for character, and excellent skill in portrayal',[16] and an 1899 review of her novel *The Duenna of A Genius* describes the book as 'as pleasant a tale in a simple way as Mr Mudie's subscribers can wish for'.[17] It seems clear that Francis was careful never to write anything improper. This propriety is present even in *The Story of Mary Dunne* (1913) where Francis addresses the subject of white slave traffic. The review of *Fiander's Widow* is a typical example of the kind of praise usually bestowed on her books:

> There is a creaminess, a perfume about it, that seems to have come straight from the dairies and the countryside, which Mrs. Blundell describes with so much charm. She has as pretty a touch as any one now writing in suggesting the freshness of dawn or the cool of evening or the shady gloom of noonday beneath boughs or any mood of nature in the fields. Her characters, too, are sketched in with a clever hand, and their quaint turns of speech, denoting curious habits of ratiocination, keep one in a continual ripple of quiet laughter. For town or country reading, we can heartily recommend 'Fiander's Widow' to old and young alike.[18]

As James H. Murphy shows, the women contributors to the *Irish Monthly*—for example Rosa Mulholland, Attie O'Brien and Katherine Roche, apart from M. E. Francis—show an ambivalent attitude to nationalism in their works.[19] On the one hand, they express a deep, sometimes even fierce love of their country, but on the other, they convey a fear that the nationalist struggle will lead to social disruptions and political instability. Their treatment of gender issues follows a parallel course, so that women are generally shown to be independent and capable, yet, in the end, in need of a man's guidance, protection and support. The associations between gender and nation are especially close–and especially complex–in Francis's novel *Miss Erin*, where nationalism is constructed as naïve and feminine at the same time as nationalist activities are described as unfeminine.

The two main representations of Ireland in the nineteenth and early twentieth centuries were Erin and Hibernia. The latter was usually preferred by English journalists and cartoonists, and was fair, helpless, passive and angelic, a maiden threatened by loutish Fenians and looking to Britannia or John Bull for protection. Erin was the image chosen by Irish cartoonists, and she differs from Hibernia in that she is dark-haired, more mature and often a mother.[20] When the protagonist of Francis's novel is called Erin, she is thus implicitly linked to an ideal of Irish womanhood as well as to the nation. Born in America, Erin is pledged to Ireland by her exiled, dying father:

> 'Erin shall be her name, as the last proof of her father's love for his country an' hers. Oh, Erin!' he says, risin' his head from the pillow and tryin' to lift the child in his arms, 'I have indeed loved thee, all that I had was thine–I would joyfully have given my life for thee! Behold,' he says, 'I dedicate to thee this child, the only thing in the world that I can still call my own. With my last breath I consecrate her to thee——.'[21]

It is a romantic gesture, and recognized as such. After her father's death, the child is sent back to his family in Ireland, but the country is not particularly welcoming to her. Erin's rich uncle Fitzgerald even hopes that the child might die and relieve him of his responsibilities, and instead of taking her in, he sends her to be fostered with his tenants, the Nolans, and their nine children:

> Poor little babe, she was all unconscious that the kind bosom on which she was cradled was the only one in all her motherland in

which she had inspired feelings other than a puzzled compassion, and that no single voice except that of this poor peasant woman had been uplifted to bid her welcome home.[22]

While Erin thinks of the Nolans as her family, she is out of place in terms of class, and her difference from her foster family is emphasized. The Nolans impose a class distinction in their own household by addressing 'the little lady' as *Miss* Erin, and treating her 'with the consideration due to her rank',[23] and her mind is described as 'of a more inquiring turn than that of the others'.[24] From the beginning, Erin is portrayed as both an insider and an outsider in her community, and this hybrid status is reflected when she speaks 'in clear tones, well modulated and refined, but with a most unmistakable brogue'.[25]

Her subsequent education ensures that she is a hybrid also where gender is concerned. Brought back to her uncle's house, Erin is taught Latin and Greek, subjects which in the nineteenth century were usually reserved for men. Like Glorvina in Sydney Owenson's *The Wild Irish Girl*, Erin is taught almost entirely by men, with her uncle Fitzgerald providing her with a classical education, her foster-father Pat Nolan teaching her folkloric history and the local priest ensuring her knowledge of Catholic history. Her education makes her different from other girls her age, and the priest's housekeeper Moll Riddick chastizes her for her lack of feminine accomplishments:

> 'I never heard of a little girl that couldn't dress a doll. Is it possible ye don't know how to sew, Erin, and you getting such a big girl? Sure, that's a disgrace! 'Pon my word it is now–A great disgrace.'
>
> 'I'm learning Greek', cried the child with angry tears in her eyes, 'I can't do everything.'[26]

But while Erin is away on holiday in Kerry, the Nolans are evicted from Fitzgerald's estate. When she returns, Pat Nolan is in prison for fighting the police, and the rest of the family are in the workhouse. Upset that her uncle sees non-payment of rent as more important than the love and friendship the Nolans have given her, Erin refuses to be taught by him any longer. With the old priest Father Lalor also dead, Erin's country becomes her only family and the only thing she has to love:

> Her own recent griefs were associated with the troubles of her country–all her hopes and dreams bound up with its destiny–what wonder, then, if she now gave herself up to the vivid fancy which had taken possession of her, and which represented her mother, Ireland, as a living, beautiful being–a being to give one's life for, to love with an ardent, personal love![27]

For the young girl, to embrace the nationalist cause means to acquire a family, and when she has followed in her father's footsteps by publishing a nationalist poem, the villagers cheer her as 'the patriot's daughter'.[28] But there was little room for women in nationalist circles. Since the images of Ireland were feminine, woman represented the site of contestation, but men were the national subjects, and those women who tried to involve themselves in the fight were dismissed as pretty ideologists, romantic fanatics or viragos.[29] Margaret Ward quotes an illuminating passage from the *Belfast Newsletter* of 18 March, 1881: 'Sensible people in the North of Ireland dislike to see women out of the place she is gifted to occupy, and at no time is woman further from her natural position than when she appears upon a political platform.'[30] Women could speak in public for moral or religious reasons, advocating temperance or supporting charitable causes, for instance, but political issues were regarded as definitely unsuitable topics. Even today, as Rick Wilford says, 'neo-nationalists revert to gender stereotypes, resurrecting or reinforcing the division between male-dominated public spaces and the private spaces defined as women's domain'.[31] Hence, by taking active part in the struggle, Erin has overstepped the gender boundaries, as the new parish priest makes clear:

> 'Faith, the cause'll get on without ye, my child,' he said, as soon as he had recovered his gravity; 'sure, what do we want with little girls? If you were a woman itself–but even so, it's men's work–men's work. Pray for the cause as much as you like,' he added, more seriously, 'and do what ye can for the poor; but don't be speechifying an' talkin' to the boys at all. It's not your place, and if your poor father was alive it's the last thing he'd wish.'[32]

Erin's wish to work for her country is thus figured as childish and unfeminine, and, moreover, highly unsuitable for someone of the landlord class. This conflict between gender and political commitment is enhanced when Erin is linked to the protagonist of Sophocles's tragedy *Antigone*.

The immediate result of Erin's poetic activities is that she is sent away to school in Brussels. On the journey she meets Mark Wimbourne, the man who will become her fiancé, and their conversation clearly shows what he regards as feminine tastes and interests:

> 'Now, what sort of reading do you like best?–story-books, of course. Don't be a prig and say you like history, for I am sure you don't! Who is your favourite author–Mrs. Molesworth or Miss Yonge?'
>
> 'I have never heard of either–I think Sophocles is my favourite author–at least, I like "The Antigone" better than anything I have ever read.'[33]

The play represents a masculine kind of learning and functions to set Erin apart from other girls, but primarily it serves as a parallel that gives depth and a precedence to Erin's actions and choices. As Antigone, Joan of Arc, Erin and Dark Rosaleen, the alias she gives instead of disclosing her real name to Mark, Erin's representative role is in fact overstated. Nevertheless, the play's function is not solely to establish a correspondence between the main characters. Partly, references to classical texts 'increase the literary status of a romantic tale', as Kate Flint says.[34] The connection enhances the value of the novel's messages, since it installs an authority elsewhere and temporarily transfers that authority to the writer at hand.[35] Interacting with *Antigone* through allusions and parallels, *Miss Erin* consequently becomes more than a romance. Since the classics were connected with male culture in the nineteenth century, the intertext claims women's right to be included in that cultural sphere, and Francis's right as an author to be considered on the same terms as her male contemporaries. The correspondences with Sophocles's tragedy operate on all the levels of plot, character, theme and subtext, and since *Antigone* is a double-voiced play, open to totally contradictory interpretations, the double voice of *Miss Erin* is accentuated.

As a universal symbol of resistance, Antigone transcends history and geography, 'so real she might have lived yesterday'.[36] Like Erin, Antigone is characterized by a passionate wilfulness that causes her to defy the law of the state and bury her brother against the explicit decree of Creon, the city's ruler. For Antigone, secular law takes second place to religious duty and family loyalty, in the same way as Joan of Arc disobeys the state but obeys her voices; and Erin rejects English law for her obligations to her mother, Ireland. The intertextual connections emphasize the distinction between political state and natural country that Francis makes in *Miss Erin*, where the state is the rule of Westminster, while the country is a much more amorphous concept, founded on cultural practices, religion and nature. There is an intensely personal relationship between the people and the land, as when Erin lies down on the hillside outside her village, feeling 'as if she was lying upon her mother's bosom'.[37] Her identification with Ireland is physical, causing her to say that 'when you insult my country, I feel as though you struck me'.[38] Mark Wimbourne, on the other hand, defends his opposition to Home Rule by seeing it as a matter of party loyalty,[39] just as Creon justifies his acts by identifying with the apparatus of the state. Personal feelings like love and the demands of kinship always come second to state government:

> Creon: Yes, to me anyone who while guiding the whole city fails to set his hand to the best counsels, but keeps his mouth shut by reason of some fear seems now and has always seemed the worst of men; and him who rates a dear one higher than his native land, him I put nowhere.[40]

The crucial point is that 'native land' is a concept that does not include love for Creon, while for Antigone, the love of country and the love of family are intertwined

Like the *Antigone*, *Miss Erin* dramatizes the relationship between citizen and state as a conflict between natural and civic order, placing the woman on the side of nature and the man on the side of civilization. Another way of seeing it is that the nation is gendered female and the state is gendered male.[41] Thus, what Erin believes in and passionately wants to fight for are the mystical properties of an imagined nation, not the legislative construction of a state. This sounds like the familiar identification of woman with the irrational and man with reason, and the anti-feminist quality of this classification is only partly countered by the circumstance that nature is valorized in both Sophocles's tragedy and Francis's romance. Both Erin and Antigone are shown to be victims of patriarchal systems that have lost their connection with the divine. Antigone justifies her actions by claiming that the laws she breaks by burying her brother are only man-made:

> Antigone: Yes, for it was not Zeus who made this proclamation, nor was it Justice who lives with the gods below that established such laws among men, nor did I think your proclamations strong enough to have power to overrule, mortal as they were, the unwritten and unfailing ordinances of the gods.[42]

The disorder Antigone represents thus reflects a deeper disorder in the polis, caused by Creon's tyrannical behaviour. In a similar manner, Erin's unfeminine assertiveness is partially justified by the extremity of Ireland's plight. The link with Antigone emphasizes women's right and ability to act, but also the futility of their actions, since Antigone finally fails. As a woman, Antigone does not have the authority to challenge the city-state, and since the gods never intervene and sanction her behaviour, there is also a sense that 'Antigone herself and her subversion of the polis did not have divine approval'.[43] Likewise, Erin's political beliefs are based on a mystical communion with the land that the Westminster politicians are unable to achieve, but, at the same time, this spiritual union is downgraded as the romantic illusion of a 'passionate and imaginative little creature'.[44] As social beings, women remain inferior and, as a consequence, the causes they fight for become inferior too.

But even though Sophocles's play was sometimes used for anti-feminist purposes, as in W. F. Barry's attack on the New Woman, *The New Antigone: A Romance* (1887), both Erin and Antigone can be seen as positive figures in the feminist debate. Apart from tracing an individual's opposition to an oppressive social structure, the *Antigone* describes a woman's confrontation with patriarchy, and the protagonist loses her life as much because she is a woman who has transgressed the rules of her gender as because she has broken the law: 'Indeed, now I am no man, but she is a man, if she is to enjoy such power as this with impunity,' says Creon.[45] By taking action on her own, she 'succeeds not only in undermining Creon's authority but also questions all that he represents: the power of the throne, supreme justice, family hierarchy, and traditional male dominance',[46] and Creon's decision to execute Antigone is grounded as much in a wish to preserve the patriarchal order as to uphold the laws of the polis. In a similar manner, Erin's political engagement threatens Mark Wimbourne's position as a man as well as his role as a politician, and his chief reason for opposing her nationalist commitment is that he has 'a constitutional dislike to talking politics with women'.[47] Just as the nationalists did, he finds such activities unfeminine: 'Your lips were framed to feed on other stuff–to me there is something so incongruous between yourself and your views that I feel personally injured and affronted when I hear you discuss them.'[48] A woman in politics is an anomaly, and Mark does not even approve of the ladies of the Primrose League.[49]

Thus, while Erin sees Antigone as an ideal, and believes that 'it was grand of her to lay down her life for a sacred cause',[50] Mark takes the opposite view and views her as a rather silly character who does not belong in modern times.[51] Their controversy reflects the contradictory responses the play evoked in the nineteenth century. Although Matthew Arnold saw the ancients, and particularly Sophocles, as cultural models whose works were eminently significant for a Victorian audience, he singles out the *Antigone* as narrow and uninteresting:

> An action like the action of the *Antigone* of Sophocles, which turns upon the conflict between the heroine's duty to her brother's corpse and that to the laws of her country, is no longer one in which it is possible that we should feel a deep interest.[52]

Hegel, on the other hand, saw Antigone's deed as a prime example of ethical behaviour, and perhaps more importantly, the play as a whole as an illustration of the process of Hegelian dialectics.[53] Both these views come together in *Middlemarch*, where George Eliot uses Antigone to emphasize how limited the options were for an 'ardent soul' like Dorothea Brooke:

> Certainly those determining acts of her life were not ideally beautiful. They were the mixed result of a young and noble impulse struggling amidst the conditions of an imperfect social state, in which great feelings will often take the aspect of error, and great faith the aspect of illusion. For there is no creature whose inward being is so strong that it is not greatly determined by what lies outside it. A new Theresa will hardly have the opportunity of reforming a conventual life, any more than a new

> Antigone will spend her heroic piety in daring all for the sake of
> a brother's burial: the medium in which their ardent deeds took
> shape is for ever gone.[54]

Antigone is offered as an inspiring example, but regrettably, one whose
dedication has no place in the modern world. Both the play and its
protagonist consequently had an uncertain cultural status in the
nineteenth century, and this very uncertainty is what informs *Miss Erin*
most deeply. There is no synthesis in the play, but a complete 'collision
between two competing forces, each carrying a high spiritual value, each
equally justified in itself and rightfully claiming human allegiance; yet,
each to be blamed for violating the rights of the other'.[55]

It is perhaps no coincidence that there have been a number of Irish
adaptations and translations of Sophocles's play: Tom Paulin's *The Riot
Act: A Version of Antigone by Sophocles* (1985),[56] *Sophocles' Antigone: A New
Version by Brendan Kennelly* (1996),[57] another 'new version' by Declan
Donnellan (1999),[58] and Seamus Heaney's translation *The Burial at
Thebes: Sophocles's Antigone*,[59] specially commissioned for the centenary of
the Abbey Theatre in 2004.[60] An aspect of the play that gains particular
significance in an Irish context is the fact that Antigone is punished for
obeying the gods. In Heaney's translation she is condemned:

> And condemned for what?
> For practising devotion,
> For a reverence that was right.[61]

The conflict between divine and human law becomes particularly
poignant against the background of Irish history.

The final comment from the Chorus seems to vindicate Antigone and
endorse her choice since it makes clear that Creon is responsible for his
own tragedy by putting the laws of the state above the proper observance
of religion:

> Chorus: Good sense is by far the chief part of happiness; and we
> must not be impious towards the gods. The great words of
> boasters are always punished with great blows, and as they grow
> old teach them wisdom.[62]

To interpret the play only in terms of its final lines is to simplify it too far, however. *Antigone* is most of all a *mélange* of oppositional voices. The play is thoroughly double-voiced, and the conflicts between civic and cosmic order, state and citizen, man and woman are only presented, never solved. The same is true of *Miss Erin*, where right and truth can be found on both sides and unacceptable opinions are voiced by sympathetic characters.

Mark and Erin represent extreme political positions, and there is no sense that their political views can be reconciled. As a Tory politician, Mark proposes a solution to the Irish land problem that ought to define him as the villain rather than the hero of the piece:

> 'I know how I should like to deal with it', said Mark laughing. 'I should serve out Maxim guns gratis to both sides of the National party, and let the Parnellites and Anti-Parnellites mow each other down at their leisure. In course of time the Unionists would have it all to themselves, and we should have a nice, loyal, peaceable little Ireland.'[63]

Less flippantly, he sees England as Ireland's benevolent guardian, only controlling the country for its own good, like a parent who refuses 'to put a knife in the hands of the child who is not to be trusted with it'.[64] This latter view was quite common among the gentry, Catholic or Anglo-Irish, and is frequently expressed in the novels published in the *Irish Monthly*.[65] Yet, Francis offers it only as yet another of the positions negotiated in the novel, and Mark's opinions are always countered by a nationalist argument from Erin. But while English prejudice is ruthlessly exposed, the vulgarity of nationalist rhetoric is also conceded, from the cant phrases of journalists to Erin's banal poetry and the harp-decorated green covers of partisan history books. Their disagreements reinforce the separation between the natural country and the political state as an opposition between female and male principles, where the female emerges as emotional and somewhat naïve, while the male is callous and impersonal. Neither position surfaces as the correct one, and neither is allowed to stand undisputed.

Both Mark and Erin refuse to yield to the other's conviction, and this is where the conflict between the tradition of the national tale and that of the popular romance becomes most obvious. In accordance with the genre conventions of the romance, Mark expects Erin to change, while she, following the conventions of the national tale, expects him to come round to her point of view. The result is that the budding love affair is interrupted:

> Oh, what a fool she had been–what a blind fool! She understood all now–all his talk of love, and the power of love, and the changes which it might effect were meant to apply to her. It was she who was to change, who was to give up her convictions, to suffer her principles to be swept away.[66]

Instead of staying in England to support Mark's political campaign, Erin returns to Ireland and becomes involved in resisting an eviction in the north-west of the country. But her dream of leading her people like a new Joan of Arc is shattered by the violence she experiences, and she is wounded by one of her own when she stands between Mark and a blow aimed to kill him.

In the end, it does seem as if love is stronger than politics, and Mark interprets Erin's attempt to save him accordingly: 'Erin, you would have died for me–we cannot forget it. If you had died of that wound, remember you would not have given your life for your country, but for me.'[67] Still, Erin refuses to marry him unless he gives up his political career, and their final union is only made possible by their respective failures–Mark's defeat in the parliamentary election and Erin's realization that the violence entailed in the struggle for liberation will prevent her from ever becoming a national leader. Erin thus gives up her struggle against the state apparatus, while Mark promises to love Ireland because it is her country, precisely like Lord Colambre in *The Absentee*, the Earl of Glenthorn in *Ennui* and Horatio in *The Wild Irish Girl*: 'Where Eve is', he said, 'must always be my Paradise!'[68] A significant difference between Mark Wimbourne and the male protagonists of the other novels, however, is that he has not really changed his political attitudes towards Ireland. He has only lost his opportunity to implement them.

Julia Anne Miller argues that the marriages that conclude the national tales of Maria Edgeworth and Sydney Owenson rely on the women's complete submission, and that, as narrative tropes, they serve to uphold the Act of Union and 'diffuse rebellion by redrawing the boundaries of conflict from an external to an internal struggle.'[69] Any future insurrection will be contained within the home, in other words. The outcome of *Miss Erin* is more ambiguous, since there is no final compromise, no unconditional submission and no real resolution. Instead, the process of negotiation continues until the last page, and the result is a kind of moral equilibrium, where both sides are partly right, partly wrong.

In Sophocles's play, Creon's son and Antigone's fiancé, Haemon, functions as the voice of reason, urging tolerance and understanding:

> Do not wear the garment of one mood only, thinking that your opinion and no other must be right! For whoever think that they themselves alone have sense, or have a power of speech or an intelligence that no other has, these people when they are laid open are found to be empty.[70]

Mark offers a similar comment when he tries to convince Erin that everybody's motives are to some extent impure, and one's point of view affects one's interpretation of circumstances: 'If you doubt the good, you can also doubt the evil. If your standard is not too high, it can be wider, more tolerant. Everything in this world is a mixture of good and evil.'[71] Creon's inability to accept any other opinion than his own is what causes the final tragedy when his whole family, as well as Antigone, are destroyed. *Miss Erin* rewrites this tragic ending by suggesting the possibility of co-existence despite difference of opinion, and what emerges as the final answer is the awareness that there is no such thing as absolute truth. If this message is embraced, it becomes possible to be both a patriot's daughter and a politician's wife.

Acknowledgement

The research for this article was made possible by a grant from the Helge Ax:son Johnson Foundation, for which I wish to express my sincere gratitude.

Ireland:

The Terra Incognita *of the New Woman Project*

Tina O'Toole

When literature and culture in the 1890s in Ireland are addressed, the focus tends to be on the Celtic Revival, and the group of writers whose work and politics we associate with it. Although this essay examines Irish writing in the 1890s, it does so from the perspective of quite a different cultural and social project. Here, I address the work of a group of writers at the end of the nineteenth century who problematized the binaries of Irish/British definition by exploring Scandinavian texts, and addressing revolutionary politics in Italy and Poland. These writers deconstructed gender binaries and disrupted the heterosocial economy by opening up subjects such as women's sexual expression and the construction of gender identities in their work. In addressing the work of the 'New Woman' project, I refer to writers such as George Egerton, Sarah Grand, 'Iota' (Kathleen Mannington Caffyn), and E. L. Voynich (Ethel Lillian Boole). These writers have been almost completely obscured by the writing of Irish literary history in the intervening century, but to draw the conclusion that their work was sub-standard, or obscure and unpopular in its own day and that this is why we know nothing of these writers, would be misguided. Apart from writing best-selling fiction, the 'New Woman' writing was also critically acclaimed at the end of the nineteenth century, and the experimental work of writers such as George Egerton changed the face of writing in the pre-modernist period.

Much critical work has been done in recent years on the New Woman project; however, scholars have neglected the Irish dimension to this work, which I propose to focus on here. Those critics who have examined the work of New Woman writers such as George Egerton, Sarah Grand and others,[1] have tended to overlook or underestimate the importance of an Irish perspective to the work of these artists. In fact the celebrated Sarah Grand, central to the New Woman project, was born in Ireland, where she lived until the age of seven, and her deployment of her experiences there, particularly in her novel *The Beth Book*, illustrates the effect of Irish social and cultural mores on her later political perspectives. I argue below that an understanding of George Egerton's use of her Irishness as a subversive tool to disrupt the ideological matrix, holding both women and men in place, is vital for any reading of her work.[2]

The contribution made by this New Woman fiction to a feminist history of ideas cannot be underestimated. Locating their work in the context of a wider reading of Irish, British and European culture in the early 1890s exemplifies the impact made by their radical fictions. Although the scope of this essay does not enable me to discuss the work of these writers in detail, I will begin by briefly outlining the New Woman project, using as an example the work of Sarah Grand, a key figure in this New feminist wave. I then move on to examine the narratives of George Egerton, whose work is my main focus here.

1893 was the key year in the history of this feminist literary revolt, the year when Egerton and Grand published their most important works, *Keynotes* and *The Heavenly Twins*. The intersection between the new roles imagined for women in New Woman texts, and the advances made by political feminists during the 1890s is crucial to our understanding of this literature.[3] We know, for example, that Olive Schreiner's *Dreams* (1890), another New Woman text, was read by the suffragette prisoners in Holloway Prison as 'a sort of bible'.[4]

Sarah Grand was a key writer and activist in the 1880s and 1890s, giving this new construct, the New Woman, a name in 1894.[5] In her feminist trilogy, *Ideala* (1888), *The Heavenly Twins* (1893) and *The Beth Book* (1897), she developed a feminist aesthetic in fiction that involved a rethink of traditional gender roles and posed a radical challenge to society and culture at the end of the century.[6] Grand's influence on later writers and feminist activists both in Ireland and abroad is legendary.[7] Her deployment of the figure of the New Woman, a woman who was assertive, strong and intelligent, while highly feminine and attractive to men as well as to other women, broke the mould as far as contemporary depictions of feminists were concerned. Versions of this character in fiction and cartoons tended to be used to demonize feminists; caricatures in late nineteenth-century periodicals such as *Punch* were meant to belittle and thus nullify the threat posed by feminism.[8] Grand created a feminist figure who could stand up to societal pressure, exploiting the growing fissure between women's potential and the roles foisted upon them in a patriarchal society. Her tactic of taking the reader into her confidence revolutionized the way in which feminism was viewed by society in the late Victorian period. The assumption made by her narrators that they are addressing reasonable, progressive adults empowers her readers to take up the struggle on their own behalf. Part of Grand's project was the construction of a powerful critique of Victorian patriarchy. Analysing the composition of a social hierarchy based on gender difference, her writings illustrate the ways in which women are bound to their social roles by a systematic process of financial inequality, physical abuse and sexual exploitation.[9] Misogyny was widespread during the period,[10] thus the impact of these arguments on the body politic was fiercely resisted, and the New Woman, both in fiction and in life, was represented as both a sexless monster and an anarchist.

Published in 1893, George Egerton's first short story collection proved to be the keynote of its time. John Lane recognized at once its potential for the 'New' marketplace he was then establishing for the Bodley Head. Commissioning an Aubrey Beardsley cover for the book, which was lavishly produced, he shuffled the contents to put the most provocative story first.[11] *Keynotes* was an immediate hit. Within the next six months it was reprinted twice,[12] and had lent its name to the Keynotes series of books[13] also published by John Lane, testimony to the influence of Egerton's fictions during the period, as well as the marketing power of her work as a 'brand'. Egerton wrote a story for the first issue of *The Yellow Book* (the notorious journal at the centre of the Decadent movement in London), for which she was lampooned by *Punch*. The toast of the literary set, Egerton moved to London and mixed with other *fin de siècle* artists, including Arthur Symons and Richard Le Gallienne. Havelock Ellis made a favourable impression on her and she went to tea with W. B. Yeats–whom she later dismissed as a *poseur*.[14] As I will demonstrate, the transgressive nature of her writing in the short stories in *Keynotes* and in her second collection, *Discords* (1894), deconstructs gender roles and relationships between the sexes.

Egerton began her writing career after Grand, who had published *Ideala* in 1888. By the time she put pen to paper, several other New Woman novels had already been published, particularly Olive Schreiner's *The Story of an African Farm*, and Grand's *Ideala* (1888). We cannot prove Egerton's familiarity with these earlier works, but the chances are that she was familiar at least with the popular representation of the early feminist movement in the early 1890s. A key influence on Egerton's early work and her career as a writer was the context in which her literary education began. In the late 1880s, she eloped to Scandinavia with a man named Henry Higginson.[15] Having moved in literary circles there, she started her education as a writer from debates by the feminist movement in Scandinavia. That her material (which examines the social world from a woman's position) was influenced by Scandinavian writers such as Hamsun and Hansson locates her texts outside the binary of British/Irish definition. Reconstructing women's subjectivity from their own perspective, discussing taboo subjects such as venereal disease, and developing a feminist literary aesthetic, Egerton's work certainly won't fit received ideas of 'Anglo-Irish writing'.

In her work, Egerton provides us with many of the characteristics of the New Woman prevalent in the cartoons and stereotypes of the period. Discussing the New Woman figure in France, Jennifer Waelti-Walters has depicted her as 'a woman with a bicycle, a divided skirt, a packet of cigarettes, and a teaching licence'.[16] There are very few differences between this description and the received notion of the New Woman in Anglophone culture. Egerton's characters are outspoken, educated, cigarette-smoking, bicycle-riding and they have their own latch-keys—a symbolic gesture of their independence.

A pioneer in the contemporary move to 'tell the truth about sexuality',[17] Egerton made self-conscious efforts to construct a feminine subjectivity in fiction, which put her work on a par with that of many later feminist writers. Her New Woman characters have clear views on sexual equality, they struggle with moral choices alone, they take lovers, have unexpected pregnancies and get on with day-to-day living without much help from their male partners. Yet her own views on feminism are unclear, and she frequently distanced herself from the feminist movement of her own day. Her investment in essentialism, along with so many of her peers, and the commitment to eugenics in her work on motherhood, has contributed to the neglect of her work by feminist critics, a detailed discussion of which is beyond the scope of this essay.

If there could be said to be a specific geographical context to the New Woman project, it is probably that of the city. The late Victorian city–specifically London–was the centre of much feminist activism during this period. Throughout much of the nineteenth century, simple activities such as taking a stroll in the city could not be undertaken by a 'respectable' woman on her own. For a woman to be seen wandering the streets was an indication of sexual availability, as Virginia Woolf commented in *The Pargiters*: 'To be seen alone in Piccadilly was equivalent to walking up Abercorn Terrace in a dressing gown carrying a sponge.'[18] By the 1890s, this had begun to change, and women of the middle and upper classes were seen for the first time walking unaccompanied down city streets, emerging at last from the private sphere to take buses and trams, to go shopping and to stroll with friends. The suffrage movement took to the streets to demand the vote, and women students in ever greater numbers began to criss-cross the city to attend public lectures and college courses. Many New Woman authors relocated to London–as did George Egerton following the success of her second collection, *Discords*. The 'city of dreadful delight' as Judith Walkowitz has described it,[19] became not only home to many New Woman figures but also to the narratives they penned. Just as women began to occupy the public sphere, the late nineteenth-century urban landscape became the location of much New Women fiction, where the action takes place in railway stations, hospitals, city streets, department stores and colleges.

However, this more usual 'New' urban landscape is not the backdrop to Egerton's narratives. While she certainly did explore it in one or two short stories ('Gone Under' from *Discords* is one such), she tends to locate her narratives in a variety of social contexts far beyond the confines of London. Where she does make use of urban settings, they tend to be Dublin or Christiania (Oslo) rather than London. Her narratives move between a variety of cultural and social settings, establishing transcultural connections between Irish and European literary practice, and thus address a wider European audience at the end of the nineteenth century.

Egerton's early short stories with Scandinavian settings are by far the best known of her material–stories such as 'The Spell of the White Elf', 'Now Spring Has Come', and the 'Under Northern Sky' trilogy, all from *Keynotes*, tend to be the main texts reprinted and anthologized. As a result of this, and of her writing style, her work has tended to be associated with Northern European scholars and texts. Her early education as a writer has its roots in the period at the end of the 1880s that she spent in Scandinavia after she had eloped with Higginson to live in Norway in 1887. There, the couple lived on a small property in Langesund where she learned Norwegian, read Ibsen, Strindberg, Bjornsen and Hamsun,[20] and discovered Hansson[21] and, through him, Nietzsche. The experiments of Ibsen and Nietzsche influenced her own writing career later on. Returning to London two years later, Egerton began to translate Hamsun's *Sult,* and the influence of this on her own early work is apparent. Elements of Hamsun's style and, at times, his ideologies and techniques come through in the work that Egerton was about to begin in her own name.[22]

Anka Ryall discusses the treatment of Norway in nineteenth-century British travel narratives, pointing out that the country tends to be depicted as a border zone on the margin of the civilized world–'the complete antithesis of the urban civilization of the southern metropolis'. Despite her frequent use of Scandinavian settings as a backdrop to the struggles of her New Woman characters, Egerton is aware that this decision to locate her narratives outside mainstream society is a risk. This is evident in the way in which those of her protagonists who have chosen to make their lives in Norway are called upon in her texts to justify this move away from the 'centre' of the world, as London was then depicted by New Woman writers, among others. As one character in the *Discords* collection comments, comparing Christiania (Oslo) with London: 'There's more real life here, or at least you can see it more plainly [. . .]. Friendship in London costs a tremendous lot, you have to pay very dearly for your social whistle, and it's only a tin one when you get it.'[23]

Egerton often points up her deliberate employment of such settings to illustrate the ways in which her characters, isolated from mainstream culture and society, make their own way in the world. In 'A Shadow's Slant', she sets the scene in a remote part of rural Norway thus:

> A strip of blue fjord and a background of dark mountains, with the cool ice-kisses of the snow queen still resting on their dusky heads, can be seen at intervals through the fir and pine trees. A squirrel scrambles up a rowan tree and a cattle bell tingles far in the distance.[24]

The narrative is that of a woman living in thrall to a boorish older man in the countryside who nonetheless manages to establish her own power and autonomy in the face of his bullying, despite the fact that she has no neighbours or kin to call on to protect her. He accuses her thus: 'You wait on me, ay, no slave better, and yet–I can't get at you, near you; that little soul of yours is as free as if I hadn't bought you, as if I didn't own you, as if you were not my chattel, my thing to do with as *I please*.'[25] Disconnecting from the mainstream is crucial, Egerton seems to suggest, if women are to be independent of mind and spirit.

To shift our perspective somewhat from the New Woman project, another late nineteenth-century genre was making travel writing and adventure fiction more popular. Following in the footsteps of Schreiner's *The Story of an African Farm*, the 'dialect novel'[26] and the 'quest novel',[27] based in distant and 'exotic' locations, were at a peak in the second half of the nineteenth century. Grand's location of part of the narrative of *The Beth Book* in the west of Ireland is a good example of this. Similarly, Egerton's use of Scandinavian landscapes in her stories gave a touch of the exotic to her work, and remind us of Ethel Tweedie's accounts of her travels in the Nordic countries at the end of the nineteenth century. In 'The Regeneration of Two', for example, Egerton locates parts of the narrative in the splendour of the northern winter, describing:

> Snow everywhere! A white world wrapped in a snowy shroud, under a grey-white sky [. . .] A twig crackling in the wood, the brittle snap of a branch under its weight of snow; the rattling rush of icicles as it crashes to the ground, the hoarse startled call of a capercailzie; every sound is as crisply distinct in the clear stillness as a sibilant whisper in a hushed room. Every touch of colour, the crimson in a little lad's muffler, as he drags his newly painted kjelke [hand-sled] up the hill, strikes warmly to one as the light in the window to a wayfarer on a murky night.[28]

Of course, there is a further, quite self-conscious strategy at play in Egerton's use of Scandinavian settings in many of her short stories. The work of Ibsen and others was beginning to make an impression on British culture at this point, and the association of 'Scandinavian' ideas with Egerton's work marked her out as one of a new generation of writers. When Egerton had first submitted her work anonymously for publication to T.P. Gill, who ran a literary column for the discovery of new talent, he rebuked this young man–as he thought–for his baldness of expression, calling on 'him' to tone down:

these mere effects of starkness and of appeals to the sexual sense. What is gained to your purpose [. . .] of that passage in 'The Cross Line' where the husband falls on his knees over the wife and then takes her up and carries her off in his arms "to their own room"? Is this not inviting the public a little too far inside one's premises? [. . .]. To put it brutally you would not (however Scandinavian your ideas may be) invite your coachman, or even your bosom friend, to 'assist' you while you and your wife were engaged in the sacred mysteries.[29]

The implication of scandal, or sexually explicit ideas with all things Scandinavian is clearly understood. By allying her work with the Nordic writers, Egerton states her intent to contribute to this new frankness about sexual matters in fiction. Furthermore, by invoking the names of renowned Scandinavian artists, as she does in 'The Spell of the White Elf', Egerton allies herself with this emerging cultural élite:

> Christiania is a singular city if one knows how to see under the surface [. . .] It was a fine clear day, and Karl Johann was thronged with folks [. . .] Everybody who is anybody may generally be seen about that time. Henrik Ibsen—if you did not know him from his portrait, you would take him to be a prosperous merchant—was just going home to dine; but Bjornsterne Bjornson, in town just then [. . .] was standing near the Storthing House with a group of politicians, probably discussing the vexed question of separate consulship.[30]

Unlike her Scandinavian work, the Irish aspect of Egerton's work has tended to be somewhat neglected by scholars. As Scott McCracken points out, this has long remained the unknown quantity at the centre of her narratives.[31] In fact, most late nineteenth-century readers of her work tended to think of this author as a Nordic writer or, at least, an English writer living in Scandinavia. Similarly, modern day readers of *fin de siècle* fiction often assume Egerton to be English. Considering the explosive effect of her first literary collection, *Keynotes*, on the literary and social world in 1893, those curious about the unknown author might have been surprised by the rather mundane circumstances of their gestation. That these texts, subverting the Victorian social and domestic world as they did, were written by a woman determined to preserve her own domestic establishment is curious, if not uncommon at that time. Unable to survive financially, she and her husband, who were then living in Cork, were about to emigrate to South Africa when Egerton hit on the idea of writing for a living. She later told her nephew, Terence de Vere White, that she had written the stories 'straight off': "The Little Grey Glove' on the back of an upturned teatray after supper in the gauger's cottage near Millstreet, County Cork'.[32] So who was George Egerton, and how did she come to start a literary career in a gauger's cottage in Cork?

George Egerton was born Mary Chavelita Dunne in 1860[33] in Melbourne, Australia, and as Katherine Tynan tells us: 'On her father's side she comes of a Roman Catholic stock of unmixed Irish descent [. . .] On the spindle side she is Welsh, her mother was a Miss George Bynon, a Vale of Gower woman [. . .].'[34] Her father was an army man, whose occupation caused frequent upheavals for the Dunne family when she was a young child. Before settling in Dublin in 1868, according to Tynan, the Dunnes had lived in New Zealand, Chile and Wales. Despite her early childhood experience of a rootless existence in many different countries, Egerton's narratives convey a strong, albeit oblique, sense of an Irish national identity imparted to her by her father. Perhaps we might refer to this today as a diasporic identity. From the age of eight to her mid-teens, Egerton lived in Dublin with her family, and there is no doubt but that she considered this home territory.

Some of her stories have Dublin settings, and reflect Dublin street life, in particular, in the latter half of the nineteenth century. From what we do know about the Dunnes' family background, it is clear that Captain Dunne was an improvident father, still living the life of a bachelor despite his family responsibilities. De Vere White tells us that he was cashiered from the army in early life and that from then on: 'he lived, with a large family, on air and other people for the greater part of his life. From two prison governorships–[. . .] the only appointments he ever had–he had to be relieved on account of his debts to local shop-keepers.'[35] As the eldest daughter, Egerton frequently visited her father in the debtor's prison, and helped her mother struggle to make ends meet in their tenement home. She later used some of these experiences in her fiction. The death of her mother in the mid-1870s had an indelible impact on her, not least because, after this, she and her siblings were separated between different schools and relatives. She herself was sent away to work as a language assistant at a school in Germany in 1875, where she spent two unhappy years. The fecklessness of her father was a constant worry to her during these years; nevertheless, she adored and supported him for the greater part of his life. There appears to be little information about Egerton's life over the next ten years. From *The Wheel of God* it is clear that she spent at least two years working in New York on her own, before returning to London to work in the mid-1880s. Tynan sets these dates as 1880–3. White mentions that she spent some time nursing in a London hospital, which presumably was when she returned from New York. However, the events of 1887 which culminated in her emigration to Scandinavia, as mentioned above, were to have a crucial impact on the rest of Egerton's life and career. On her return to London following Higginson's death in 1889, she met and married a Newfoundlander, George Egerton Clairmonte. The couple lived in penury as a result of Clairmonte's profligacy, and in order make ends meet they moved to Ireland, where they lived in Millstreet, County Cork. It was there that Egerton began to write, in an effort to earn her keep.

The Irish contexts of Egerton's work are not immediately obvious, and while a definition of Egerton's sense of her own national identity is a reasonably straightforward affair, critical discussion of its effect on her work is quite another. Today, Egerton's work is generally included in a specifically British genre of fiction, the New Woman novel. Yet her writing consistently addresses questions of national identities, kinship loyalties and, more significantly, outsider perspectives on different cultural practices. By virtue of her family background, which was Irish, Catholic and nationalist, Egerton was an outsider to the political and cultural hegemony of the late nineteenth century. Commenting on what he refers to as 'the history of her marginalisation', McCracken discusses Egerton's deliberate positioning of her work within the Decadent movement, in other words, on the margins of 'respectable British society'.

As we know, imperialist ambitions in the late nineteenth century focused on attempts to make English a world language. The fear that the language would be contaminated by indigenous tongues as a result of the spread of the empire caused a major emphasis to be placed not only on the speaking of English, but on its 'correct' pronunciation. As Dowling notes: 'the only safeguard for the English language seemed to lie in linguistic and literary vigilance of the most assiduous and unsleeping sort'.[36] New Woman novelists were frequently accused of contributing to the degeneration of the language, because of their lack of education, and frequent difficulties with grammar. I would argue that the work of New Woman writers such as Egerton and Grand challenged the dominant culture in their very use of language. Grand's references to the Irish language in *The Beth Book*, and the fact that Beth is punished for speaking Irish, is just one example of this. Similarly, Egerton's characters frequently use dialect, or introduce the Scandinavian languages, as well as placenames in Ireland and northern Europe that are not consistent with 'pure' English. For example, in the story 'The Child', from *Discords*, the school the girls attend is in Rathmines, and Egerton's use of Hiberno-English idiom locates it just as squarely in Dublin as the place name given. Egerton makes it clear that while her protagonist 'speaks without a trace of an accent',[37] her schoolmates all have quite strong Irish accents: '"Never mind dear; ma says you can't help exaggeratin'; for pa says your father's the biggest loiar out!"'[38] The interpolation of barbarous language and dangerous (often sexual) knowledge in their texts, and thus into the lives of their women readers, is radical in itself.

Some of Egerton's protagonists have strongly nationalist viewpoints (particularly Mary in her novel, *The Wheel of God*), and many of her early stories give hints as to the origins of their author.[39] Several of the stories evoke the Irish countryside in their setting, although they may not be geographically located in any specific way. While fishing with a stranger in just such a dislocated landscape, the protagonist in 'A Cross Line' observes: '"I fancy most of these flies are better for Scotland or England,"'[40] (i.e. these fishing flies are not so useful in the current situation–this suggests that although the landscape may *seem* like that of a Scottish or English riverside, the location is elsewhere). Later, the narrator homes in a little closer in terms of territory: 'She is stretched on her back on the short heather-mixed moss at the side of a bog stream [. . .]. Bunches of bog-wool nod their fluffy heads, and through the myriad indefinite sounds comes the regular scrape of a strickle on the scythe of a reaper in a neighbouring meadow [. . .]';[41] before finally telling us where we are: 'she can feel now, lying in the shade of Irish hills [. . .]'.[42] This fusion of Irish regionalism and a more elusive, impressionistic perspective on landscape often appears in Egerton's work. She frequently uses a specifically delineated locale as a basis for an imaginative leap into the aesthetic. In other stories, she sketches a particularly Irish *social* landscape. In 'Gone Under' she describes an Irish dock labourer in New York who is 'sending home the rent to Kerry'.[43] Her stories define Irish identity in social terms that fit in with her own childhood experience of deriving her national identity from the songs and stories she learned from her father, while living far away from a homeland she had never seen.

More importantly, the overall perspective of her fiction is that of an outsider. Having established psychological depth in her protagonist in 'The Child', Egerton goes on to show that such depth marks out the individual from the crowd. Among her playmates, the nameless child is a star: 'They are waiting for her, for is she not the most daring, the most individual amongst them?'[44] However, this singularity ceases to be an asset as the child grows up. In the second part of this story, 'The Girl', Egerton comments: '[The girl] is too sharp-tongued, too keen-eyed, too intolerant of meanness and untruth to be a favourite with her classmates–too independent a thinker, with too dangerous an influence over weaker souls to find favour with the nuns.'[45] Freedom of choice, the chance for an individual intellect to choose its own path, is seen as potentially seditious by one of the nuns in this Dublin school: 'For to the subdued soul of this still young woman who has disciplined thoughts and feelings and soul and body into a machine in a habit, this girl is a *bonnet-rouge*, an unregenerate spirit, the embodiment of all that is dangerous.'[46]

Egerton would have been familiar with Irish customs and, more importantly, traditional Irish narratives, thanks to her Irish father, who was famous for his storytelling ability, according to different sources. Angela Bourke discusses the methods employed by Irish storytellers of the nineteenth century, whom she describes as 'the artists and intellectuals of a tradition that was not amenable to the rules of the logical and literate nineteenth and twentieth centuries'. She writes: 'They used vivid imagery and repetition to make facts, techniques and ideas memorable [. . .]. Their stories often hinge on what has come to be known as "lateral thinking", the solving of problems by indirect, or apparently illogical means.'[47] The use of such lateral approaches to social problems by writers such as Egerton, posing a direct challenge to the late nineteenth-century hegemony, could be said to have come from her engagement with dominant discourses from the position of a cultural outsider who grew up in the colonies. Similar traits can be found in the work of Olive Schreiner, who grew up in South Africa.

In 'The Spell of the White Elf', Egerton puts both her knowledge of Irish narratives, and this element of lateral thinking to work, in a story about surrogacy. This story involves three women, their attitudes to sexuality and maternity, and the unusual domestic arrangement they arrive at for the rearing of a child. It begins, as many of Egerton's tales do, as a life story recounted by one woman to another on a sea voyage. She tells the story of a bitter enmity between herself and another woman, who had once been a friend. As a result of this hostility, the main protagonist becomes quite seriously ill, following which she is told that she can never have children: 'I am one of the barren ones; they are less rare than they used to be.'[48] Here, Egerton is alluding to the celibacy or chosen barrenness of many of the New Women during this period, against which conservative social commentators such as Eliza Lynn Linton were fulminating. The woman's maid Belinda has a deep-seated hatred of men and is childless as a result, unequivocally stating: 'if only one could have child ma'am without the horrid men and the shame.'[49]

Throughout the feuding, her ex-friend had been carrying a child, and the narrator tells us: 'all the time she was carrying the elf, she was full of simmering hatred, and she wished me evil often enough.'[50] In one of those strange, supernatural twists found regularly in Egerton's stories (to which I will return), the child born of this hatred is quite singular: 'It was a wretched, frail little being with a startling likeness to me. It was as if the evil the mother had wished me had worked on the child, and a constant thought of me stamped my features on its little face [. . .].'[51] As part of Egerton's rendering of all aspects of a woman's reaction to pregnancy and maternity, the new mother suffers from post-natal depression and rejects her child. In a neatly dovetailed movement, her sworn enemy, who has since met a man and married, forms an immediate bond with this child: 'when I looked at it, I could see how like we were.'[52] They undertake to rear 'the elf' as their own.

The similarity between this woman and the new-born child extends beyond a mere physical resemblance in the story. This baby is never referred to in the story as a human child, but always as an 'elf' which adds to the charged atmosphere around its birth. From the moment it is born, the child is characterized as uncanny and odd-looking. No doubt to a Victorian audience, the fact that its biological mother had rejected the child would have been enough to confirm its unnaturalness. Writing about the New Woman, Elliott comments: 'Emancipated females who demanded increasing social, political, educational and economic opportunities were considered as freakish as those who openly flaunted their sexuality in the pursuit of careers.'[53] That Egerton's heroine fits into this category is a point to which I will return later. Suffice it to say, her bond with the child is partially comprised of this mark of identification between them–they were both regarded as freaks of nature.

Another possible reading of this aspect of the text is to examine it in the light of a very different tradition familiar to Egerton. Writing on the Cork–Kerry border at the end of the nineteenth century, she was surrounded by a tradition quite different from the one for which her work was intended: that of Irish oral culture. By the 1890s, this tradition had been colonized by an English, literate mode of discourse. Nonetheless, aspects of the submerged culture created fissures in the dominant discourse of this late nineteenth-century Irish writer.[54] The full menace of the woman's ex-friend having 'wished [her] evil often enough' makes more sense when read against the backdrop of a culture steeped in a subtext of folklore, where this kind of threat is tangible enough.[55] In fact, within this context, the woman's barrenness could have been seen as the result of this evil wish. To the reader versed in oral accounts of the changeling, or even the Yeats poem 'The Stolen Child', the parallels between these discourses and 'The Spell of the White Elf' are striking. I mentioned the heightened atmosphere around the birth of this child, who, it then transpires, is quite unlike its mother in appearance. Add to this the constant repetition of the name 'elf' to refer to the child, and any reader versed in Irish oral culture will immediately jump to the conclusion that the child is a changeling. Angela Bourke describes the belief that fairies had stolen children from their cradles, often at birth, replacing them with withered, cantankerous changelings (that is, fairy offspring).[56] Thus, subtly blending elements of a familiar tale from oral culture with a new theme, surrogacy, Egerton weaves her own fairy spell around the complexities of maternity.

The underlying belief that womanhood consists of a series of roles, most enforced rigidly by society, is borne out in 'The Spell of the White Elf'. Having already created an irregular arrangement for the upbringing of a child, that it be raised by a childless couple completely unrelated to the birth mother, and a woman with whom she has no affinity furthermore, Egerton goes on to add to the oddness of their domestic arrangement. Her main protagonist is a career woman, a writer whose occupation causes her to travel widely. At the beginning of the story, a male observer describes her somewhat caustically as: 'a very learned lady; she has been looking up referats in the university bibliothek [. . .] I suppose her husband he stay at home and "keep the house"' (*sic*).[57] Egerton delights in informing us, a little later on, that this is the case. She says: "'Positions are reversed, they often are nowadays. My husband stays at home and grows good things to eat and pretty things to look at, and I go out and win the bread and butter.'"[58] As such, Egerton creates an early picture of a career woman with a baby. Reassuringly, unlike other New Woman novelists who introduce a child to the life experience of a New Woman, for example Iota's *A Yellow Aster*, Egerton's protagonist is enabled to have both family and career. Certainly, the arrival of the 'white elf' brings changes to her life, but these do not include the denial of her professional aspirations, and Egerton's approval of this state of affairs permeates the narrative.

Another Irish writer whose work was influenced by the narrative tradition he grew up with, and his position as an outsider, was Oscar Wilde. During the Wilde trials, the paper the *Speaker* referred to the New Women as 'creatures of Mr. Oscar Wilde's fantasy'. The effects of the scandal created by the Wilde trials in 1895 were far reaching, and a backlash against dissident voices quickly gathered force. It was (incorrectly) reported in the press that Wilde had been carrying *The Yellow Book* when arrested, and stones were thrown through the windows of the Bodley Head in Vigo Street.[59] Needless to say, this growing conservatism affected the work of the New Woman writers, particularly that of Egerton, as John Lane began to suggest changes to her work and reject her more radical experiments. Lane no longer wanted to publish anything that might bring public opprobrium on the Bodley Head and, accordingly, Egerton was asked to tone down her subject matter, presumably to suppress the sexual content of her stories. While working on her third collection, *Symphonies*, she expressed her dismay in a letter to Lane dated November 1896:

> You did not say you wished a 'milk and water' book on entirely different lines to that which made the success of *Keynotes* when we made our autumn arrangements, and now on the eve of completing my book it comes as a backhander [. . .]. I have had to change a great deal, out of concession to the new Bodley Head policy and this has necessitated much rewriting and rearrangement, as merely erasing paragraphs would not do.[60]

Symphonies was published in 1897 and in one review of this collection, the reviewer comments: 'Just at the moment, George Egerton's fortunes are low.'[61] Unfortunately for her, in terms of her new family responsibilities–she had just had a baby boy and Clairmonte had finally walked out on her–this ebb could not have come at a worse time. Used to living on her wits, Egerton temporarily abandoned the short-story form, which she was having difficulties selling to publishers, and began examining other forms, not with much success. In fact, in the months following Wilde's sentence, *Punch* announced triumphantly on the front cover: 'The End of the New Woman has Come at Last.'[62]

Discussing the Wilde trials, Bourke reminds us that they reveal a lot about the ways in which societies treat their marginal members: 'rendering them invisible; driving them underground; consigning them to the wild or barren areas of the shared landscape; punishing them viciously when they refuse to disappear.'[63] Although the New Woman writers did not suffer the same fate as Wilde or some of his fellow aesthetes, his imprisonment and disgrace meant that their literary careers effectively were also forced 'underground'. This period shows Egerton alienated from the literary scene following the Wilde trial–the backlash expelled both sexually degenerate and foreign influences–when imperial conservatism reasserted itself. This marginalization consistently finds voice in her fiction, particularly in her later stories such as 'The Well of Truth' from *Fantasias*, in which she writes of the predicament of a radical woman writer during that period:

> Poor V. finished a book just at this time [. . .]. There was an astonishing change in the atmosphere, all the book vendors wore clean overalls [. . .]. Of course, her unfortunate vision made it clear to her that they wore just the same suits underneath [. . .]. All the nursery windows were filled with Nursery Idylls, the subject of men and women had become positively indecent: all the new editors inserted parsley bed or gooseberry bush, wherever there had been a mention of a lying-in or crib, these latter being too suggestive–in fact, the entire reading public were going in for a milk and water diet.[64]

The contribution made by New Woman fiction to a feminist history of ideas, and to the study of Irish literature, cannot be underestimated. Writers such as Egerton created the intellectual and aesthetic space for early feminists to explore theoretical perspectives and to invest in themselves. By examining contemporary structures designed to keep these radical narratives at bay, I have illustrated the ways in which this literary project was ultimately defeated by a conservative and anti-feminist cultural establishment. Addressing the shifting locations of these narratives enables us to find new contexts for our understanding of this feminist fiction. More importantly, relocating this feminist fiction in an Irish context illuminates new paths for scholarship and understanding of late nineteenth-century writing in and about Ireland.

The Art of Politics in Somerville and Ross's Fiction with Emphasis on their Final Collection of Stories, In Mr. Knox's Country

Julie Anne Stevens

The Fox never sent a better messenger than himself.[1]

The fox is the supreme trickster in both politics and art. Edith Somerville and Martin Ross's treatment of Reynard in their writing draws upon his many aliases in history and literature to suggest a complex portrait of the late nineteenth and early twentieth-century Irish countryside. This essay traces the origins of the women writers' use of the fox in their sporting novel, *The Silver Fox* (1898), and in the most political of their three volumes of Irish R. M. stories and final collaborative work, *In Mr. Knox's Country* (1915). Focus on Reynard gives opportunity to demonstrate the significance of both an Anglo-Irish discourse as well as the broader European tradition of burlesque and beast fable in Irish writing. Even more importantly, this essay argues that the free-flying fox's passage through Somerville and Ross's country, his flight into the earth and his multiple aliases, allow him to act as a kind of vehicle of change; with Reynard we can analyse the writers' modernizing treatment of traditional material. The fox's shifting face in Somerville and Ross's novels and stories provides a key to our understanding of the development of popular Irish short fiction. As the Irish saying goes, the fox is his own messenger; his shape-changing potential manifests the possibilities of transformation in the short story.

Despite their reputation as 'hunting-stable novelists'[2] and as Anglo-Irish aficionados obsessed with the 'Sport of Kings' and 'King of Sports',[3]

Somerville and Ross did not concentrate on the hunt until well into their career. Nonetheless, their wholehearted involvement in the royal blood sport–Edith Somerville's position as Master of the West Carbery Foxhounds, their letters to each other stuffed full of detailed accounts of various runs across Ireland, the gradual dominance of the hunt in their collaborative work–has tended to secure their reputation as members of an élite Ascendancy, tediously preoccupied with outdated posturing and distant from the felt life of a politicized Irish countryside. By tackling the central symbol of British occupation in Ireland in Somerville and Ross's fiction–fox-hunting–and considering its working both inside and outside the Irish context, this essay demonstrates the writers' complex treatment of the sport. The argument reveals the multifaceted possibilities of a neglected aspect of their fiction and thus shows the need for a reconsideration of the women's writing as a whole, one that does not rely solely on the Irish context but reckons the significant influence of a wider-ranging argument.

Somerville and Ross have been situated alternatively within two central discourses: first, a feminist/sexual argument, and second, the Anglo-Irish tradition of country-house writing. Early critical biographies of the women writers established these two avenues of approach. Maurice Collis speculated on the writers' sexual orientation in *Somerville and Ross* (1968). The response of Gifford Lewis in *Somerville and Ross: The World of the Irish R. M.* (1985) and, more recently, *Edith Somerville, A Biography* (2005) relied on careful biographical documentation to refute suggestions of homosexuality.[4] Literary criticism of Somerville and Ross confirms the writers' sexual or social significance. The writers are included in works that concentrate on sexual politics, such as *Sex, Nation and Dissent in Irish Writing* (1997) edited by Eibhear Walshe, or in studies of Big House writing, such as Vera Kreilkamp's *The Anglo-Irish Novel and the Big House* (1998).[5] The recently published *Field Day Anthology of Irish Writing* by and about Irish women confirms these two approaches rather than offering new ways of studying the writers, largely because the treatment of Irish women's fiction in the *Anthology* follows along these selfsame lines, the sexual and social.[6]

The publication of *The Edith Œnone Somerville Archive in Drishane House* by Otto Rauchbauer in 1995, and Declan Kiberd's inclusion of Somerville and Ross within a postcolonial framework in *Inventing Ireland* (1995) and *Irish Classics* (2000), indicates the potential richness of

Somerville and Ross's writings and Edith Somerville's art works.[7] The writers' interest in landscape or in children's literature, for example, suggests the possibility of various approaches to their work–eco-feminist theory, or beast fable and fairy tale analysis–that will allow us to see it in new ways.[8] Perhaps even more importantly, their regular visits to France, their inclusion of popular material in the writing and their negotiation of the demands of the English periodical press ask that the work be considered in a wider context than has been the case thus far.

This discussion looks at the Irish fox to explore how his various aliases in Somerville and Ross's writing–the Celtic fox, Dan Russel and Reynard–invigorate his representation and politicize the authors' works. In so doing, the argument moves in and out of the Irish context to demonstrate the workings of the popular European beast fable alongside Irish concerns. In a similar way, the argument takes out of context Somerville and Ross's final collection of stories, normally considered within the Irish R. M. stories as a whole, to illustrate a larger argument and show the development of the writers' short fiction.

Before stepping out of context, however, to consider the possible political significance of Somerville and Ross's Irish fox, we might first consider the manner in which the Irish material was received in Great Britain. A summary of the reception of the texts will show popular attitudes towards the use of Irish politics in fiction, the demand for suitable Irish material by the reading public, and how the periodical press initially perceived these women writers.

*

The reception of Somerville and Ross's first novel, *An Irish Cousin*, in 1889 was generally marked by the English reviewers' relief that the writers had avoided Irish politics. Somerville and Ross's novel, as the *Observer* noted, managed to provide a 'picture of ramshackle Irish provincial society' with 'the additional merit of being absolutely unpolitical'.[9] Magazines and newspapers like the *Spectator*, *St James Gazette* and the *Sunday Times* delighted in the novel's comic scenes, its Irishness ('redolent of the soil'), while avoiding unpleasant realities. As the *Graphic* put it, '[t]here is nothing–welcome relief!–about politics, or agrarian outrage, or the Coercion Act'.[10]

One longer review of the novel in the Scottish periodical, the *Old*

Saloon, treated the work at greater length and alongside a novel that did not avoid politics, Robert Louis Stevenson's *The Master of Ballantrae* (a novel Somerville and Ross admired). While the reviewer found the absence of politics in the Irish novel a 'wonderful relief', the final effect was disconcerting:

> The peculiarity of the book [. . .] is that though supposed to be a picture of Ireland in the present day, there is not a word of politics from beginning to end, and the events of the story might be going on in Somersetshire or the Isle of Wight [. . .] instead of in the most agitated part of an agitated country.[11]

The reviewer admits to being confused. There is a church in Somerville and Ross's novel but no chapel, respectful tenants in a place 'where Captain Moonlight has never been heard of'.[12] How does one know that this countryside actually *is* Ireland?

Somerville and Ross must have taken the criticism to heart, for their next novel, *Naboth's Vineyard*, dealt directly with agrarian outrage and Irish Catholicism in a small village called Rossbrin, the fictional counterpart of Edith Somerville's home, Castletownshend, West Cork. Boycotting, the maiming of cattle and the threats of Captain Moonlight provided the central action of the work. The novel was admired, however, for its 'impartiality'. Though the ladies' magazine *Black and White* noted that the authors took the 'Unionist view of the situation', magazines like the *Saturday Review* praised the 'neutrality' of the text and felt that the 'boycotting scenes [were] but picturesque accessories'.[13] In the words of a reviewer in the *Daily Express*, the point of Irish politics in Irish fiction such as *Naboth's Vineyard* was not whether or not it should be included but how best it might be managed:

> Novelists satiated with the intricacies of London society or the matchless sunsets of the Scottish Highlands are beginning to find that Ireland with her smiles and her tears can, when properly managed, make excellent 'copy'.[14]

It wasn't until the publication of *The Real Charlotte* in 1894 that the British reviewers uneasily admitted to a disturbing element in the fiction. The *Graphic* side-stepped the issue, describing the book as an 'unconventional novel', while some reviewers ignored the troubling portrait of Charlotte Mullen and concentrated on the 'charming' and 'rattling' depiction of pretty Francie Fitzpatrick.[15] The *Westminster Gazette*, however, did not hesitate to describe the book as 'one of the most disagreeable novels we have ever read'.[16] Particularly unsettling was the nature of the action in the text, events that sat uneasily under the safe heading of the picturesque. 'The book is marked throughout', says the reviewer, 'by a persistent preference for ugly incident whenever possible.' As the *Lady's Pictorial* notes with ladylike unease, 'English people who read this novel will be confirmed in their mistaken idea that Ireland is a nation of barbarians [. . .] The book winds up in unrelieved gloom.'[17] It seems as though the unsavoury element could no longer be overlooked.

The writers' intent to reveal more clearly the dark side of Irish life may have been precipitated by Martin Ross's increasing interest in Irish politics. A year before the appearance of *The Real Charlotte*, Martin published a political essay in the *World* that described in stark and uncompromising terms the conditions for the Irish poor—women especially—in an increasingly nationalist Ireland. Appropriately named 'The Terror in Ireland', the article depicts the fear of those who attempt to support the movement against Home Rule (provoked by Gladstone's second Home Rule bill). An elderly woman signs the Unionist Alliance petition and, a day later, begs that her name be removed or '"they'll smell it out, and the house'll be burnt over us! The priest in ——— cursed it from the altar. I'm not able to dhraw a breath nor ate a bit this day. I'm near dead with the fright!"' Martin's profile of the Irish people in the article emphasizes their diversity and dissension and thus attacks the notion of a unified Irish Catholic population mobilized against the upper-class Protestant Irish population. The same argument drives the plot of Somerville and Ross's 'impartial' novel, *Naboth's Vineyard*, but in the later essay, energized no doubt by the re-emergence of Gladstone's bill, the emphasis is on England's ignorance of the inner workings of the Irish population. There are, claims Martin with Unionist fervour, many Roman Catholic peasants who dread Home Rule:

> for the reason that so many of [this] kind secretly dislike; it would
> bestow the power of the country on the farmers and the priests;
> who may, by blood and bringing up together, count as one class;
> and it would probably oust the 'gintry', to whom affections

turned with the force of old association. [. . .] [The Irish peasant] hated the farmers with a hate thickened by jealousy of their prosperity, and by experience of their dealings with those beneath them.

Catholic Irish self-hate, mutual distrust and fear fester beneath the larger arguments abroad in relation to politics and religion in Ireland. Martin's article reveals the voices of an unheard underclass whose feelings darken the lives of those who live in the country:

> Far below the surface of that Ireland which comes to English breakfast-tables in special correspondence and party speeches; almost as deep as the shadowy wrecks and memorials of human death agony that lie below the feet of the tourist while he reads his paper on the deck of a Channel steamer, and feels pleasantly aware of his position and general advantages.[18]

Martin Ross's intent in 'The Terror of Ireland' is to reveal the deep and dark underbelly of Irish life to readers interested in Irish affairs. Active involvement in politics (collecting signatures for the Unionist Alliance) directs her interests. The publication of *The Real Charlotte* a year later met with mixed reviews in England because of the novel's representation of a world that escaped patronizing and complacent notions of Irishness. The novel showed a countryside where 'the smile and the tear' had a darker meaning than what may have been hitherto accepted as palatable across the water.

*

Somerville and Ross started writing the Irish R. M. stories in 1898, the same year they published their fourth novel, *The Silver Fox*, a work that recalls Bram Stoker's *Dracula*, which also appeared this year.[19] Both novels elaborate on a concept their authors introduced in earlier works, *Naboth's Vineyard* and *The Snake's Pass* (1890): the Irish landscape conceals dark and dangerous depths that contain hints of supernatural forces. In *The Silver Fox* and *Dracula*, the concept becomes a dominating metaphor so that the plots of both works revolve around the literal notion of 'going to earth', to use the hunting term. An animal–fox or wolf–embodies the soul of a human and escapes into the ground like some witch or demon of the underworld, recalling the Celtic myth recorded by Sir James Frazer in his *Golden Bough*. The demon/witch transforms itself into a fox, an animal traditionally burnt in the midsummer festival fires.[20] The 'witch or fairy' fox of Somerville and Ross's novel is appropriated from Irish fairy folklore collected in Galway and West Cork. The writers' lifelong interest in oral culture may have been sharpened in the late 1890s by the notorious incident of 'witch-burning' in Tipperary in 1895, a case that was well documented and discussed in the English and Irish papers of the time, as surveyed in Angela Bourke's study, *The Burning of Bridget Cleary: A True Story*.[21] In *The Silver Fox*, Irish folklore is grafted on to Anglo-Irish traditions and the New Woman novel through the device of the fox. In other words, the animal functions as a fairy for the local people, a familiar of the New Woman Slaney Morris, and also belongs firmly within the sporting world of the Anglo-Irish Ascendancy. At the same time, Somerville and Ross's silver witch works as a device in the novel, a means of enticing the hunters onto the dangerous boggy terrain of Ireland's West. The fox enters the dreams of characters and manifests unknown dimensions of the Irish countryside that an Englishman's reckless improvements (the attempt to lay a railway line across the bog) have stirred up. The silver fox exists on the interface of reality (the land) and the unknown (underground), and its natural environment is a suitably mixed element, the 'spongy gravel' of the bogland.[22]

In the first two collections of R. M. stories, *Some Experiences of an Irish R. M.* (1898) and *Further Experiences of an Irish R. M.* (1908), various invisible foxes create mayhem and elude capture, flying down crannies and crevices in the Irish countryside like ghosts or fairies. With their second sporting novel of 1911, *Dan Russel The Fox*, Somerville and Ross introduced a most potent kind of fox into their writing, a 'soldier of fortune': 'that good-looking gentleman of many aliases, Dan Russel the Fox.'[23] Sir Russel Fox of Chaucer's 'Nun's Priest's Tale'[24] enters the Irish countryside with his own political pistolry, and his introduction indicates the writers' interest in using political allegory in their later short fiction, *In Mr. Knox's Country*.[25] The fabulist qualities of Reynard would have especially attracted Edith Somerville, who wrote and illustrated a number of children's stories and evidently enjoyed the satirical potential of the beast material.[26] *The Story of the Discontented Little Elephant* published in 1912 relied on bold pictures of humanized animal figures for comic effect.

Most striking of all her children's books must be her undated, handmade book, *Growly-Wowly or the Story of the Three Little Pigs*.[27] Brightly illustrated and with a plot in which the youngest female pig gains the upper hand over the wolf, Growly-Wowly, it turns the familiar tale on its head. A later publication, *Little Red-Riding Hood in Kerry* (1934), shows her appropriating another international fairy tale for her own purposes.[28] Somerville's children's books gave her an opportunity to include her comic illustrations with her writing, but she was also strongly attracted to the allegorical possibilities of fables and exploited familiar stories in both children's and adult fiction.

As a keen theatre-goer and lover of pantomime, Martin Ross may have noted the fox's connection to Harlequin (who sometimes wore the fox's brush), and probably enjoyed the 1898 edition of Ben Jonson's *Volpone*, illustrated by Aubrey Beardsley in 1897–8. As a political critic and admirer of Goethe's work, she undoubtedly appreciated the possibilities of the Reynard fable during a period of Home Rule revival. Goethe published his satire on the French Revolution, *Reineke Fuchs*, in 1793. In 1887, in the midst of popular interest in Goethe, Thomas J. Arnold published a translation of Goethe's version of the beast fable. In his introduction to the translation, beautifully illustrated with the original designs and pictures by Wilhelm Von Kaulbach and Joseph Wolf, Arnold suggests that the revived interest in the Reynard material in Britain originated with the Great Exhibition of 1851.[29] Whatever the case, by the time Somerville and Ross had started writing their ultimate collaborative work, *In Mr. Knox's Country*, they had established a strong interest in the beast epic, 'Reynard the Fox.' The final stories transport the allegory, with its connection to the *commedia dell' arte* demonstrated by *Volpone*, onto Irish terrain, telling the old story in a new way so that the politics of the original fable are re-charged with a different tradition.

As I have pointed out, the first two collections of R. M. stories are sandwiched between two less successful novels, *The Silver Fox* and *Dan Russel The Fox*, which concentrate on the hunt. In the earlier novel and as already noted, the fox is a magical and rather sinister creature, most likely a fairy figure drawn from local folk stories collected by the writers.[30] In the later novel, however, Sir Russel Fox comes from a broader folk tradition. Characters manifest the attributes of animals in the opening scenes of the novel, an indicator not only of the writers' love of caricature but also of their growing interest in the use of fables in their fiction. As a result, in the final collection of stories, *In Mr. Knox's Country*, Flurry Knox and his wife Sally have settled into the background, the clown Slipper has disappeared, and Flurry's role as the trickster subsides. A battalion of animals enters the lists: varieties of dogs and horses, donkeys, a peacock, turkey-cock, a bull, wood-pigeons, rats, rabbits, cows, goats, plenty of bees and ducks, and an animal frequently masquerading as cat or dog–the fox. From the midst of the beasts, old Mrs Knox of Aussolas Castle emerges as a challenge to the rising middle class and her sidekick, the fox, aids her subterfuge.

The fox in the novel works as contrivance or part of the picturesque background, but the fox enters the R. M. stories as if he is coming home–he becomes an integral part of the form. The fox of the R. M. series, especially the final collection, addresses both the contents of the stories and the shape they take. There is no contrivance because the stories are suspended within an Irish chronotope–carnival time when animals and humans have equal significance, when dogs, horses and donkeys can nearly talk and the fox is in his element. The fox lives underground and frequently leads his pursuers downwards, to the centre not only of his universe but also that of comic satire with its hell-bent, thrusting force. Reynard runs through *In Mr. Knox's Country* disappearing and reappearing, like harlequin effecting amazing transformations, in this case with a flick of the tail, and carrying within himself the essence of folk laughter. In the R. M. stories, he is part of the Irish countryside, a feature of the landscape, as well as being an integral aspect of the fable form and a natural conduit for satire. He also unites the different traditions Somerville and Ross introduce into their short fiction, combining within his presence the attributes of the folklore, stage and Anglo-Irish tradition. In other words, as a cypher of burlesque or as a figure of the royal hunt, he recalls more than one discourse.

The fox belongs as much to the royal hunt as he does to Celtic mythology, a hidden Gaelic Ireland, or European beast fable. The fox and his brush rouse the *furor venaticus* just as Harlequin and his wand introduce '*la frontière du merveilleux*'.[31] The fox, however, is also a vital aspect of the material world. In pursuit of him, the hunt transgresses physical borders: stone walls, closed gates, turf banks. The hunt ignores boundaries and embraces the Irish landscape as its own.

By its very nature, fox-hunting calls upon the united efforts of the countryside to participate in the landlord's sport. Without willing farmers and an affable peasantry, the sport could not succeed. As a result, the hunt emerged as an opportunity to exercise passive resistance on the part of Land League sympathizers. In 1881 and 1882, for instance, the Land League campaign against fox-hunting employed massed groups of people to tramp through the countryside and disturb any possible prey. The game was ruined but the people had not broken the law.[32]

The repeated summoning of the hunt in Somerville and Ross's later fiction has provoked the sharpest criticism of their work. These 'hunting-stable novelists', as Susan Mitchell dismissed them in 1919, 'whipped-up all life into a froth, piling it lightly over the tragic and dark in Ireland, obscuring reality and, with the most amiable of intentions, inflicting a lasting hurt upon the character of their country'.[33] The pageantry of the hunt smacked of triumphalism. Its ability to cover large tracts of land, the farmer's grazing fields and the tenant's smaller plots, in the pursuit of casual delights belittled the land's allotment to the hard-working folk. The proprietary tone of loud voices atop fine horses ranging across a struggling land seemed to assert prior ownership and to disdain the new land laws. More generally, constant reference to the Irish hunt provoked a feeling that Somerville and Ross remained at odds with the times, clinging to outdated representations of Ireland that belonged more rightly to the illustrated cartoons of *Punch* in the previous century than the altered political landscape of the period.

However, nationalists like Susan Mitchell understood that the struggle for Irish land in early twentieth-century Ireland took place as much on the page as it did in the fields or courtroom. The Ireland that was to advance forward into the twentieth century as an independent nation could hardly countenance a landscape that included the quintessentially royal sport of riding to hounds. Daniel Corkery suggests something similar when he asserts in *Synge and Anglo-Irish Literature* that those who did not belong (or whom Corkery could not see as belonging) amongst the crowds attending an Irish hurling match could not possibly write about those who did.[34]

The additional affront of a comic treatment of the hunt, laughing landlords blissfully ignorant of the serious business of Irish political landscaping, gave fuel to smouldering nationalist hearts. The suspicion that the tomfoolery of the R. M. stories provides a deceptively charming picture concealing aristocratic greed may have contributed to the determination to erase the remnants of an Anglo-Irish tradition from the plundered land, to return to a Celtic Eden, or, at least, to present an Irish landscape emptied of Protestant Ascendancy myths. In 1903, the year

Edith Somerville took up her five-year position as Master of the West Carbery Foxhounds, the Wyndham Act promised to accelerate the transfer of ownership of the land from landlord to tenant through the encouragement of the sale of entire estates.[35] The land was changing hands, and the R. M. stories of this period might be considered a series of landscapes heavily inscribed by distinctly Anglo-Irish *Weltanschauung* that takes imaginative possession of Ireland's green fields.[36]

*

In Mr. Knox's Country initially focuses upon Flurry Knox's decrepit and ancient grandmother, old Mrs Knox of Aussolas Castle. The first two stories concentrate upon her reign as an Anglo-Irish autocrat of a feudalistic estate who still appears to hold sway in the Irish countryside. The middle stories elaborate upon the increasing significance of a middle-class Dublin family, the McRorys, who have bought into Knox country. One of these McRorys, young and pretty Larkie McRory, wins over Major Yeates and company with her cheeky vitality, her 'street-boy quality of being in the movement'.[37] Thus in the penultimate story of the series, 'The Comte de Pralines', we are not too surprised to discover that the young Dubliner wins the ultimate hunt prize, the fox's brush. However, the parody of the rise of the metropolitan middle class–which Larkie McRory represents–is not the final comment of this collection. The last story, 'The Shooting of Shinroe', continues to satirize the hunting process with a final, wonderfully bathetic conclusion to the collection. This essay concentrates on the initial stories of the collection to draw attention to the use of the fox.

In the earlier stories, Mrs Knox controls house, servants and family through personality and guile. In the second story, 'The Finger of Mrs. Knox', she confronts her ex-tenants in a play for supremacy. Though no longer owning the land and close to her deathbed, she still exercises considerable influence. One of the most pathetic of her ex-tenants, whining and nearly destitute Stephen Casey, petitions her aid to save him from the mercenary reckoning of Goggins, the gombeen man. Old Mrs Knox drives out with Major Yeates in his new motor car to confront Goggins, a successful merchant, who has built his property on the 'blood-money'[38] of the local woods, trees planted by his own grandfather as tenant of the Knox family. Goggins is about to claim Stephen Casey's remaining livelihood, a few starving animals, in return for money owed.

In the midst of Mrs Knox's high-handed demands that Goggins reduce his claim and Goggins' servile but evasive response, Flurry Knox's hunting party arrives on the scene. A sighting of the fox causes such a hullabaloo that everyone, including Stephen Casey's animals, joins the chase. Major Yeates and Mrs Knox take the car but everyone else sprints off on foot, hoof, or paw after the fox. As always in the R. M. stories, except for 'The Comte de Pralines' where the beast is slaughtered, the fox escapes. The hounds start chasing Casey's donkey, and Yeates mistakes a dog for a fox. By the end of the tale, Yeates finds himself gulled twice, once by Mrs Knox, who leaves the British civil servant to pay Casey's debt, and once by the fox. Luckily for Yeates, he has no money. So, as a final and clever twist in the story, Mrs Knox suggests that Goggins lend Yeates the money owed. Goggins ends up paying himself.

The fox and Mrs Knox are equal in their stratagems and sleight of hand. Both slip away from the various traps set for them, and each ends up tricking the trapper. Time ignores them. At age ninety-plus, Mrs Knox's existence spans the nineteenth century and she has chased and plotted against many a fox in her time. They collaborate at this stage. Various biographers, following the lead of Lady Gregory who first noted the resemblance, draw comparison between Mrs Knox and Martin Ross's mother.[39] Mrs Martin's maiden name, Fox, could suggest a connection between the fictional representatives of the old-Irish world, Mrs Knox and the fox, a connection elaborated upon below. For the moment, however, and more significant to this argument, we will note Somerville and Ross's treatment of the story of Reynard the Fox in 'The Finger of Mrs. Knox'. A brief consideration of a popular late nineteenth-century translation of Goethe's version of the Reynard material will highlight the Anglo-Irish writers' appropriation of the political allegory in their short fiction.

The stories of the Reynard cycle satirize feudal society through the trickster-hero's ability to outwit established authority. The folk material is the stuff of carnival, when the individual and his anarchic stratagems overcome order and introduce momentary mayhem into the normal state of affairs. The fox is the villain, the lion is the king, the wolf the dupe and the donkey the victim. Reynard is also devilishly clever and takes on the role of unmasker in *Reineke Fuchs*; the fox exposes greed and ambition within the kingdom. His name, as Goethe's translator, Thomas Arnold, points out, comes from the German, *Reinhart*, and the Flemish, *Reinart*, and means 'counsellor' or 'adviser'. His fortress, Malpertuis, means 'an evil hole'.[40]

Various animals complain to King Noble about Reynard's tricks, pleading for his intercession and help. While some of their stories are true, others are half-fabrications; either they blame the fox for their own misdeeds or mask the fact of their contribution to his unlawful acts. Reynard is the source of envy and resentment amongst many of his fellow subjects because first, he is the shrewdest amongst a clever bunch, and second, he has set himself apart from their society. He is an outlaw. When the king sends a series of royal messengers to bring Reynard to justice at court, the fox tricks and humiliates each one of them. Each trick–Reynard fooling Bruin the bear by appealing to his gluttony for honey; Reynard tricking Tybalt the cat into the trap that has been set for Reynard himself–tells its own story. Finally, Reynard's friend the badger brings him to court and Reynard arrives believing he can fool them all, even the king himself.

Reynard has few sympathizers and is quickly sentenced to death. But the wily fox manages once more to trick everyone by hinting at a wondrous hidden treasure, a secret stash concealed deep in the darkness of the earth. Seduced by his own covetousness, the king lets Reynard go, but instead of finding treasure for the king, the fox gobbles up one of the royal messengers and sends his skin back to court. There never was any secret treasure; nonetheless, the lure of diamonds and gold compels the king to heed Reynard's hints. The fox's ultimate trick, then, is to promise wondrous treasure; that promise proves to be the bait that no animal, not even a lion, can resist. However much the king might doubt the existence of the treasure, to ignore the lure is to lose the promise of untold riches.[41]

Various connections between the fable and *In Mr. Knox's Country* might be drawn. Bruin the bear's gluttony, for instance, is repeated in the Englishman, Chichester, in 'A Friend of Her Youth'. This 'well-fed [. . .] schoolboy'[42] dines on heather honey like some greedy bear, and he falls into foolishness because of his own stomach. In another story, 'Harrington's', the hidden secrets and 'the thrill of possible treasure-trove'[43] at the auction situated next to a disused gold mine remind us of Reynard's imaginary treasure. The riches of the Irish auction prove just as elusive when Yeates ends up bidding for and buying his own ladder. Throughout the R. M. stories, Somerville and Ross capitalize on the notion of the hidden Ireland as a place of treasure, a source of ultimate truth and lost glory, which, however distant or vague, must be respected by the authorities that be. The treasure in the R. M. stories lurks behind the shifting face of the Irish terrain, safeguarded by an Irish fox.

It is not my intention to list the numerous links between the folk tale and Somerville and Ross's stories, however. Suffice to say that the fable–and especially the wily fox–reverberates throughout their final collection. This politicized material with its connection to the carnivalesque and its use of allegory–a kind of masking–addresses universal questions about society and power. Goethe's version, as popularized by Thomas Arnold, sets up an argument between the forces of the aristocracy and those of democracy.[44] Reference to the beast fable gives resonance and depth to the Irish material. We might keep in mind, then, that the story of Reynard deals with attempts to control the kingdom, and in Somerville and Ross's short fiction the various visiting English characters to Mrs Knox's/Fox's Castle might be seen as royal envoys attempting to control the wily old trickster. Knox/Fox acts as an outsider in 'The Finger of Mrs. Knox', resented for the cleverness and brutality that has given her the upper-hand amongst the king's subjects, and suspected of holding vast reservoirs of treasure in her decrepit house.

Significantly, Mrs Knox's position repeats that of the hero of an earlier story by Martin Ross's older brother, Robert Martin, called 'St. Patrick's Day in the Morning' (1899). However, in Robert Martin's semi-autobiographical tale, the Anglo-Irish landlord, debt-ridden and forced by a changing social system to evacuate his castle, sees himself as victim rather than master of the situation:

> This hunting season is over, and for the last run of the season the Master is the fox. The Hard Time Hounds will soon run him from scent to view, and there is nothing for him but to look for another country for some seasons to come.[45]

Like his hero in 'St. Patrick's Day in the Morning', Robert Martin also left his 'country' (the Martin territory of Galway), pursued by 'the Hard Time Hounds' (Parnell's pack). Unfortunately, he did not discover a pot of gold in Australia with which to recover his estate, as the hero of his fiction does. Somerville and Ross knew both the dream and the reality of his position.

One might argue that Somerville and Ross, like Robert Martin, reverse Reynard's role in their short story. In the beast fable, the fox symbolizes the cleverness of the enlightened individual by demonstrating the stratagems of the royal hunt's prey. By placing autocratic Mrs Knox in Reynard's position, by making the hunter the hunted in the new Ireland, Somerville and Ross appear to subvert the fabulist material. Such a supposition would fall in with Terry Eagleton's observation on the paradoxical reversal of the Irish Ascendancy's perception of itself as victim in works such as Maturin's *Melmoth the Wanderer* or Stoker's *Dracula*. Eagleton reads the alienated and doomed Melmoth as a symbol of the Irish Protestant governing class:

> Their sense of persecution, in part at least, is a dread of the vengeance of those they have persecuted. Estranged from the populace by culture and religion, the élite can easily mistake itself for the marginal, and so misperceive itself as a mirror image of the people themselves. The hunters become the hunted: and this is surely one reason why the figure of the self-lacerating Satanic hero can strike such a powerful resonance.[46]

The exploiter, says Eagleton, 'has put himself beyond the pale of humanity, and so is curiously on terms with those he dispossesses'.[47]

In a similar way, Bram Stoker's *Dracula* has been read as an expression of colonial anxiety. The 'old fox', as Van Helsing describes the vampire, is put to the chase by his pursuers when they 'sterilize his lairs, so that he cannot use them of old'.[48] The hunter becomes in the course of the novel the prey of new-world 'knights of the Cross'.[49] In broken English, Van Helsing tells his fellow Christian huntsmen that they will go and '"do what our friend Arthur [Godalming] call, in his phrases of hunt 'stop the earths' and so we run down our old fox–so? Is it not?"'[50] The reversal of the vampire's role makes him go to ground, like a fox, and assists in Eagleton's perception of the figure as Anglo-Irish Ascendancy: 'The Ascendancy, too, will evaporate once their earth is removed from them, though to wrench it from them will demand rather more than a sprig of garlic and rather less than a stake through the heart.'[51]

Somerville and Ross's treatment of the Reynard material does not demonstrate this neat reversal. The writers parody an Anglo-Irish trope as depicted in Robert Martin's story by turning *their* fox into a stage figure. Instead of a misplaced psychological perception that transforms the colonizer into an outlawed figure, the exploiter into the exploited, as

Eagleton suggests, I would argue that the adoption of marginalized figures like the fox (or Harlequin or Mephisto or even Dracula) derives from a burlesque tradition. If we consider the role of the hunted in Ben Jonson's *Volpone*, for instance, popularized at the end of the nineteenth century by Beardsley's illustrations, we discover that the prey has become the hunter in the burlesque form. Such a rehabilitation of the beast fable material does not demonstrate a suppressed anxiety regarding Britain's role in Europe so much as put into action a fundamental satirical device: everything is turned upside down.

Like Volpone in Jonson's play, Mrs Knox with her suspected (and coveted) wealth/position is a manipulator in her own right. If there is any reversal at all in 'The Finger of Mrs. Knox', it is that the fox has become the hunter; she has turned the tables on her pursuers. In *Volpone*, we recall that various animal-like characters covet the fox's treasure, his gold: Voltore, the lawyer-vulture; Corvino, the merchant-crow and Corbaccio, the old man-raven. The treasure as bait and the fox's stratagems, aided by the devilish Mosca (the Hellequin of medieval folklore) become artful manipulations whereby the middle class is exposed in all its gullibility and greed. Somerville and Ross's treatment of the beast fable works in a similar manner. Mrs Knox and the fox use themselves as bait to expose Goggins' greed. As in Goethe's version of the Reynard story, the fox is the trickster, a comic cousin of Harlequin, rather than a victim of the 'Hard Time Hounds' let loose by Irish nationalist politics. Indeed, to discover the possible political purpose of Somerville and Ross's later story, we might consider its context when it first appeared in 1913 rather than rely on a comparison to the earlier and rather obvious comic stories of the Irish landowner, Robert Martin.

As already noted, 'The Finger of Mrs. Knox' pits the craft and authority of a weakened Anglo-Irish autocracy against the opportunistic usury of gombeenism, and thus it is frequently cited as the most political of the R. M. stories.[52] *Blackwood's* published the story in June, 1913; it followed a series of articles debating Asquith's Home Rule bill introduced in April of the previous year. In 1912 and 1913, *Blackwood's* published four sustained attacks on the bill. Sir John Pentland Mahaffy of Trinity College Dublin wrote three of these articles. 'What is Nationality?' in February 1912 argued that nationality, a sentiment of brotherhood supported by a supposed commonality of race, home, language and religion, cannot be ascribed to by the Irish in all their differences. The resurgence of the Gaelic language, Mahaffy's pet hate, is a backward step towards isolationism and ultimately stifles progress. 'Will Home Rule Be Rome Rule?' published the following August, stated the arguments of the minority Irish Protestants and the educated Roman Catholics against the power of the Catholic Church in Ireland as it would be affected by Home Rule. Then, in February 1913, Mahaffy's 'Who Wants Home Rule?' outlined for the *Blackwood's* reader what he saw as dubious support for Home Rule in Ireland and argued against a too precipitous, almost reckless, voting in of the measure. Those who want Home Rule consist of 'Jackeens, Buckeens, horse-dealers, Gombeen men, idle sons of strong farmers or of respectable shopkeepers, insubordinate school-teachers, editors of local newspapers, leader writers in the same, patriot poets, bankrupt traders. To all such a new vista of success is opened.'[53] Additional arguments against the Home Rule bill appeared in editorial commentary and in an article published in January 1913 by the imperialist Arthur Page called 'Ireland and the Empire'. Particular attention in these pieces is given to the Ulster Unionists who will be 'under the heel' of nationalists if Home Rule goes through.

Somerville and Ross's story responds directly to the ongoing Home Rule debate in *Blackwood's Magazine*, but to what extent does the comic fiction support either side of the argument? The direct allusion to the usurpation of the landed gentry through the Irish Land Acts of the early twentieth century in 'The Finger of Mrs. Knox', leads analysts to read the story as a critique of the emergence of adept profiteering in the new Ireland.[54] Direct juxtaposition of the old world (Mrs Knox in Aussolas Castle) and the new (Major Yeates's car, reference to cinematography) appears to confirm the sense in this story that a golden feudal age has passed. For example, in 'Comedy and the Land: Somerville and Ross's Irish R. M.', Joseph Devlin reads 'The Finger of Mrs. Knox' as a romanticization of the 'old feudal order' and Mrs Knox as an expression of the writers' 'desired status' to be female autocrats: 'Faced with the evaporation of landlord control and their own double marginality as unattached women, Somerville and Ross created an all-powerful female character able to hold her own, and able to hold the land.'[55] Yet the story's context in *Blackwood's* suggests a gentle dig at Mahaffy's entrenched and biased position, while the deployment of the fox/Harlequin material demands that we ask to what extent the feudal backdrop facilitates form. The longing for a Golden Age–as *Volpone* shows with its *commedia dell'arte* figures whose craving for the fox's treasure satirizes the Renaissance ideal–is echoed in the romantic depiction of past Anglo-Irish glories. In short, though the story is located within an ongoing argument related to land ownership and Home Rule (an argument already shown to be of particular interest to Martin Ross), it presents a complex version that parodies as much as it propagates the Unionist position. More important than sentimental musings on the Anglo-Irish past is the modernizing treatment of form.

'The Finger of Mrs. Knox' creates an Irish feudal landscape, not to mull over the passage of Ascendancy rule, but to incorporate within the short fiction the beast fable material. The antique setting furthers the sense of timelessness we identify with carnival and, more recently, the short story form. The political commentary lies in the authors' reworking of the Reynard fable rather than their depiction of Ireland as feudal landscape. All those elements perceived to be indicative of the authors' lament for the aristocratic past could also be seen as aesthetic devices used to generate the developing genre of short fiction (which *Blackwood's* encouraged) as well as providing an implicit, if uneasy, commentary on the Anglo-Irish role. Aussolas Castle and Mrs Knox, her sycophantic, whining ex-tenant, the hunt and the hounds, 'like creatures in a tapestry hunting scene',[56] the variety of animal and human life, 'from goat to gombeen man',[57] and above all the trickery of both Mrs Knox and the fox directly recall the fable of Reynard. The material is carefully set in the new world so that Yeates and Mrs Knox chase the hunt by car and Anglo-Irish 'rule' possesses no real meaning in modern Ireland. Thus the story recreates the fabulist material and continues its aims by parodying exaggerated perceptions of Ascendancy rule (Mrs Knox possesses no real power), British authority in Ireland (Yeates remains bewildered) and nationalist ideals of the rising middle class (Goggins swindles the poor).

Consideration of the different sources of Reynard both inside and outside the Irish world presents a multifaceted picture of reality in the later stories. The ever-shifting angles of Somerville and Ross's final collaborative work, what Martin Ross believed to be the best of their three collections of Irish R. M. stories,[58] displays the art of the fox who lies at the heart of the short fiction. The stories express a modern ambiguity in their elusive handling of character and situation. Ambivalence emerges as a necessary tension between tradition and progress, between the impulse to retain the past and the drive to admit change. The free-flying fox's passage through these stories, his flight into the earth and multiple aliases, demonstrates the inability of the fiction to capture or to enclose the various masks/traditions of the Irish landscape. The short story form finds its greatest proponent in the furtive fox–timeless, evasive, the very essence of political strategy in a tricky world.

Bibliography

Adams, J. R. R., *The Printed Word and the Common Man: Popular Culture in Ulster 1700–1900*, Belfast: The Institute of Irish Studies, Queen's University Belfast, 1987

Albion and Ierne; A Political Romance, by an Officer, London and Belfast: Marcus Ward, 1886

Anderson, Carol and Riddell, Aileen M., 'The Other Great Unknowns: Women Fiction Writers of the early Nineteenth Century', in Douglas Gifford and Dorothy McMillan (eds), *A History of Scottish Women's Writing*, Edinburgh: Edinburgh University Press, 1997, pp. 179–95

Archives of the Royal Literary Fund, London, 1984

Ardis, Anne L., *New Women, New Novels: Feminism and Early Modernism*, New Brunswick: Rutgers University Press, 1990

Armstrong, Nancy, *Desire and Domestic Fiction: A Political History of the Novel*, Oxford: Oxford University Press, 1987

Arnold, Matthew, 'Preface to Poems (1853)', in Stephen Greenblatt (gen. ed.), *Norton Anthology of English Literature* vol. 2, 8th ed., New York: Norton, 2006, pp. 1374–84

Arnold, Thomas J., 'Introductory Letter (1855)' in *Reynard the Fox, After the German Version of Goethe*, illustrated by Wilhelm Von Kaulbach and Joseph Wolf, London: John C. Nimmo, 1887, pp. xiii–xxvii

Baker, Ernest, *A Guide to the Best Fiction in English*, London: Routledge, 1913

Barbauld, Anna Laetitia, No title, *Monthly Review* 60, Oct. 1809, pp. 217–18

Baudelaire, Charles, *Oeuvres Complètes*, vol. 2, ed. Claude Pichois, Paris: Editions Gallimard, 1976

Belanger, Jacqueline (ed.), *The Irish Novel in the Nineteenth Century*, Dublin: Four Courts Press, 2005

Benger, Elizabeth, *Memoirs of the Late Mrs. Elizabeth Hamilton*, 2 vols., London: Longman & Co., 1818

Bermingham, Ann, 'Elegant Females and Gentlemen Connoisseurs: The Commerce in Culture and Self-Image in Eighteenth-Century England', in Ann Bermingham and John Brewer (eds), *The Consumption of Culture 1600–1800: Image, Object, Text*, London: Routledge, 1995, pp. 489–513

Berrow, June Hilary, 'Somerville and Ross: Transitional Novelists', unpublished thesis, University College Dublin, Jan. 1975

Bhabha, Homi K., *The Location of Culture*, London: Routledge, 1994

Bjørhovde, Gerd, *Rebellious Structures*, Oslo: Norwegian University Press, 1987

Blackburne (Casey), Elizabeth Owens, *The Heart of Erin: An Irish Story of Today*, 3 vols., London, 1882

Blanton, Casey, *Travel Writing: The Self and the World*, New York: Twayne, 1997

Blessington, Marguerite, *Grace Cassidy or The Repealers*, 3 vols., London: Bentley, 1833

Blundell, Margaret, *M. E. Francis: An Irish Novelist's Own Story*, Dublin: Catholic Truth Society of Ireland, 1935

Boland, Eavan, 'A Kind of Scar: The Woman Poet in a National Tradition', in *A Dozen Lips*, Dublin: Attic Press, 1994, pp. 72–92

Bourke, Angela, Siobhán Kilfeather, Maria Luddy, Margaret Mac Curtain, Gerardine Meaney, Máirín Ní Dhonnchadha, Mary O'Dowd and Clair Wills (eds), *Field Day Anthology of Irish Writing: Women's Writing and Traditions*, vols. 4 and 5, Cork: Cork University Press, 2002

Bourke, Angela, *The Burning of Bridget Cleary: A True Story*, London: Pimlico, 1999

Bric, Maurice J., 'The Whiteboy Movement in Tipperary 1760–80', in W. Nolan and T. G. McGrath (eds), *Tipperary: History and Society*, Dublin: Geography Publications, 1985, pp. 148–184

Brodhead, Richard, *Cultures of Letters: Scenes of Reading and Writing in Nineteenth-Century America*, Chicago: University of Chicago Press, 1993

Brown, Stephen J., *Ireland in Fiction: A Guide to Irish Novels, Tales, Romances and Folklore*, 1915; 2nd ed. 1919; Shannon: Irish University Press, 1969

Brown, Stephen J., *Ireland in Fiction: A Guide to Irish Novels, Tales, Romances, and Folk-Lore* Dublin: Maunsel, 1919

Bull, Philip, *Land, Politics and Nationalism: A Study of the Irish Land Question*, Dublin: Gill & Macmillan, 1996

Bunbury, Selina, *A Summer in Northern Europe, Including Sketches in Sweden, Norway, Finland, The Aland Islands, Gothland, &c.*, London: Hurst & Blackett, 1856

Bunbury, Selina, *Evelyn: or a Journey from Stockholm to Rome in 1847–48*, London: Richard Bentley, 1849

Bunbury, Selina, *Life in Sweden; with Excursions in Norway and Denmark*, London: Hurst & Blackett, 1853

Butler, Marilyn, 'Edgeworth's Ireland: History, Popular Culture, and Secret Codes', *Novel* 34.2, Spring 2001, pp. 267–92

Butler, Marilyn, 'Irish Culture and Scottish Enlightenment: Maria Edgeworth's Histories of the Future', in Stefan Collini, Richard Whatmore and Brian Young (eds), *Economy, Polity, and Society: British Intellectual History 1750–1950*, Cambridge: Cambridge University Press, 2000, pp. 158–80

Butler, Marilyn, *Maria Edgeworth: A Literary Biography*, Oxford: Clarendon Press, 1972

Buzard, James, *The Beaten Track: European Tourism, Literature and Ways to 'Culture' 1800–1918*, Oxford: Clarendon Press, 1993

Campbell, Mary, *Lady Morgan: The Life and Times of Sydney Owenson*, London: Pandora, 1988

Chaucer, Geoffrey, *The Canterbury Tales*, trans. Nevill Coghill, Baltimore, Maryland: Penguin, 1952

Clay, Edith (ed.), *The Idler in Naples*, London: Hamilton, 1979

Clyde, Tom, *Irish Literary Magazines: An Outline History and Descriptive Bibliography*, Dublin: Irish Academic Press, 2003

Collini, Stefan, Donald Winch and John Burrow, *That Noble Science of Politics: A Study in Nineteenth-Century Intellectual History*, Cambridge: Cambridge University Press, 1983

Collis, Maurice, *Somerville and Ross*, London: Faber & Faber, 1968

Connely, Willard, *Count D'Orsay: Dandy of Dandies*, London: Cassell, 1952

Connor, Jennifer J., 'The Irish Origins and Variations of the Ballad "Molly Bawn"', *Canadian Folk Music Journal* 14, 1986, pp. 10–18

Corbett, Mary Jean, *Allegories of Union in Irish and English Writing, 1790–1870*, Cambridge: Cambridge University Press, 2000

Corkery, Daniel, *Synge and Anglo-Irish Literature*, Cork: Mercier, 1966

Costello-Sullivan, Kathleen, 'Novel Traditions: Realism and Modernity in *Hurrish* and *The Real Charlotte*', in Jacqueline Belanger (ed.), *The Irish Novel in the Nineteenth Century*, Dublin: Four Courts Press, 2005, pp. 150–66

Cowman, Roz, 'Lost Time: The Smell and Taste of Castle T', in Eibhear Walshe (ed.), *Sex, Nation and Dissent in Irish Writing*, Cork: Cork University Press, 1997, pp. 87–102

Cummins, Geraldine, *Dr. E. Œ. Somerville*, London: Andrew Dakers, 1952

Cunningham, Bernadette and Máire Kennedy (eds), *The Experience of Reading: Irish Historical Perspectives*, Dublin: Rare Books Group of the Library Association of Ireland and Economic and Social History Society of Ireland, 1999

Curtis Jr., L. P., 'Stopping the Hunt, 1881–1882', in C. H. E. Philpin (ed.), *Nationalism and Popular Protest in Ireland*, Cambridge: Past and Present Society, 1987, pp. 349–402

Darnton, Robert, *The Kiss of Lamourette: Reflections in Cultural History*, New York and London: W. W. Norton, 1990

Davies, Mark A., *A Perambulating Paradox: British Travel Literature and the Image of Sweden c. 1770–1865*, Malmö: Lunds Universitet, 2000

Davis, Lennard J., *Factual Fictions: The Origins of the English Novel*, Philadelphia: University of Pennsylvania Press, 1986, 1991

de Vere White, Terence, *A Leaf From the Yellow Book: The Correspondence of George Egerton*, London: Richards, 1958

Devlin, Joseph, 'Comedy and the Land: Somerville and Ross's Irish R. M.' *Studies in Anglo-Irish Fiction and Balladry*, Working Papers in Irish Studies, 94–1, Fort Lauderdale, Florida: Nova University, 1994, pp. 1–30

Dictionary of Irish Literature A-L., rev. and expanded ed., Robert Hogan (ed.), Westport, Conn.: Greenwood Press, 1996

Donnelly Jr., James J., 'The Whiteboy Movement, 1761–5', *Irish Historical Studies* 21, Mar. 1978, pp. 20–54

Dowling, Linda, 'The Decadent and the New Woman in the 1890s', *Nineteenth Century* vol. 33, 1979, pp. 434–53

Dunne, Tom (ed.), *The Writer as Witness: Literature as Historical Evidence*, Cork: Cork University Press, 1987

Dunne, Tom, 'Ireland, Irish and Colonialism', *Irish Review*, vol. 30, 2003

Eagleton, Terry, 'Afterword', in Jacqueline Belanger (ed.), *The Irish Novel in the Nineteenth Century*, Dublin: Four Courts Press, 2005, pp. 222–28

Eagleton, Terry, *Crazy John and the Bishop, and Other Essays on Irish Culture*, Critical Conditions series, Cork: Cork University Press, in association with Field Day, 1998

Eagleton, Terry, *The Function of Criticism: From* The Spectator *to Post-Structuralism*, 1984; London: Verso, 1997

Eagleton, Terry, *Heathcliff and the Great Hunger: Studies in Irish Culture*, London: Verso, 1995

Eagleton, Terry, *Scholars and Rebels in Nineteenth-Century Ireland*, Oxford: Blackwell, 1999

Edgeworth, Maria, 'Mrs. Elizabeth Hamilton', *Edinburgh Evening Courant*, 1 Aug 1816, p. 4

Edgeworth, Maria, *Castle Rackrent* and *Ennui*, ed. Marilyn Butler, London: Penguin Books, 1992

Egerton, George, *Discords*, London: Elkin Mathews & John Lane, 1894

Egerton, George, *Fantasias*, London: John Lane, 1897

Egerton, George, *Keynotes*, London: Elkin Mathews & John Lane, 1893

Eliot, George, *Middlemarch*, ed. W. J. Harvey, 1871–72; Harmondsworth: Penguin, 1985

Elliott, Bridget, 'New and Not So New Women on the London Stage: Aubrey Beardsley's *Yellow Book* Images of Mrs. Patrick Campbell and Rèjane', *Victorian Studies* vol. 3.1, 1987, pp. 33–57

Ezell, Margaret, *Writing Women's Literary History*, Baltimore: Johns Hopkins University Press, 1993

Felski, Rita, *The Gender of Modernity*, Cambridge MA: Harvard University Press, 1995

Ferris, Ina, 'Narrating Cultural Encounter: Lady Morgan and the Irish National Tale', *Nineteenth-Century Literature* vol. 51.3, 1996, pp. 287–303

'Fiction, Poetry, Sketches of Travel, and Humorous Works', *Harper's New Monthly Magazine* vol. 92, May 1896, pp. 11–20

Finke Laurie, *Feminist Theory, Women's Writing*, Ithaca: Cornell University Press, 1992

Flint, Kate, *The Woman Reader, 1837–1914*, Oxford: Clarendon Press, 1993

Fludernik, Monika, Introduction, in Monika Fludernik (ed.), *Hybridity and Post-Colonialism: Twentieth-Century Indian Literature*, Tübingen: Stauffenberg-Verlag, 1998, pp. 9–18

Foster, Shirley, *Across New Worlds: Nineteenth Century Women Travellers and their Writing*, New York: Harvester Wheatsheaf, 1990

Francis, M. E. [Mrs. Francis Blundell or Mary Sweetman], *Miss Erin*, London and New York: Benziger, 1898

Francis, M. E., *Miss Erin*, London: Methuen, 1898

Francis, M. E., *Molly's Fortunes*, London: Sands, 1905?

Frazer, James, *The Golden Bough*, New York: Macmillan, 1947

Frye, Northrop, *Anatomy of Criticism: Four Essays*, Princeton: Princeton University Press, 1957

Gallaher, Fannie, *Thy Name is Truth* 3 vols., London, 1884

Garber, Marjorie, *Quotation Marks*, New York: Routledge, 2003

Garside, Peter and Schöwerling, Rainer (eds), *The English Novel 1770–1829*, 2 vols. Oxford: Oxford University Press, 2000

Garside, Peter, 'Popular Fiction and National Tale: Hidden Origins of Scott's *Waverley*', *Nineteenth-Century Literature* vol. 46.1, Jun. 1991, pp. 30–53

Gill, Pat, 'The Way of the Word: Telling Differences in Congreve's *Way of the World*', in K. M. Quinsey (ed.), *Broken Boundaries: Women and Feminism in Restoration Drama*, Kentucky: University Press of Kentucky, 1996, pp. 164–81

Grogan, Claire 'Crossing Genre, Gender and Race in Elizabeth Hamilton's *Translation of the Letters of a Hindoo Rajah*', *Studies in the Novel* 34, Spring 2002, pp. 21–42

Grøndahl, Illit and Raknes, Ola, *Chapters in Norwegian Literature*, London: Gyldendal, 1923

Grosz, Elizabeth, *Space, Time, and Perversion: Essays on the Politics of Bodies*, New York: Routledge, 1995

Gubar, Susan, *Critical Condition: Feminism at the Turn of the Century*, New York: Columbia University Press, 2000

Gustafson, Alrik, *A History of Swedish Literature*, Minneapolis: Minnesota University Press, 1971

Haberstroh, Patricia Boyle, *Women Creating Women: Contemporary Irish Women Poets*, Dublin: Attic Press, 1996

Hall, S. C., *Retrospect of a Long Life*, 2 vols., London: Bentley, 1883

Hamilton, Catherine, *Women Writers: Their Works and Ways*, 1st Series, London: Ward, Lock, Bowden & Co. 1892

Hamilton, Elizabeth, Preface, in Elizabeth Hamilton, *The Cottagers of Glenburnie*, 3rd ed., Edinburgh: Manners and Miller, 1808

Hamilton, Elizabeth, *The Cottagers of Glenburnie*, new ed., Edinburgh: Nimmo, Hay, & Mitchell, 1895

Hare, Augustus, *The Life and Letters of Maria Edgeworth*, 2 vols., London: Edward Arnold, 1894

Harris, W., 'John Lane's Keynotes Series and the Fiction of the 1890s', *PMLA* vol. 83, 1968, pp. 1407–13

Henderson, Heather, 'The Travel Writer and the Text: My Giant Goes With Me Wherever I Go', in Michael Kowalewski (ed.), *Temperamental Journeys: Essays on the Modern Literature of Travel*, Athens GA: University of Georgia Press, 1992, pp. 230–48

Holland, Joel, '"Beauty and the Beast": Depictions of Irish Female Types during the Era of Parnell, c.1880–1891', in Lawrence W. McBride (ed.), *Images, Icons and the Irish Nationalist Imagination*, Dublin: Four Courts, 1999, pp. 53–72

Hotson, J. Leslie, 'Colfox vs. Chauntecleer', in Edward Wagenknecht (ed.), *Chaucer: Modern Essays in Criticism*, New York: Oxford University Press, 1959, pp. 98–116

Houghton, Walter E. *et al* (eds), *The Wellesley Index to Victorian Periodicals*, 5 vols., Toronto and Buffalo: University of Toronto Press, 1966-

Howes, Marjorie, 'Discipline, Sentiment and the Irish-American Public: Mary Ann Sadlier's Popular Fiction', *Éire-Ireland* vol. 40.1–2, 2005, pp. 140–69

Hume, R. D., 'The Myth of the Rake in 'Restoration' Comedy', *Studies in the Literary Imagination* 10, 1977, pp. 25–55

Hungerford, Mrs. [Margaret], *Molly Bawn*, 1878; London: Herbert Jenkins, n. d.

Innes, C. L., *Woman and Nation in Irish Literature and Society, 1880–1935*, Athens, Georgia: University of Georgia Press, 1993

Jeffrey, Francis, Rev. of *The Cottagers of Glenburnie*, by Elizabeth Hamilton, *Edinburgh Review* 12, Jul. 1808, n. p.

Jones, Ann H., *Ideas and Innovations: Best Sellers of Jane Austen's Age*, New York: AMS Press, 1986

Jordan, Ellen, 'The Christening of the New Woman: May 1894', *Victorian Newsletter* 48, 1983, pp. 19–21

Joseph, Gerhard, 'The *Antigone* as Cultural Touchstone: Matthew Arnold, Hegel, George Eliot, Virginia Woolf, and Margaret Drabble', *PMLA* 96.1, 1981, pp. 22–35

Kelleher, Margaret, '*The Field Day Anthology* and Irish Women's Literary Studies', *Irish Review*, 30, 2003, pp. 82–94

Kelleher, Margaret, 'Writing Irish Women's Literary History', *Irish Studies Review* vol. 9.1, 2001, pp. 5–14

Kelly, Gary, *Women, Writing, and Revolution, 1790–1827*, Oxford: Clarendon Press, 1993

Kiberd, Declan, *Inventing Ireland*, London: Jonathan Cape, 1995

Kiberd, Declan, *Irish Classics*, London: Granta, 2000

Kilfeather, Siobhán, 'Sex and Sensation in the Nineteenth-Century Novel', in Margaret Kelleher and James H. Murphy (eds), *Gender Perspectives in Nineteenth-Century Ireland*, Dublin: Irish Academic Press, 1997, pp. 83–92

Kingsley, Mary, *Travels in West Africa. Congo Français, Corisco and Cameroons*, 1897; Boston: Beacon Press, 1988

Kreilkamp, Vera, *The Anglo-Irish Novel and the Big House*, New York: Syracuse University Press, 1998

Kunitz, Stanley J. (ed.), *British Authors of the Nineteenth Century*, New York: Wilson, 1964

Lady Blessington's Conversations of Lord Byron, ed. with an introduction by Ernest Lovell Jr., Princeton NJ: Princeton University Press, 1969

Laird, Heather, *Subversive Law in Ireland 1879–1920*, Dublin: Four Courts Press, 2005

Lawrence, Karen R., *Penelope Voyages: Women and Travel in the British Literary Tradition*, Ithaca: Cornell University Press, 1994

Ledger, Sally, *The New Woman: Fiction and Feminism at the Fin de Siècle*, Manchester: Manchester University Press, 1997

Leerssen, Joep, 'How *The Wild Irish Girl* Made Ireland Romantic', in C. C. Barfoot and Theo D'haen (eds), *The Clash of Ireland: Literary Contrasts and Connections*, Amsterdam: Rodopi, 1989, pp. 98–117

Leppert, Richard, 'Social Order and the Domestic Consumption of Music: The Politics of Sound in the Policing of Gender Construction in Eighteenth-Century England', in Ann Bermingham and John Brewer (eds), *The Consumption of Culture 1600–1800: Image, Object, Text*, London: Routledge, 1995, pp. 514–34

Lewis, Gifford, *Edith Somerville, A Biography*, Dublin: Four Courts Press, 2005

Lewis, Gifford, *Somerville and Ross, The World of the Irish R. M.*, 1985; London: Penguin, 1987

Linn, William, 'The Life and Works of the Hon. Emily Lawless, First Novelist of the Irish Literary Revival', unpublished thesis, New York University, 1971

Lloyd, David, 'Afterword: Hardress Cregan's Dream', in Jacqueline Belanger (ed.), *The Irish Novel in the Nineteenth Century*, Dublin: Four Courts Press, 2005, pp. 228–37

Lloyd, David, *Anomalous States: Irish Writing and the Post-Colonial Moment*, Dublin: Lilliput, 1993

Lloyd, David, *Nationalism and Minor Literature: James Clarence Mangan and the Emergence of Irish Cultural Nationalism*, California: University of California Press, 1987

Longley, Edna, *From Cathleen to Anorexia: The Breakdown of Irelands*, Dublin: Attic Press, 1990

Luddy, Maria (ed.), *Irish Women's Writing, 1839–1888*, 6 vols., London: Routledge/Thoemmes Press, 1998

Lynch, Rachel Jane, 'The Crumbling Fortress: Molly Keane's Comedies of Anglo-Irish Manners', in Theresa O'Connor (ed.), *The Comic Tradition in Irish Women Writers*, Gainesville: University Press of Florida, 1996, pp. 73–98

Lyons, F. S. L., *Ireland Since the Famine*, London: Fontana, 1971

Mac Anna, Ferdia, Introduction, in Ferdia Mac Anna (ed.), *An Anthology of Irish Comic Writing. Selected and Introduced by Ferdia Mac Anna*, London: Michael Joseph, 1995, pp. xi–xxi

MacDonagh, Oliver, '*Sanditon*: a Regency Novel?', in Tom Dunne (ed.), *The Writer as Witness*, Cork: Cork University Press, 1987, pp. 114–32

Madden, R. R., *Literary Life and Correspondence of the Countess of Blessington*, 3 vols., London: Newby, 1855

Mahaffy, Sir John Pentland, 'Who Wants Home Rule', *Blackwood's Magazine* cxciii. mclxviii, Feb. 1913, pp. 245–53

Martin Ross, 'The Terror in Ireland', *World*, 5 Apr. 1893, pp. 22–23

Martin, Robert, *Bits of Blarney*, London: Sands, 1899

McClintock, Letitia, *A Boycotted Household*, London, 1881

McCracken, Scott, 'George Egerton's *Wheel of God*', in Tadhg Foley *et al* (eds), *Gender and Colonialism*, Galway: Galway University Press, 1995, pp. 139–57

'M. E. Francis', *Times* 11 Mar. 1930, p. 18 col. B

'M. E. Francis', *Times* 15 Mar. 1930, p. 17 col. B

Merish, Lori, *Sentimental Materialism: Gender, Commodity Culture and Nineteenth-Century American Literature*, Durham and London: Duke University Press, 2000

Miller, Julia Anne, 'Acts of Union: Family Violence and National Courtship in Maria Edgeworth's *The Absentee* and Sydney Owenson's *The Wild Irish Girl*', in Kathryn Kirkpatrick (ed.), *Border Crossings: Irish Women Writers and National Identities*, Dublin: Wolfhound, 2000, pp. 13–37

Mills, Sara, *Discourses of Difference: An Analysis of Women's Travel Writing and Colonialism*, London: Routledge, 1991

Molloy, Joseph Fitzgerald, *The Most Gorgeous Lady Blessington*, 2 vols., London: Downey & Co., 1896

Moynahan, Julian, *Anglo-Irish*, New Jersey: Princeton University Press, 1995

Murphy, James H., *Catholic Fiction and Social Reality in Ireland, 1873–1922*, Westport, Conn: Greenwood Press, 1992

Murphy, James H., 'Insouciant Rivals of Mrs Barton: Gender and Victorian Aspiration in George Moore and the Women Novelists of the *Irish Monthly*', in Margaret Kelleher and James H. Murphy (eds), *Gender Perspectives in Nineteenth-Century Ireland*, Dublin: Irish Academic Press, 1997, pp. 221–28

Murphy, James H., '"Things Which Seem to You Unfeminine": Gender and Nationalism in the Fiction of Some Upper Middle Class Catholic Women Novelists, 1880–1910', in Kathryn Kirkpatrick (ed.), *Border Crossings: Irish Women Writers and National Identities*, Dublin: Wolfhound, 2000, pp. 58–78

Mussell, Kay, *Fantasy and Reconciliation: Contemporary Formulas of Women's Romance Fiction*, London: Greenwood Press, 1986

Ní Dhomhnaill, Nuala, 'What Foremothers?', in Theresa O'Connor (ed.), *The Comic Tradition in Irish Women Writers*, Gainesville: University of Florida Press, 1996, pp. 8–20

No title, *Freeman's Journal*, 10 Oct. 1881, n. p.

No title, *Freeman's Journal*, 20 May 1881, n. p.

Nulty, Thomas, *The Land Question: Letter of the Most Rev. Dr. Nulty to the Clergy and Laity of the Diocese of Meath*, Dublin: Joseph Dollard, 1881

Ó Ciosáin, Niall, *Print and Popular Culture in Ireland, 1750–1850*, Basingstoke: Palgrave, 1997

O'Connor, Theresa, 'Introduction: Tradition and the Signifying Monkey', in Theresa O'Connor (ed.), *The Comic Tradition in Irish Women Writers*, Gainesville: University Press of Florida, 1996, pp. 1–7

O'Donoghue, D. J., *The Poets of Ireland: A Biographical Dictionary*, Dublin: Hodges Figgis & Co, 1912

Obituary of Elizabeth Owens Blackburne, *Athenaeum*, 14 Apr. 1894, p. 480

Paulin, Tom, *The Riot Act: A Version of Antigone by Sophocles*, London: Faber & Faber, 1985

Pettman, Jan Jindy, *Worlding Women: A Feminist International Politics*, London: Routledge, 1996

Powell, Violet, *The Irish Cousins*, London: Heinemann, 1970

Power, Thomas P., *Land, Politics and Society in Eighteenth Century Tipperary*, Oxford: Clarendon Press, 1993

Pyle, Hilary, *Red-Headed Rebel: Susan L. Mitchell, Poet and Mystic of the Irish Cultural Renaissance*, Dublin: Woodfield Press, 1998

Rauchbauer, Otto (ed.), *The Edith Œnone Somerville Archive in Drishane House*, Dublin: Irish Manuscripts Commission, 1995

Read, Charles A. (ed.), *The Cabinet of Irish Literature*, 4 vols., London, 1879–1880

'Recent Novels', *The Times*, 30 Aug. 1901, p. 5 col. A

'Recent Novels', *The Times*, 6 Jan. 1899, p. 4 col. E

Reilly, Eileen, 'Beyond Gilt Shamrock: Symbolism and Realism in the Cover Art of Irish Historical and Political Fiction, 1880–1914,' in Lawrence W. McBride (ed.), *Images, Icons and the Irish Nationalist Imagination*, Dublin: Four Courts, 1999, pp. 95–112

Rev. of *A Boycotted Household*, by Letitia McClintock, *Athenaeum* 2812, 17 Sep. 1881, p. 365

Rev. of *The Cottagers of Glenburnie*, by Elizabeth Hamilton, *Belfast Monthly Magazine* 2, May 1809, pp. 379–83

Rev. of *The Cottagers of Glenburnie*, by Elizabeth Hamilton, *British Critic* 32, Aug. 1808, pp. 116–18

Rev. of *The Heart of Erin*, by Elizabeth Owens Blackburne, *Athenaeum* 2847, 20 May 1882, p. 632

Rev. of *Hurrish: A Study*, by Emily Lawless, *Nation* 20 Feb. 1886, n. p. Clipping in the Lawless papers, Marsh's Library, Dublin

Rev. of *An Irish Cousin*, by Somerville and Ross, *Graphic*, Sep. 1889, n. p.

Rev. of *An Irish Cousin*, by Somerville and Ross, *Observer*, Sep. 1889, n. p.

Rev. of *An Irish Cousin*, by Somerville and Ross, *Old Saloon*, Nov. 1889, pp. 702–05

Rev. of *The Earl of Cork*, by Madame Genlis, *Belfast Monthly Magazine* 2, 31 Jan. 1809, p. 57

Rev. of *Life in Sweden*, by Selina Bunbury, *Littell's Living Age* vol. 38, 24 Sept. 1853, pp. 793–96

Rev. of *Naboth's Vineyard*, by Somerville and Ross, *Black and White*, 19 Dec. 1891, n. p.

Rev. of *Naboth's Vineyard*, by Somerville and Ross, *Daily Express*, 2 Nov. 1891, n. p.

Rev. of *Naboth's Vineyard*, by Somerville and Ross, *Daily Graphic*, 5 Oct. 1891, n. p.

Rev. of *Naboth's Vineyard*, by Somerville and Ross, *Saturday Review*, 21 Nov. 1891, n. p.

Rev. of *Popular Essays*, by Elizabeth Hamilton, *Critical Review*, fourth ser., 5, Mar. 1814, p. 225

Rev. of *The Real Charlotte*, by Somerville and Ross, *Athenaeum*, 9 Jun. 1894, n. p.

Rev. of *The Real Charlotte*, by Somerville and Ross, *Graphic*, 20 Oct. 1894, n. p.

Rev. of *The Real Charlotte*, by Somerville and Ross, *Lady's Pictorial*, 19 May 1894, n. p.

Rev. of *The Real Charlotte*, by Somerville and Ross, *Liverpool Mercury*, 23 May 1894, n. p.

Rev. of *The Real Charlotte*, by Somerville and Ross, *Westminster Gazette*, n. d., n. p.

Rev. of *Self-Control*, by Mary Brunton, *Eclectic Review* 8, Jun. 1812, p. 605

Rev. of *Woman; or, Ida of Athens*, by Sydney Owenson, *Belfast Monthly Magazine* 2, Feb. 1809, p. 141

Richards, Shaun, Foreword, in Scott Brewster, Virginia Crossman, Fiona Becket and David Alderson (eds), *Ireland in Proximity: History, Gender Space*, London: Routledge, 1999, pp. xi–xv

Ryan, W. P., *The Irish Literary Revival: Its History, Pioneers, and Possibilities etc.*, London: printed by the author, 1894

Sadleir, Michael, *Blessington-d'Orsay: A Masquerade*, 2nd ed., London: Constable, 1947

Sadleir, Michael, *Blessington-d'Orsay: A Masquerade*, London: Constable, 1933. American edition *The Strange Life of Lady Blessington*, Boston: Little, Brown & Co., 1933

Schama, Simon, *Landscape and Memory*, London: Fontana, 1995

Scheff, Thomas J., 'Shame and the Social Bond: A Sociological Theory', <http://www.soc.ucsb.edu/faculty/scheff> Access date 20 Sept. 2002

'Selina Bunbury', *Irish Book Lover* vol. 7, Jan. 1916, pp. 105–07

Shattock, Joanne (ed.), *The Cambridge Bibliography of English Literature*, vol. 4, 3rd ed., Cambridge: Cambridge University Press, 1999

Showalter, Elaine, *Sexual Anarchy: Gender and Culture at the Fin de Siècle*, London: Virago, 1992

Sillard, P.A., 'A Notable Irish Authoress', *New Ireland Review* 27, Aug. 1907, pp. 369–72

Smith, Barbara Herrnstein, *Contingencies of Value: Alternative Perspectives for Critical Theory*, 1988; Cambridge, MA: Harvard University Press, 1991

Smyth, Ailbhe, (ed.), Introduction, in Ailbhe Smyth (ed.), *Wildish Things: An Anthology of New Irish Women's Writing*, Dublin: Attic Press, 1989, pp. 7–16

Somerville Edith Œ., 'Hunting in Ireland', *Irish Travel*, Oct. 1927, p. 295

Somerville, Edith Œ., Letter to James Pinker, 18 Nov. 1911, no. 3330–1, Manuscripts Department, Trinity College Library, Dublin

Somerville, Edith, *Little Red Riding-Hood in Kerry*, London: Peter Davies, 1934

Somerville, Edith Œ., *The Sweet Cry of Hounds*, London: Methuen, 1936

Somerville, Edith Œ. and Ross, Martin, *Collection of Irish Anecdotes, 1885–1945*, no. 881, Special Collections, Queen's University Library, Belfast

Somerville, Edith Œ. and Ross, Martin, *Dan Russel, The Fox*, London: Methuen, 1911

Somerville, Edith Œ. and Ross, Martin, *The Irish R. M.*, London: Abacus, 1992

Somerville, Edith Œ. and Ross, Martin, *The Silver Fox*, 1898; London: Longmans, Green & Co., 1918

Sophocles Antigone in a new version by Declan Donnellan, London: Oberon Books, 1999

Sophocles, *Antigone; The Women of Trachis; Philoctetes; Oedipus at Colonus*, ed. and transl. Hugh Lloyd-Jones, Cambridge, MA: Harvard University Press, 1994

Sophocles' Antigone: A New Version by Brendan Kennelly, Highgreen: Bloodaxe, 1996

Sourvino-Inwood, Christiane, 'Assumptions and the Creation of Meaning: Reading Sophocles' *Antigone*', *Journal of Hellenic Studies* 109, 1989, pp. 134–48

Staves, Susan, *Players' Scepters: Fictions of Authority in the Restoration*, Lincoln: University of Nebraska Press, 1979

Stephenson, Roger H., 'The Political Import of Goethe's Reineke Fuchs', in Kenneth Vartry (ed.), *Reynard the Fox: Social Engagement and Cultural Metamorphoses in the Beast Epic from the Middle Ages to the Present*, New York: Berghahn, 2000, pp. 191–207

Stetz, Margaret Diane and Lasner, Mark Samuels, *England in the 1890s: Literary Publishing at the Bodley Head*, Washington: Georgetown University Press, 1990

Stevens, Julie Anne, *Writing and Illustrating Ireland: The Somerville and Ross Exhibition Catalogue*, Trinity College Library Dublin, November to December 2002, Dublin: Paceprint, 2002

Stevenson, Lionel, *The Wild Irish Girl: The Life of Sydney Owenson, Lady Morgan*, London: Chapman & Hall, 1936

Stewart, Bruce, 'Bram Stoker's *Dracula*: Possessed by the Spirit of the Nation?', *Irish University Review* vol. 29.2, autumn/winter 1999, pp. 238–55

Stoker, Bram, *Dracula*, 1898; New York: W. W. Norton, 1997

Sturgis, Matthew, *Passionate Attitudes: The English Decadence of the 1890s*, London: Macmillan, 1995

Sullivan, Niamh, 'The Iron Cage of Femininity: Visual Representations of Women in the 1880s Land Agitation', in Tadhg Foley and Seán Ryder (eds), *Ideology and Nineteenth-Century Ireland*, Dublin: Four Courts, 1998, pp. 238–55

The Burial at Thebes: Sophocles's Antigone, transl. Seamus Heaney, London: Faber & Faber, 2004

Thompson, Nicola Diane, *Reviewing Sex: Gender and the Reception of Victorian Novels*, Basingstoke: Macmillan, 1996

Todd, Janet, *Mary Wollstonecraft: A Revolutionary Life*, London: Weidenfeld & Nicolson, 2000

Tracy, Robert, 'Maria Edgeworth and Lady Morgan: Legality versus Legitimacy', *Nineteenth-Century Fiction* vol. 40.1, 1985, pp. 1–22

Trumpener, Katie, *Bardic Nationalism: The Romantic Novel and the British Empire*, Princeton, N.J.: Princeton University Press, 1997

Tsappa, Lilian, '*Antigone*: A Case of Political Remedy', *Classical and Modern Literature* vol. 19.1, 1998, pp. 17–33

Ty, Eleanor, 'Female Philosophy Refunctioned: Elizabeth Hamilton's Parodic Novel', *Ariel* 22, 1991, pp. 111–29

Wakefield, Edward, *An Account of Ireland, Statistical and Political*, 2 vols., London: Longman & Co., 1812

Walkowitz, Judith, *City of Dreadful Delight: Narratives of Sexual Danger in Late-Victorian London*, London: Virago, 1992

Walters, Jennifer Waelti and Hause, Stephen C., *Feminisms of the Belle Époque*, Lincoln: University of Nebraska Press, 1994

Ward, Margaret, *Unmanageable Revolutionaries: Women and Irish Nationalism*, 1983; London: Pluto Press, 1995

Watts, Ian, *The Rise of the Novel*, 1957; Berkeley: University of California Press, 1984

Welsh, Charles, McCarthy, Justin *et al* (eds), *Irish Literature: Irish Authors and Their Writings in Ten Volumes*, Philadelphia: Morris, 1904

Wilde, Jane Francesca, *Notes on Men, Women and Books*, London: Ward & Downey, 1891

Wilford, Rick, 'Women, Ethnicity and Nationalism: Surveying the Ground', in Rick Wilford and Robert L. Miller (eds), *Women, Ethnicity and Nationalism: The Politics of Transition*, London: Routledge, 1998, pp. 1–22

Women, Education and Literature: The Papers of Maria Edgeworth, 1768–1849, Adam Matthew Publications, 2001

Woolf, Virginia, *The Pargiters*, ed. Mitchell A. Leaska, London: Hogarth Press, 1978

Yeats, W. B., 'Irish National Literature, II: Contemporary Prose Writers–Mr. O'Grady, Miss Lawless, Miss Barlow, Miss Hopper, and the Folklorists', in John P. Frayne (ed.), *Uncollected Prose by W. B. Yeats 1: First Reviews and Articles 1886–1896*, London: Macmillan, 1970, pp. 366–73

Notes and References

Introduction

1. While there are many women's names missing from the history of poetry in Ireland, poets were more highly esteemed than novelists in the nineteenth and early twentieth centuries, which means that more women poets than women novelists have been remembered. Poetry is also more easily anthologized, and thus more likely to remain in print than the long novels. See, however, Nuala Ní Dhomhnaill, 'What Foremothers?', in Theresa O'Connor (ed.), *The Comic Tradition in Irish Women Writers* (Gainesville: University of Florida Press, 1996), pp. 8–20 for a discussion of women poets writing in Irish and how they have been represented.

2. Shaun Richards, Foreword, in Scott Brewster, Virginia Crossman, Fiona Becket and David Alderson (eds), *Ireland in Proximity: History, Gender Space* (London: Routledge, 1999), p. xiv

3. Elizabeth Grosz, *Space, Time, and Perversion: Essays on the Politics of Bodies* (New York: Routledge, 1995), p. 54

4. Ailbhe Smyth, Introduction, in Ailbhe Smyth (ed.), *Wildish Things: An Anthology of New Irish Women's Writing* (Dublin: Attic Press, 1989), p. 8

5. Edna Longley, *From Cathleen to Anorexia: The Breakdown of Irelands* (Dublin: Attic Press, 1990), p. 23

6. Eavan Boland, 'A Kind of Scar: The Woman Poet in a National Tradition', in *A Dozen Lips* (Dublin: Attic Press, 1994), pp. 90–92

7. Margaret Kelleher, 'Writing Irish Women's Literary History', *Irish Studies Review* vol. 9.1, 2001, p. 10

8. Rita Felski, *The Gender of Modernity* (Cambridge MA: Harvard University Press, 1995), p. 33

9. Terry Eagleton, Preface, *Scholars and Rebels in Nineteenth-Century Ireland* (Oxford: Blackwell, 1999), n. p.

10. Declan Kiberd, *Irish Classics* (London: Granta, 2000), p. ix

11. Kiberd, pp. ix–x

12. Barbara Herrnstein Smith, *Contingencies of Value: Alternative Perspectives for Critical Theory* (1988; Cambridge, MA: Harvard University Press, 1991). See particularly Chapter 3, pp. 30–53

13. Laurie Finke, *Feminist Theory, Women's Writing* (Ithaca: Cornell University Press, 1992), p. 172

14. Finke, p. 172

15. See W. B. Yeats, 'Irish National Literature, II: Contemporary Prose Writers–Mr. O'Grady, Miss Lawless, Miss Barlow, Miss Hopper, and the Folklorists', in John P. Frayne (ed.), *Uncollected Prose by W. B. Yeats 1: First Reviews and Articles 1886–1896* (London: Macmillan, 1970), pp. 366–373; Rev. of *Hurrish: A Study*, by Emily Lawless, *Nation* 20 Feb. 1886, n. p. Clipping in the Lawless papers, Marsh's Library, Dublin. Also quoted in William Linn, 'The Life and Works of the Hon. Emily Lawless, First Novelist of the Irish Literary Revival', diss., New York University, 1971, pp. 74–75

16. Finke, pp. 16–17

17. Boland, p. 88

18. Patricia Boyle Haberstroh, *Women Creating Women: Contemporary Irish Women Poets* (Dublin: Attic Press, 1996), p. 6

19. Susan Gubar, *Critical Condition: Feminism at the Turn of the Century* (New York: Columbia University Press, 2000), p. 44

20. Terry Eagleton, *The Function of Criticism: From* The Spectator *to Post-Structuralism* (London: Verso, 1984, 1997), p. 9

21. Eagleton, *The Function of Criticism*, pp. 35–38

22. Margaret Ezell, *Writing Women's Literary History* (Baltimore: Johns Hopkins University Press, 1993), p. 99

23. Ezell, p. 93

24. See Nicola Diane Thompson, *Reviewing Sex: Gender and the Reception of Victorian Novels* (Basingstoke: Macmillan. 1996)

25. Eagleton, *Scholars and Rebels*, p. 22

26. Robert Tracy, 'Maria Edgeworth and Lady Morgan: Legality versus Legitimacy', *Nineteenth-Century Fiction* vol. 40.1, 1985, pp. 1–22

27. Terry Eagleton, *Heathcliff and the Great Hunger: Studies in Irish Culture* (London: Verso, 1995), p. 201

28. Joep Leerssen, 'How *The Wild Irish Girl* Made Ireland Romantic', in C. C. Barfoot and Theo D'haen (eds), *The Clash of Ireland: Literary Contrasts and Connections* (Amsterdam: Rodopi, 1989), p. 115

29. Ina Ferris, 'Narrating Cultural Encounter: Lady Morgan and the Irish National Tale', *Nineteenth-Century Literature* vol. 51.3, 1996, p. 303

'Improvement is a Nation's Blessing'

1. Robert Darnton, 'What is the History of Books?', in Robert Darnton, *The Kiss of Lamourette: Reflections in Cultural History* (New York and London: W. W. Norton, 1990), p. 135

2. Niall Ó Ciosáin, *Print and Popular Culture in Ireland, 1750–1850* (Basingstoke: Palgrave, 1997). See also the essays in Bernadette Cunningham and Máire Kennedy (eds), *The Experience of Reading: Irish Historical Perspectives* (Dublin: Rare Books Group of the Library Association of Ireland and Economic and Social History Society of Ireland, 1999)

3. Katie Trumpener, *Bardic Nationalism: The Romantic Novel and the British Empire* (Princeton University Press, 1997), p. 17

4. Marilyn Butler, 'Irish Culture and Scottish Enlightenment: Maria Edgeworth's Histories of the Future', in Stefan Collini, Richard Whatmore, and Brian Young (eds), *Economy, Polity, and Society: British Intellectual History 1750–1950*

(Cambridge University Press, 2000), p. 166. For similar comments, see Marilyn Butler, 'Edgeworth's Ireland: History, Popular Culture, and Secret Codes', *Novel* 34.2, Spring 2001, pp. 267–292

5.   I am grateful to Professor Peter Garside, my colleague at Cardiff University, for these observations.

6.   See Peter Garside, 'Popular Fiction and National Tale: Hidden Origins of Scott's *Waverley*', *Nineteenth-Century Literature* vol. 46.1, Jun. 1991, pp. 30–53 (esp. pages 46–47)

7.   Anna Laetitia Barbauld, *Monthly Review* 60, Oct. 1809, pp. 217–18. A number of recent critics have argued that Hamilton's work is equally difficult to categorize along either generic or political lines. Claire Grogan has characterized Hamilton's writings as 'multigeneric', blending fiction with ostensibly factual discourses such as history, ethnography, and political polemic. Similarly, recent critical attention to Hamilton's work also highlights the perils of identifying her with any one political or ideological position. While generally classified as an anti-Jacobin author, critics such as Gary Kelly and Eleanor Ty argue that Hamilton's works are far more nuanced in their engagement with the major political, social and cultural issues of the fraught post-Revolutionary decades than they might at first appear. See Claire Grogan 'Crossing genre, gender and race in Elizabeth Hamilton's *Translation of the Letters of a Hindoo Rajah*', *Studies in the Novel* 34, Spring 2002, pp. 21–42; Eleanor Ty, 'Female Philosophy Refunctioned: Elizabeth Hamilton's Parodic Novel', *Ariel* 22, 1991, pp. 111–29. See also Gary Kelly's chapters on Hamilton, by far the best sustained treatment of Hamilton's work available, in *Women, Writing, and Revolution, 1790–1827* (Oxford: Clarendon Press, 1993)

8.   Elizabeth Hamilton, *The Cottagers of Glenburnie*, new ed. (Edinburgh: Nimmo, Hay, & Mitchell, 1895), p. 82. For the reception of *Glenburnie* in England, see Elizabeth Benger, *Memoirs of the Late Mrs. Elizabeth Hamilton*, 2 vols. (London: Longman & Co., 1818), vol. 1, p. 170

9.   Francis Jeffrey, unsigned rev. of Elizabeth Hamilton, *The Cottagers of Glenburnie*, *Edinburgh Review* 12, Jul. 1808, p. 402

10. The preface to *Castle Rackrent* states that 'Thady's idiom is incapable of translation'. Maria Edgeworth, *Castle Rackrent* and *Ennui*, ed. Marilyn Butler (London: Penguin, 1992), p. 63

11. In the *Edinburgh Review*, Jeffrey highlighted the need for a cheap edition of *Glenburnie*, so that the reforms advocated in the text could reach the appropriate audience.

12. *Glenburnie* is also listed in the 1838 catalogue of Hodgson's New Circulating Library in Belfast, and in the 1819 catalogue of Kempston's Library in Dublin. I am grateful to Rolf Loeber for the information about *Glenburnie*'s presence in the Lough Fea library, and for other information about Irish editions of *Glenburnie*.

13. Benger, vol. 1, p. 180

14. Joanne Shattock (ed.), *The Cambridge Bibliography of English Literature*, vol. 4, 3rd ed. (Cambridge University Press, 1999), p. 926. There appears to be some confusion about whether the 1840 edition was published in Dublin by C. M. Warren, or in Belfast by Sims and M'Intyre. According to Adams, Sims and M'Intyre often seemed to co-publish works with Warren, so editions appear with Dublin imprints which are given in publisher's lists as Sims and M'Intyre publications. See Adams, *The Printed Word and the Common Man: Popular Culture*

in Ulster 1700–1900 (The Institute of Irish Studies, Queen's University Belfast, 1987) esp. chapter 8 and pp. 194–99

15. Edward Wakefield, *An Account of Ireland, Statistical and Political,* 2 vols. (London: Longman & Co., 1812), vol. 2, p. 416

16. *Belfast Monthly Magazine* 2, May 1809, pp. 379–80

17. Tom Clyde, *Irish Literary Magazines: An Outline History and Descriptive Bibliography* (Dublin: Irish Academic Press, 2003), p. 79

18. *Belfast Monthly Magazine* 2, 31 Jan. 1809, p. 57

19. Rev. of Sydney Owenson, *Woman; or, Ida of Athens, Belfast Monthly Magazine* 2 (Feb. 1809), p. 141.

20. Elizabeth Hamilton, Preface, *The Cottagers of Glenburnie,* 3rd ed. (Edinburgh: Manners & Miller, 1808), pp. viii–ix

21. *Belfast Monthly Magazine* 2, May 1809, p. 379

22. *Belfast Monthly Magazine* 2, May 1809, p. 380

23. *Belfast Monthly Magazine* 2, May 1809, p. 380

24. Rev. of Elizabeth Hamilton, *The Cottagers of Glenburnie, British Critic* 32, Aug. 1808, p. 116, p. 118

25. Letter from Elizabeth Hamilton to Mrs. Gregory, quoted in Benger, vol. 1, p. 126

26. Carol Anderson and Aileen M. Riddell, 'The Other Great Unknowns: Women Fiction Writers of the early Nineteenth Century', in Douglas Gifford and Dorothy McMillan (eds), *A History of Scottish Women's Writing* (Edinburgh University Press, 1997), p. 181

27. Benger, vol. 2, p. 68. Hamilton sits as easily in Scottish literary anthologies as Irish ones. Extracts from Hamilton's *Letters from a Hindoo Rajah* are included in Angela Bourke, Siobhán Kilfeather, Maria Luddy, Margaret Mac Curtain, Gerardine Meaney, Máirín Ní Dhonnchacha, Mary O'Dowd and Clair Wills (eds), *Field Day Anthology of Irish Writing: Women's Writing and Traditions,* vol. 4 (Cork University Press, 2002). Hamilton is also included in a forthcoming bibliographic study by Rolf Loeber and Magda Stouthamer-Loeber entitled *A Guide to Irish Fiction, 1650–1900: A Mirror of the Times.* Hamilton figures equally in histories of Scottish writing. See, for example, Carol Anderson and Aileen M. Riddell, cited above.

28. Hamilton, *The Cottagers of Glenburnie,* new ed., p. 203

29. Rev. of Elizabeth Hamilton, *The Cottagers of Glenburnie, British Critic* 32, Aug. 1808, p. 116

30. *The Dictionary of National Biography,* quoting Manson

31. *Belfast Monthly Magazine* 2, May 1809, p. 383

32. See Janet Todd, *Mary Wollstonecraft: A Revolutionary Life* (London: Weidenfeld & Nicolson, 2000), pp. 126–29. As Todd notes, Wollstonecraft's former pupil Margaret King, later Lady Blessington, 'Presumably [. . .] read the work of her charismatic governess since she assumed the name of Mrs. Mason when she disgraced her family and passed as a commoner' (p. 467, note 4)

33. Marilyn Butler, *Maria Edgeworth: A Literary Biography* (Oxford: Clarendon Press, 1972), p. 199. Long before she read *Glenburnie,* Edgeworth had encountered and enjoyed Hamilton's works, most notably Hamilton's satirical novel *Memoirs of Modern Philosophers* (1800).

34. Letter from Maria Edgeworth to Charles Sneyd Edgeworth, 16 Dec 1808 and 30 Dec 1808, *Women, Education and Literature: The Papers of Maria Edgeworth, 1768–1849* (Adam Matthew Publications, 2001) part 2, reel 5, nos. 651 and 653

35. Letter from Maria Edgeworth to Margaret Ruxton, 2 Feb 1809, *Women, Education and Literature*, part 2, reel 5, no. 667. In the edition of Edgeworth's selected correspondence edited by Augustus Hare, the words 'in Ireland' are omitted from the comments about *Glenburnie*, so that Edgeworth's statement merely reads 'I think it will do a vast deal of good, and besides [. . .]'. *The Life and Letters of Maria Edgeworth*, 2 vols., ed. Augustus J. C. Hare (London: Edward Arnold, 1894) vol. 1, p. 160

36. Letter from Maria Edgeworth to Margaret Ruxton, 1 Feb. 1809, *Women, Education and Literature*, part 2, reel 5, no. 671. Charles Sneyd Edgeworth, writing from Edinburgh in Nov 1808, also praises *Glenburnie* and expresses the hope that 'Kitty, who has shown all the goodness that a valuable servant possesses [. . .] shd have the reward of reading this book'. Letter from Charles Sneyd Edgeworth to Charlotte Sneyd, Nov 1808, *Women, Education and Literature*, part 2, reel 5, no. 649

37. *Critical Review*, fourth ser., 5, Mar. 1814, p. 225

38. Kelly, p. 279

39. The former United Irishman William Drennan, who was the editor of the *Belfast Monthly Magazine* and possibly the author of the review of *Glenburnie* for that magazine, was also a pupil of Stewart's at Edinburgh. This link would further help to explain why the stress in the article (and in the journal generally) is laid so heavily on improvement as the true expression of patriotism. For Maria Edgeworth's use of Stewart's theories, I am heavily indebted to Marilyn Butler's essay 'Irish Culture and Scottish Enlightenment: Maria Edgeworth's Histories in the Future', in Stefan Collini, Richard Whatmore, and Brian Young (eds), *Economy, Polity, and Society: British Intellectual History 1750–1950* (Cambridge University Press, 2000), pp. 158–80

40. Butler, *Maria Edgeworth*, p. 198

41. For a discussion of Hamilton's and Jeffrey's relationship, I am grateful to Dr Pam Perkins of the University of Manitoba for allowing me to read her unpublished conference paper 'Jeffrey Reading Women, Women Reading Jeffrey', delivered at the 2002 'Places of Exchange' conference at Glasgow University.

42. Quoted in Benger, vol. 2, pp. 72–73

43. Stefan Collini, Donald Winch, and John Burrow, 'The system of the North: Dugald Stewart and his pupils', in Stefan Collini, Donald Winch, and John Burrow, *That Noble Science of Politics: A study in nineteenth-century intellectual history* (Cambridge University Press, 1983), p. 39, p. 42

44. Maria Edgeworth, *Castle Rackrent* and *Ennui*, ed. Marilyn Butler (London: Penguin, 1992), p. 189

45. Hamilton, *The Cottagers of Glenburnie*, new ed., p. 111

46. Ann H. Jones, *Ideas and Innovations: Best Sellers of Jane Austen's Age* (New York: AMS Press, 1986), pp. 42–43

47. Ó Ciosáin, p. 137

48. Adams, p. 100

49. Ó Ciosáin, p. 150

50. Rev. of Mary Brunton, *Self-Control*, *Eclectic Review* 8, Jun. 1812, p. 605

51. Letter from Mary Leadbeater to Mrs. Trench, 17 May 1810, *The Leadbeater Papers*, in Maria Luddy (ed.), *Irish Women's Writing, 1839–1888*, vols. 2 and 3 (London: Routledge/Thoemmes Press, 1998) vol. 3, p. 189

52. Maria Edgeworth, 'Mrs. Elizabeth Hamilton', *Edinburgh Evening Courant*, 1 Aug 1816. The obituary initially appeared in *The Gentleman's Magazine*, supplement,

1816, pp. 623–43. The article in the *Edinburgh Evening Courant* indicates that it is reprinted from an Irish newspaper, so it is likely that the obituary appeared in at least three publications. It is also quoted at length in Benger.

53.   Butler, 'Irish Culture and Scottish Enlightenment', p. 171

Travels of a Lady of Fashion

1.   Joseph Fitzgerald Molloy, *The Most Gorgeous Lady Blessington*, 2 vols. (London: Downey & Co., 1896). Lady Blessington was also the subject of the more soberly entitled *Literary Life and Correspondence of the Countess of Blessington*, 3 vols. (London: Newby, 1855), ed. R. R. Madden. See also Michael Sadleir, *Blessington-d'Orsay: A Masquerade* (London: Constable, 1933). A second London edition of 1947 contains corrections and additions. The American edition of Sadleir's biography was entitled *The Strange Life of Lady Blessington* (Boston: Little, Brown & Co., 1933)

2.   Jane Francesca Wilde, *Notes on Men, Women and Books* (London: Ward & Downey, 1891), p. 127

3.   R. R. Madden, *The Literary Life and Correspondence of the Countess of Blessington*, 2nd ed., 3 vols., (London: Newby, 1855) vol. 1, p. 499. Unless otherwise indicated, references will be to this edition. The first edition is also dated 1855. The page references vary slightly between the editions.

4.   Madden gives an extended account of the trials and executions in an appendix: 'The Fate of the Sheehys in 1765 and 1766', vol. 1, pp. 484–522. Mrs James Sadlier published a novel called *The Fate of Father Sheehy* in New York in 1845, although it is not known if Lady Blessington ever saw it. Recent historical studies of these incidents include James J. Donnelly Jr, 'The Whiteboy Movement, 1761–5', *Irish Historical Studies* 21, Mar. 1978, pp. 20–54; Maurice J. Bric, 'The Whiteboy Movement in Tipperary 1760–80', in W. Nolan and T. G. McGrath (eds), *Tipperary: History and Society* (Dublin: Geography Publications, 1985); Thomas P. Power, *Land, Politics and Society in Eighteenth Century Tipperary* (Oxford: Clarendon Press, 1993), pp. 183–87, pp. 238–71. The relative by marriage of Edmund Burke was James Nagle of Garnavilla.

5.   Madden, vol. 1, pp. 12–14

6.   From 'Memoir of the Countess of Blessington by Miss Power' [niece of Lady Blessington], quoted by Madden, vol. 1, p. 12

7.   Madden. vol. 1, pp. 20–21

8.   Madden, vol. 1, p. 19. Donoughmore 'was the chief spokesman in favour of relief in the [Irish] House of Lords' during the debate on the Catholic Relief Bill of 1793. See Power, pp. 292–97

9.   Madden, vol. 1, pp. 19–23

10.   Madden, vol. 1, pp. 23–27 and Appendix vol. 1, pp. 476–83. See also Catherine Hamilton, *Women Writers: Their Works and Ways*, 1st Series (London: Ward, Lock, Bowden & Co. 1892), p. 266

11.   Madden, vol. 1, pp. 31–36. Madden quotes an account given to him personally by Lady Blessington on 15 October 1843, about the violence of her first marriage and her return home after three months.

12.   Michael Sadleir, *Blessington-d'Orsay: A Masquerade*, 2nd ed. (London: Constable, 1947), p. 17, pp. 19–23. Unless otherwise specified, all references will be to this

edition. Madden does not refer to the period of several years during which Marguerite lived with Capt. Jenkins, merely saying: 'In 1807 she was living at Cahir, in the County Tipperary, separated from her husband; in 1809 she was sojourning in Dublin; a little later she was residing in Hampshire; in 1816, we find her established in Manchester Square, London; and at the commencement of 1818, on the point of marriage with an Irish nobleman.' Madden, vol. 1, p. 38

13. Of this event Sadleir remarks: 'In 1816 he was created Earl of Blessington, for reasons so little obvious that they must have been financial.' Sadleir, p. 26

14. Gardiner's first wife was born Mary Campbell, and married Lieutenant William Brown, of the Light Dragoons in 1804. Brown was a friend of Gardiner, who bailed him out financially several times. In 1809 William Brown, to escape his debts, accepted a commission as major in a regiment in the West Indies, but left his wife in England where she quickly became the mistress of Gardiner. Their first two children, Charles John (1810) and Emily Rosalie (1811), were illegitimate. William Brown died in May 1812, and Gardiner and Mary Brown married in July. Their subsequent children, Harriet Anne (August 1812) and Luke Wellington (1813, died 1823) were therefore legitimate. Mary died in September 1814. See Sadleir, pp. 27–33, pp. 86–87

15. See extract in Angela Bourke, Siobhán Kilfeather, Maria Luddy, Margaret Mac Curtain, Gerardine Meaney, Máirín Ní Dhonnchacha, Mary O'Dowd and Clair Wills (eds), *Field Day Anthology of Irish Writing: Women's Writing and Traditions*, vol. 5 (Cork University Press, 2002), pp. 870–73

16. Sadleir, p. 126

17. Madden, vol. 1, p. 231

18. Wilde, p. 145

19. Madden, vol. 1, p. 273

20. Madden, 1st edition vol. 1, pp. 232–33

21. Sadleir, pp. 287–91, pp. 334–35

22. Letter to Mrs. Brookfield quoted in Willard Connely, *Count D'Orsay: Dandy of Dandies* (London: Cassell, 1952), p. 499. Apart from 'Wanaty Fair', Thackeray used other colloquialisms in this letter.

23. Margaret Kelleher, '*The Field Day Anthology* and Irish Women's Literary Studies', *The Irish Review*, 30, 2003, p. 92

24. For a list of Blessington's chief writings, seen *Field Day Anthology*, vol. 5, pp. 893–94

25. *Lady Blessington's Conversations of Lord Byron*, ed. with an introduction by Ernest Lovell Jr. (Princeton University Press, 1969). Selections from *The Idler in Italy* have been republished as *The Idler in Naples*, ed. Edith Clay (London: Hamilton, 1979)

26. Lovell, Introduction, pp. 3–8

27. Lovell, Introduction, pp. 112–13

28. Lovell, Introduction, pp. 42–43

29. Blessington, *Conversations*, ed. Lovell, p. 68, p. 71

30. Lovell, Introduction, pp. 102–03

31. Blessington, *Conversations*, ed. Lovell, pp. 52–53

32. Letter from Byron to Lady Hardy, 10 June 1823, and from Lady Hardy to Byron, 17 June 1823. Lovell, Introduction, p. 62

33. Willard Connely lists three Byron sketches included in the Gore House auction lot of 260 portrait sketches by D'Orsay: Byron full-length, Byron half-length, and Byron seated writing. *Count D'Orsay*, p. 265

34. Madden, 1st ed. vol. 1, p. 258

35. Blessington, *Conversations*, ed. Lovell, p. 43

36. Wilde, p. 154

37. Madden, vol. 1, p. 12

38. 'My colleen dhas': *mo chailín deas*, my dear girl; 'na bochlis': *ná bac leis*, don't mind that; 'cuishlamachree': *a chuisle mo chroí*, literally 'heartbeat of my heart'.

39. Marguerite Blessington, *Grace Cassidy or The Repealers*, 3 vols. (London: Bentley, 1833), vol. 2, pp. 185–86. Further references to this novel will be included in the text. I prefer the abbreviation *Grace Cassidy* to *The Repealers*, used by earlier commentators.

40. 'Extracts from a Memoir of the Countess of Blessington by Miss Power', Madden, vol. 1, p. 18. According to Madden's calculations, Marguerite would have been seven or eight years old when the family moved from their country home to Clonmel.

41. In 1826 a novel in three volumes called *Almack's* was published anonymously in London (written by Marianne Spencer Hudson). A 'Key to Almack's' was published in the *Literary Gazette*, 9 Nov. 1826. See *The English Novel 1770–1829*, ed. Peter Garside and Rainer Schöwerling, 2 vols. (Oxford: Oxford University Press, 2000), vol. 2, pp. 27–28

42. Madden, 1st ed. vol. 1, pp. 258–59. Madden notes that the Key was written in 1833, the year of publication, by Lady Blessington

43. Sadleir, 1st ed., p. 208

44. S. C. Hall, *Retrospect of a Long Life*, 2 vols. (London: Bentley, 1883), vol. 2, p. 113. Sadleir quotes a letter from Byron to Lady Hardy: 'I had heard that she had been a mistress of some kind or other before she espoused the Earl of Blessington.' Sadleir, p. 78, see also pp. 18–27

45. Mary Campbell, *Lady Morgan: The Life and Times of Sydney Owenson* (London: Pandora, 1988), p. 228

46. Lionel Stevenson, *The Wild Irish Girl: The Life of Sydney Owenson, Lady Morgan* (London: Chapman & Hall, 1936), pp. 300–01

47. Edward George Stanley, later Earl of Derby, also established the Board of Works, instituted the Shannon navigation improvements, and brought in the Education Act of 1831, during his tenure as Chief Secretary for Ireland, 1830–33. See *Dictionary of National Biography* (London: 1898), vol. 54, pp. 54–5.

48. Sadleir, pp. 191–94. There is no identification for Abberville in the 'Key to The Repealers'.

49. Madden, vol. 1, pp. 135–6

50. Tom Dunne, 'Ireland, Irish and Colonialism', *Irish Review*, vol. 30, 2003, p. 96

The Art of Bookmaking

1. In many encyclopaedias of Irish and English literature she is ignored, and when she is mentioned it is seldom in favourable contexts. See for example *Dictionary of Irish Literature* A-L., rev. and expanded ed., ed. Robert Hogan (Westport, Conn.: Greenwood Press, 1996), p. 199. Neither is she mentioned in critical works about travel literature.

2. Quoted in 'Selina Bunbury', *Irish Book Lover*, vol. 7, Jan. 1916, pp. 105–06. The second statement in the quotation is found in the preface to the seventh edition of her book.

3. 'Selina Bunbury', p. 106

4.   'Selina Bunbury', p. 107

5.   Selina Bunbury, *Evelyn: or a Journey from Stockholm to Rome in 1847–48* (London: Richard Bentley, 1849); *Life in Sweden; with Excursions in Norway and Denmark* (London: Hurst & Blackett, 1853); *A Summer in Northern Europe, Including Sketches in Sweden, Norway, Finland, The Aland Islands, Gothland, &c.* (London: Hurst & Blackett, 1856). In the discussion I will refer to the two volumes of *Evelyn* as *E* I and *E* II, to the two volumes of *Life* as *L* I and *L* II, and to the two volumes of *Summer* as *S* I and *S* II.

6.   Rev. of *Life in Sweden*, by Selina Bunbury, *Littell's Living Age*, vol. 38, 24 Sept. 1853, p. 793

7.   *Littell's Living Age*, vol. 38, p. 793

8.   *Littell's Living Age*, vol. 38, p. 796

9.   Shirley Foster, *Across New Worlds: Nineteenth Century Women Travellers and their Writing* (New York: Harvester Wheatsheaf, 1990), p. 6

10. Foster, p. 6. See her description of William Carey's introduction to the diary of Annie Taylor's journey in Tibet for an apt illustration of this. For valuable discussions about the contemporary shift in how women travellers are, and should be, viewed, see Sara Mills, *Discourses of Difference: An Analysis of Women's Travel Writing and Colonialism* (London: Routledge, 1991)

11. Karen R. Lawrence, *Penelope Voyages: Women and Travel in the British Literary Tradition* (Ithaca: Cornell University Press, 1994), p. 24

12. Lawrence, p. 24

13. Casey Blanton, *Travel Writing: The Self and the World* (New York: Twayne, 1997), p. 15. The rise of Western Romanticism and the formulation of Romantic subjectivity influenced the emphasis on the individual's experiences and responses.

14. James Buzard, *The Beaten Track: European Tourism, Literature and Ways to 'culture' 1800–1918* (Oxford: Clarendon Press, 1993), pp. 160–61

15. I am not suggesting that any journey can be the first. Previous narratives, whether oral or written, previous travellers, whether foreign or native to the area always exist, thus in a sense supplying the known or unknown, visible or invisible footsteps that the traveller is faced with negotiating.

16. This feature is also connected to ethnography and anthropology, and it is worth pointing out that these were fields of study considered suitable even for early women travellers. Subjectivity, first-hand knowledge and empirical work are mirrored in other female travellers' work. One example is Mary Kingsley who writes that: 'I have written only things that I know from personal experience and very careful observation. I have never accepted an explanation of a native custom from one person alone, nor have I set down things as being prevalent customs from having seen one single instance.' Mary Kingsley, *Travels in West Africa. Congo Français, Corisco and Cameroons* (1897; Boston: Beacon Press, 1988), p. xx

17. The different variants of spelling may in part be due to historical changes, that is, a place name's spelling may have changed over time, but at times Bunbury offers alternate spellings within the same text. In *Summer*, for example, Gotland is spelled Gothland in the title, and Gottland elsewhere (e. g. *S* I, p. 171). Motala is erroneously spelled Mottala in *Evelyn*, but with a single t in *Summer*. In this article, outside of quotations, the spelling of place names are contemporary Swedish–Dalarna, instead of Dalecarlia, for instance, and I have not attempted to correct Bunbury's varied spelling.

18. I do not intend to discuss potentially hierarchical differences between travellers and tourists here, but merely state that I do not privilege one over the other.

19. The past as a redeemer as is the case, at times, with Rome, is seldom to be found in Bunbury's descriptions of Scandinavia. 'In Sweden antiquity seldom, if ever, meets you; you may look for it and find traces sometimes, but your general impression is that you are in a modern but a very backward age' (*S* II, p. 58). This, again, may have less to do with actual 'antiquity' than with the absence of previous texts on which to 'hang' the narrative, with which to compare Bunbury's present experiences.

20. In *A Perambulating Paradox: British Travel Literature and the Image of Sweden c. 1770–1865* (Malmö: Lunds Universitet, 2000) Mark Davies identifies eighty-nine texts depicting Sweden and the Swedes, published in Great Britain between 1769 and 1865. It needs to be pointed out, however, that Bunbury does not specifically refer to previous texts about the Northern countries in the same manner as she comments on previous writings regarding the Continent.

21. For instance, she remarks 'we went to one dedicated to the evening amusements of the lower orders of the people of Christiania. I like to see the arrangements made for the recreation and amusements of a people, being very long convinced that they stand in closer connection with their civilization and morality, that we in England have the habit of believing' (*L* I, p. 113) Later on, she has the following to say: 'The other day I dined in a much humbler way, with persons who are quite out of either high or rich life. I enjoy this diversity very much, and the lowlier rank of the persons who invite me, the more pleased I am to go' (*L* II, p. 92)

22. Buzard, p. 120

23. A parallel can be drawn here to the earlier discussion about Bunbury preparing the reader for what he or she will experience by likening the lesser known northern cities to their continental counterparts.

24. Heather Henderson, 'The Travel Writer and the Text: My Giant Goes With Me Wherever I Go', in Michael Kowalewski (ed.), *Temperamental Journeys: Essays on the Modern Literature of Travel* (Athens GA: University of Georgia Press, 1992), pp. 231–32

25. Henderson, p. 238

'Factual Fictions'

1. Siobhán Kilfeather, 'Sex and Sensation in the Nineteenth-Century Novel', in Margaret Kelleher and James H. Murphy (eds), *Gender Perspectives in Nineteenth-Century Ireland* (Dublin: Irish Academic Press, 1997), p. 85

2. Important exceptions include the essays by Claire Connolly, Helen O'Connell, Kathleen Costello-Sullivan and Rolf Loeber and Magda Stouthamer-Loeber in Jacqueline Belanger (ed.), *The Irish Novel in the Nineteenth Century* (Dublin: Four Courts Press, 2005)

3. In addition to McClintock, Blackburne and Gallaher's novels, discussed below, these were *Marcella Grace* (1886) by Rosa Mulholland, *Hurrish* (1886) by Emily Lawless, *The Plan of Campaign* (1888) by English author and historian Frances Mabel Robinson, *A Ruined Race; or The Last MacManus of Drumroosk* (1889) by Hester Sigerson, *Boycotted* (1889) by Mabel Morley and *The Lloyds of Ballymore* (1890) by Edith Rochfort. Also published during this period were William Upton's *Uncle Pat's*

Cabin (1882), Anthony Trollope's *The Landleaguers* (1883), Edward Moran's *Edward O'Donnell* (1884), George Moore's *A Drama in Muslin* (1886), Amos Reade's *Norah Moriarty; or, Revelations of Irish Life* (1886) and William O'Brien's *When We Were Boys* (1890). Later novels on the land topic include E. Noble's *An Irish Decade* (1891), William Ryan's *The Heart of Tipperary* (1893), Edna Lyall [Ada Bayly]'s *Doreen* (1894), M. E. Francis's *Miss Erin* (1898), J. J Moran's *Two Little Girls in Green* (1898), Rosa Mulholland's *Onora* (1900) and H. H. Penrose's *Burnt Flax* (1914). Stephen J. Brown's *Ireland in Fiction: A Guide to Irish Novels, Tales, Romances and Folklore* (1915; 2nd ed. 1919; Shannon: Irish University Press, 1969) is an invaluable guide to this and other nineteenth-century Irish fiction.

4.　See James H. Murphy's article on 'Insouciant Rivals of Mrs Barton: Gender and Victorian Aspiration in George Moore and the Women Novelists of the *Irish Monthly*', in Margaret Kelleher and James H. Murphy (eds), *Gender Perspectives in Nineteenth-Century Ireland* (Dublin: Irish Academic Press, 1997), pp. 221–28. Brief approving references to *Hurrish* are made by Terry Eagleton in his *Heathcliff and the Great Hunger* (London: Verso, 1995). The complexity of the novel has been explored recently by Heather Laird in *Subversive Law in Ireland 1879–1920* (Dublin: Four Courts Press, 2005), pp. 43–59 and by Kathleen Costello-Sullivan in her comparative study 'Novel Traditions: Realism and Modernity in *Hurrish* and *The Real Charlotte*', in Belanger (ed.), *The Irish Novel in the Nineteenth Century*, pp. 150–66

5.　Lennard J. Davis, *Factual Fictions: The Origins of the English Novel* (1986; Philadelphia: University of Pennsylvania Press, 1991), pp. 212–13

6.　Letitia McClintock, *A Boycotted Household* (London, 1881), p. 89

7.　This refers to the official valuation of land for tax purposes which was carried out between 1853–65, under the direction of Richard Griffith.

8.　McClintock, p. 13, p. 31

9.　McClintock, p. 67

10.　McClintock, p. 229

11.　The novel was published by Smith & Elder, one of the more reputable Victorian publishers: founders of the *Cornhill Magazine*, the *Pall Mall Gazette* and the *Dictionary of National Biography*.

12.　Review of *A Boycotted Household*, *Athenaeum* 2812, 17 Sep. 1881, p. 365.

13.　McClintock, pp. 310–9, p. 313

14.　See the entries for McClintock in *The Wellesley Index to Victorian Periodicals*, 5 vols., ed. Walter E. Houghton *et al* (Toronto and Buffalo: University of Toronto Press, 1966), vol. 5, p. 488

15.　*Irish Literature: Irish Authors and Their Writings in Ten Volumes*, ed. Charles Welsh, Justin McCarthy *et al* (Philadelphia, 1904), vol. 6

16.　Allibone's dictionary and the British Library Catalogue credit McClintock with a total of eight other titles: most of these appear to be collections of children's stories, some of which went into a number of editions.

17.　See also, for example, Mabel Morley's *Boycotted* (1889), Edith Rochfort's *The Lloyds of Ballymore* (1890) and H.H. Penrose's *Burnt Flax* (1914). For a discussion of Morley's novel, see Eileen Reilly, 'Beyond Gilt Shamrock: Symbolism and Realism in the Cover Art of Irish Historical and Political Fiction, 1880–1914', in Lawrence W. McBride (ed.), *Images, Icons and the Irish Nationalist Imagination* (Dublin: Four Courts, 1999), pp. 107–10

18. Elizabeth Owens Blackburne Casey (1848–94) was born in Slane, County Meath. In 1873 she moved to London where she became a journalist and novelist, writing under the pen-name E. Owens Blackburne. Towards the end of her life, she returned to Dublin where she died in 1894. Blackburne was the author of six novels, two collections of tales and the two-volume *Illustrious Irishwomen* (1877) comprising biographical sketches of 'some of the most notable Irishwomen from the earliest ages to the present century'. See the biographical note provided in *The Cabinet of Irish Literature*, 4 vols., ed. Charles A. Read (London, 1879–1880), vol. 4, p. 277; also P.A. Sillard, 'A Notable Irish Authoress', *New Ireland Review* 27, Aug 1907, pp. 369–72

19. Elizabeth Owens Blackburne (Casey), *The Heart of Erin: An Irish Story of Today* 3 vols. (London, 1882), vol. 1, p. 238

20. Blackburne vol. 2, pp. 136–37

21. Blackburne vol. 2, pp. 134–35

22. Rev. of *The Heart of Erin* by Elizabeth Owens Blackburne, *Athenaeum* 2847, 20 May 1882, p. 632

23. *Athenaeum* 2847, p. 632

24. See Blackburne vol. 3, ch. 10

25. Blackburne vol. 2, p. 49; Bishop Thomas Nulty, *The Land Question: Letter of the Most Rev. Dr. Nulty to the Clergy and Laity of the Diocese of Meath* (Dublin: Joseph Dollard, 1881)

26. Blackburne vol. 2, ch. 7

27. Hall later rescinded his reference and Walter Besant also warned the fund against supporting Blackburne, claiming 'she is a great drunkard [. . .] they took away her ticket for the Reading Room at the Museum [. . .] and she really was once a fairly good writer'. Blackburne's own letters to the fund emphasize her earlier successes as a writer, earning between £120–160 a year at the peak of her career. See File No. 2269, *Archives of the Royal Literary Fund* (London, 1984)

28. *Athenaeum*, 14 Apr. 1894, p. 480

29. Fannie Gallaher, *Thy Name is Truth* 3 vols. (London, 1884)

30. Brown, *Ireland in Fiction*, p. 113

31. See Gallaher vol. 2, pp. 115–22 and *Freeman's Journal*, 20 May 1881; also Gallaher vol. 3, pp. 295–302 and *Freeman's Journal*, 10 Oct. 1881

32. A small number of Catholic girls attended the Church of Ireland Alexandra College, following its opening in 1866; this was especially the case prior to the establishment of Dominican convents such as Eccles Street (1883) and before a Catholic University College (St Mary's) was opened for women in 1893. Gallaher's comments on women's education also refer implicitly to the (unsuccessful) efforts by the Intermediate Board in 1882–83 to establish a separate educational programme for girls.

33. Gallaher vol. 1, pp. 131–34. For a discussion of very different contemporary representations of the Ladies Land League, see Niamh Sullivan, 'The Iron Cage of Femininity: Visual Representations of Women in the 1880s Land Agitation', in Tadhg Foley and Seán Ryder (eds), *Ideology and Nineteenth-Century Ireland* (Dublin: Four Courts, 1998), pp. 181–96; also Joel Holland, '"Beauty and the Beast': Depictions of Irish Female Types during the Era of Parnell, c.1880–1891', in Lawrence W. McBride (ed.), *Images, Icons and the Irish Nationalist Imagination* (Dublin: Four Courts, 1999), pp. 53–72

34. Gallaher vol. 3, pp. 290–91

35.   My thanks to Carla King for her illuminating comments on this issue.

36.   *Marcella Grace* was reissued by Maunsel (Washington) in 2001, in an edition edited and introduced by James H. Murphy. Murphy has uncovered the source for much of the novel, specifically its story of wrongful accusation, in a real-life event of the time; see his introduction. See also his discussion of Rosa Mulholland's work in his *Catholic Fiction and Social Reality in Ireland, 1873–1922* (Westport, Conn, USA: Greenwood Press, 1992)

37.   See also M. E. Francis [Mrs. Francis Blundell or Mary Sweetman], *Miss Erin* (London and New York: Benziger, 1898)

38.   Murphy very persuasively argues that the 'polemical agenda' at work in *Marcella Grace* and other novels like it, is 'advocacy of a new Catholic gentry as the solution to Ireland's land problems'.

39.   Gallaher vol. 1, ch. 3

40.   David Lloyd, 'Afterword: Hardress Cregan's dream', in Belanger (ed.), *The Irish Novel in the Nineteenth Century*, p. 235

41.   Lloyd, 'Afterword', p. 234

42.   Tom Dunne (ed.), *The Writer as Witness: Literature as Historical Evidence* (Cork University Press, 1987)

43.   Oliver MacDonagh, '*Sanditon*: a Regency Novel?', in Tom Dunne (ed.), *The Writer as Witness*, pp. 114–32

44.   MacDonagh, pp. 130–31

45.   Eagleton, *Heathcliff and the Great Hunger*, p. 147

46.   Eagleton, 'Afterword', in Belanger (ed.), *The Irish Novel in the Nineteenth Century*, p. 233. The quotation first appeared in *Heathcliff and the Great Hunger*, p. 154

47.   'Political instability is the ruin of disinterested representation, and as such a significant curb on a major literary realism': Eagleton, *Heathcliff and the Great Hunger*, p. 149

48.   David Lloyd, *Anomalous States: Irish Writing and the Post-Colonial Moment* (Dublin: Lilliput, 1993), p. 130

49.   Terry Eagleton, Preface, *Crazy John and the Bishop, and Other Essays on Irish Culture*, Critical Conditions series (Cork University Press, in association with Field Day, 1998). Here Eagleton criticizes the narrowness of the Irish literary pantheon and observes that 'few labourers in the field seem interested in Isaac Butt or Susan Mitchell, George Sigerson or Arthur Clery'. These examples prove to be odd choices: Butt, Clery and Sigerson receive only a passing mention in the volume and Mitchell does not appear at all.

50.   See Lloyd's comments on Mikhail Bakhtin and Benedict Anderson, *Anomalous States*, pp. 150–55

51.   See David Lloyd, *Nationalism and Minor Literature: James Clarence Mangan and the Emergence of Irish Cultural Nationalism* (University of California Press, 1987)

52.   Nancy Armstrong, *Desire and Domestic Fiction: A Political History of the Novel* (Oxford University Press, 1987), p. 3

53.   Armstrong, p. 9

54.   Lori Merish, *Sentimental Materialism: Gender, Commodity Culture and Nineteenth-Century American Literature* (Durham and London: Duke University Press, 2000), p. 3; I am indebted to Marjorie Howes for this reference.

55.   Marjorie Howes, 'Discipline, Sentiment and the Irish-American Public: Mary Ann Sadlier's Popular Fiction', *Éire–Ireland* vol. 40.1–2 (2005), p. 169

56. An exception is the work of Paige Reynolds; see her forthcoming *The Audiences of Irish Modernism* (Cambridge University Press, 2006)

57. Richard Brodhead, *Cultures of Letters: Scenes of Reading and Writing in Nineteenth-Century America* (University of Chicago Press, 1993), p. 5

58. Lloyd, 'Afterword', p. 233

59. My thanks to Carla King, James H. Murphy and Larry Geary for their valuable comments and advice on this essay.

Hybridization as a Literary and Social Strategy

1. There seems to be some confusion as to the number of novels published by Mrs Hungerford. The number given in various sources ranges from thirty to forty-six. There are, however, forty-nine titles listed in the British Library catalogue, six of which refer to collections of stories and the rest to novels.

2. S. J. Brown, *Ireland in Fiction: A Guide to Irish Novels, Tales, Romances, and Folk-Lore* (Dublin: Maunsel, 1919), p. 142.

3. Mrs [Margaret] Hungerford, *Molly Bawn* (1878; London: Herbert Jenkins, n. d.). Further references to this work are included parenthetically in the text.

4. Quoted in Stanley J. Kunitz (ed.), *British Authors of the Nineteenth Century* (New York: Wilson, 1964), p. 315

5. Ernest Baker, *A Guide to the Best Fiction in English* (London: Routledge, 1913), p. 129

6. Ferdia Mac Anna, Introduction, *An Anthology of Irish Comic Writing: Selected and Introduced by Ferdia Mac Anna* (London: Michael Joseph, 1995), p. xv

7. Theresa O'Connor, 'Introduction: Tradition and the Signifying Monkey', Theresa O'Connor (ed.), *The Comic Tradition in Irish Women Writers* (Gainesville: University Press of Florida, 1996), p. 2

8. O'Connor, p. 4

9. O'Connor, p. 3

10. Monika Fludernik, Introduction, Monika Fludernik (ed.), *Hybridity and Post-Colonialism: Twentieth-Century Indian Literature* (Tübingen: Stauffenberg-Verlag, 1998), p. 10

11. Homi K. Bhabha, *The Location of Culture* (London: Routledge, 1994), p. 219

12. Mac Anna, p. xii

13. Rachel Jane Lynch, 'The Crumbling Fortress: Molly Keane's Comedies of Anglo-Irish Manners', in Theresa O'Connor (ed.), *The Comic Tradition in Irish Women Writers*, p. 73

14. Pat Gill, 'The Way of the Word: Telling Differences in Congreve's *Way of the World*', in K. M. Quinsey (ed.), *Broken Boundaries: Women and Feminism in Restoration Drama* (Kentucky: University Press of Kentucky, 1996), p. 166

15. Northrop Frye, *Anatomy of Criticism: Four Essays* (Princeton University Press, 1957), pp. 43–52, pp. 163–186

16. Susan Staves, *Players' Scepters: Fictions of Authority in the Restoration* (University of Nebraska Press, 1979), p. 42

17. Jennifer J. Connor, 'The Irish Origins and Variations of the Ballad "Molly Bawn"', *Canadian Folk Music Journal* 14 (1986), pp. 10–18, p. 26

18. Connor, p. 12

19. Connor, p. 16

20.   R. D. Hume, 'The Myth of the Rake in 'Restoration' Comedy', *Studies in the Literary Imagination* 10 (1977), p. 29

21.   Ian Watts, *The Rise of the Novel* (1957; Berkeley: University of California Press, 1984), pp. 148–149

22.   Thomas J. Scheff, 'Shame and the Social Bond: A Sociological Theory', <http://www.soc.ucsb.edu/faculty/scheff> Access date 20 Sept. 2002

23.   Ann Bermingham, 'Elegant Females and Gentlemen Connoisseurs: The Commerce in Culture and Self-Image in Eighteenth-Century England', in Ann Bermingham and John Brewer (eds), *The Consumption of Culture 1600–1800: Image, Object, Text* (London: Routledge, 1995), p. 491

24.   Richard Leppert, 'Social Order and the Domestic Consumption of Music: The Politics of Sound in the Policing of Gender Construction in Eighteenth-Century England', Ann Bermingham and John Brewer (eds), *The Consumption of Culture 1600–1800: Image, Object, Text*, p. 515

25.   Leppert, p. 517

26.   Scheff, p. 13

27.   Kay Mussell, *Fantasy and Reconciliation: Contemporary Formulas of Women's Romance Fiction* (London: Greenwood Press, 1986), p. 181

28.   Mussell, p. 189

Patriot's Daughter, Politician's Wife

1.   *Albion and Ierne; A Political Romance, by an Officer* (London and Belfast: Marcus Ward, 1886)

2.   Mary Jean Corbett, *Allegories of Union in Irish and English Writing, 1790–1870* (Cambridge University Press, 2000), p. 3

3.   According to the information in a short biography by M. E. Francis's daughter Margaret Blundell, M. E. Francis was a very frail infant. She was immediately baptized and given only one name–Mary–since it was thought that she would die in a matter of hours. It was not considered necessary to give more than one name to a child not expected to survive. The initial E. was therefore probably added later. Margaret Blundell, *M. E. Francis: An Irish Novelist's Own Story* (Dublin: Catholic Truth Society of Ireland, 1935), p. 3

4.   'M. E. Francis', *Times* 11 Mar. 1930, p. 18 col. B

5.   James H. Murphy, '"Things Which Seem to You Unfeminine": Gender and Nationalism in the Fiction of Some Upper Middle Class Catholic Women Novelists, 1880–1910', in Kathryn Kirkpatrick (ed.), *Border Crossings: Irish Women Writers and National Identities* (Dublin: Wolfhound, 2000), p. 59

6.   *Molly's Fortunes* was first serialized in the *Irish Monthly* in 1887, and later published in book form. According to the preface, *Molly's Fortunes* was not M. E. Francis's first published work, however: 'a little tale of mine, written when I was fourteen and called Dame Grump and the Fairy Spectacles, found its way, like many another fledgling effort, to the kindly pages of the *Irish Monthly*.' M. E. Francis, Preface, *Molly's Fortunes* (London: Sands, 1905?), p. viii

7.   M. E. Francis, Preface, *Molly's Fortunes*, pp. xiii–xiv

8.   D. J. O'Donoghue, *The Poets of Ireland: A Biographical Dictionary* (Dublin: Hodges Figgis & Co 1912)

9. W. P. Ryan, *The Irish Literary Revival: Its History, Pioneers, and Possibilities etc.* (London: printed by the author, 1894), p. 117

10. Blundell, p. 29

11. 'M. E. Francis', *Times*, 11 Mar. 1930

12. M. E. Francis, Preface, *Molly's Fortunes*, p. xv

13. Blundell, p. 28

14. 'M. E. Francis', *Times*, 15 Mar. 1930, p. 17 col. B. See also Blundell, p. 29

15. Quoted in Blundell, p. 29

16. 'Fiction, Poetry, Sketches of Travel, and Humorous Works', *Harper's New Monthly Magazine* vol. 92, May 1896, p. 18

17. 'Recent Novels', *Times* 6 Jan. 1899, p. 4 col. E

18. 'Recent Novels', *Times* 30 Aug. 1901, p. 5 col. A

19. Murphy, pp. 58–61

20. C. L. Innes, *Woman and Nation in Irish Literature and Society, 1880–1935* (Athens, Georgia: University of Georgia Press, 1993), pp. 13–17

21. M. E. Francis, *Miss Erin* (New York: Benziger Brothers, 1898), p. 33. Unless otherwise stated, all further references are to this edition.

22. Francis, *Miss Erin*, p. 36

23. Francis, *Miss Erin*, p. 41

24. Francis, *Miss Erin*, p. 45

25. Francis, *Miss Erin*, p. 48

26. M. E. Francis, *Miss Erin* (London: Methuen, 1898), p. 74. This section does not appear in the Benziger edition.

27. Francis, *Miss Erin*, pp. 105–06

28. Francis, *Miss Erin*, p. 111

29. Innes, p. 3

30. Margaret Ward, *Unmanageable Revolutionaries: Women and Irish Nationalism* (1983; London: Pluto Press, 1995), p. 23

31. Rick Wilford, 'Women, Ethnicity and Nationalism: Surveying the Ground', in Rick Wilford and Robert L. Miller (eds), *Women, Ethnicity and Nationalism: The Politics of Transition* (London: Routledge, 1998), p. 19

32. Francis, *Miss Erin*, p. 112

33. Francis, *Miss Erin*, p. 125

34. Kate Flint, *The Woman Reader, 1837–1914* (Oxford: Clarendon Press, 1993), p. 258

35. Marjorie Garber, *Quotation Marks* (New York: Routledge, 2003), p. 2. Garber discusses direct quotation, but allusions and textual parallels install an authority outside the text at hand in similar ways.

36. Francis, *Miss Erin*, p. 125

37. Francis, *Miss Erin*, p. 105

38. Francis, *Miss Erin*, p. 182

39. Francis, *Miss Erin*, p. 230

40. Sophocles, *Antigone; The Women of Trachis; Philoctetes; Oedipus at Colonus*, ed. and transl. Hugh Lloyd-Jones (Cambridge, MA: Harvard University Press, 1994), p. 21

41. Jan Jindy Pettman, *Worlding Women: A Feminist International Politics* (London: Routledge, 1996), p. 49

42. Sophocles, *Antigone*, p. 45

43. Christiane Sourvino-Inwood, 'Assumptions and the Creation of Meaning: Reading Sophocles' *Antigone*', *Journal of Hellenic Studies* 109 (1989), p. 143

44.   Francis, *Miss Erin*, p. 104

45.   Sophocles, *Antigone*, p. 47

46.   Lilian Tsappa, '*Antigone*: A Case of Political Remedy', *Classical and Modern Literature* vol. 19.1, 1998, p. 24.

47.   Francis, *Miss Erin*, p. 178

48.   Francis, *Miss Erin*, pp. 178–79

49.   Francis, *Miss Erin*, p. 178

50.   Francis, *Miss Erin*, p. 125

51.   Francis, *Miss Erin*, pp. 125–26

52.   Matthew Arnold, 'Preface to Poems (1853), in Stephen Greenblatt (gen. ed.), *Norton Anthology of English Literature* vol. 2, 8th ed. (New York: Norton, 2006), p. 1382

53.   Gerhard Joseph, 'The *Antigone* as Cultural Touchstone: Matthew Arnold, Hegel, George Eliot, Virginia Woolf, and Margaret Drabble', *PMLA* 96.1 (1981), pp. 23–24

54.   George Eliot, *Middlemarch*, ed. W. J. Harvey (1871–72; Harmondsworth: Penguin, 1985), p. 896

55.   Tsappa, p. 22

56.   Tom Paulin, *The Riot Act: A Version of Antigone by Sophocles* (London: Faber & Faber, 1985)

57.   *Sophocles' Antigone: A New Version by Brendan Kennelly* (Highgreen: Bloodaxe, 1996)

58.   *Sophocles Antigone in a new version by Declan Donnellan* (London: Oberon Books, 1999)

59.   *The Burial at Thebes: Sophocles's Antigone*, transl. Seamus Heaney (London: Faber & Faber, 2004)

60.   I am grateful to Loredana Salis for alerting me to the existence of some of these works

61.   *The Burial at Thebes*, p. 41

62.   Sophocles, *Antigone*, p. 127

63.   Francis, *Miss Erin*, p. 154

64.   Francis, *Miss Erin*, p. 200

65.   Murphy, p. 59

66.   Francis, *Miss Erin*, p. 220

67.   Francis, *Miss Erin*, p. 286

68.   Francis, *Miss Erin*, p. 291

69.   Julia Anne Miller, 'Acts of Union: Family Violence and National Courtship in Maria Edgeworth's *The Absentee* and Sydney Owenson's *The Wild Irish Girl*', in Kathryn Kirkpatrick (ed.), *Border Crossings: Irish Women Writers and National Identities* (Dublin: Wolfhound, 2000), p. 14

70.   Sophocles, *Antigone*, p. 69

71.   Francis, *Miss Erin*, p. 187

Ireland: The *Terra Incognita* of the New Woman Project

1.   Interestingly, two other well-known New Woman novelists also had Irish backgrounds. Iota [Kathleen Mannington Caffyn] was from County Tipperary where she lived until she was twenty-one before emigrating to London and then

Australia, and E. L. Voynich [Ethel Lillian] was the Cork-born daughter of the mathematician George Boole and the scientist Mary Everest Boole.

2. For example, her only novel, *The Wheel of God* (1898) takes as its subject matter the story of a young Irish woman who emigrates to New York in the late nineteenth century.

3. For a more detailed discussion of the effect of the New Woman figure on the aspirations of the contemporary feminist movement, see Sally Ledger, *The New Woman: Fiction and Feminism at the Fin de Siècle* (Manchester University Press, 1997), Introduction

4. Gerd Bjørhovde, *Rebellious Structures* (Oslo: Norwegian University Press, 1987), p. 56

5. The origin of the name 'New Woman' can be found in a response to an essay by Grand. The essay, entitled 'The New Aspect of the Woman Question', threw down the gauntlet to the patriarchal *status quo*. The phrase 'New Woman' was singled out by 'Ouida' [Marie Louise de la Ramée], an anti-feminist journalist of the period, to ridicule the revolutionary aspirations of this feminist project. For further discussion of this, see Jordan, 'The Christening of the New Woman: May 1894', in *Victorian Newsletter* 48 (1983), pp. 19–21

6. Although this trilogy was not Grand's first foray into writing, these novels were her first to be published.

7. Just after the publication of *The Heavenly Twins*, Edith Somerville noted in her diary: 'All here reading Heavenly Twins–much controversy'. Gifford Lewis, *Somerville and Ross: The World of the Irish R. M.* (1985; London: Penguin, 1987), p. 66

8. The label 'New Woman' was used by *Punch,* among others, to delegitimize the radicalism of the group.

9. Prefiguring the much later work of materialist feminists such as Christine Delphy and Monique Wittig.

10. Elaine Showalter, *Sexual Anarchy: Gender and Culture at the Fin de Siècle* (London: Virago, 1992)

11. Margaret Diane Stetz and Mark Samuels Lasner, *England in the 1890s: Literary Publishing at the Bodley Head* (Washington: Georgetown University Press, 1990), p. 39

12. Matthew Sturgis, *Passionate Attitudes: The English Decadence of the 1890s* (London: Macmillan, 1995), p. 202

13. This series included works by Ella Darcy, Gertrude Dix, Grant Allen, Edith Nesbit, and Mabel Wotton

14. Terence de Vere White, *A Leaf From the Yellow Book: The Correspondence of George Egerton* (London: Richards, 1958), p. 166

15. Higginson was a friend of Captain Dunne, Egerton's father. At this point in his varied career Higginson was bigamously married to the widow of Whyte Melville, the poet, whom it is suggested he had blackmailed into marrying him (de Vere White 16). In 1887, Mrs Whyte Melville asked Captain Dunne to let his daughter travel with them as a companion to her, as a result of which Higginson and Egerton eloped together, apparently taking some of Mrs Whyte Melville's fortune with them. When Higginson died two years later, he left a small legacy to Egerton, and the property in Langesund, which was her only income for many years to come.

16. Jennifer Waelti Walters and Stephen C. Hause, *Feminisms of the Belle Époque* (Lincoln: University of Nebraska Press, 1994)

17. Anne L. Ardis, *New Women, New Novels: Feminism and Early Modernism* (New Brunswick: Rutgers University Press, 1990), p. 34

18. Virginia Woolf, *The Pargiters*, ed. Mitchell A. Leaska (London: Hogarth Press, 1978), p. 37

19. Judith Walkowitz, *City of Dreadful Delight: Narratives of Sexual Danger in Late-Victorian London* (London: Virago, 1992)

20. Knut Hamsun (1859–1952), Nobel Prize-winning Norwegian novelist, dramatist and poet; today considered the major prose writer of Norwegian literature, and one of Norway's most widely known literary figures. See Illit Grøndahl and Ola Raknes, *Chapters in Norwegian Literature* (London: Gyldendal, 1923), pp. 269–274

21. Ola Hansson (1860–1925), Swedish novelist, short story writer and esssayist. Originally a poet from the Skåne group whose early poetry collections *Dikter* (1884) and *Notturno* (1885) are heavily influenced by aestheticism and mysticism. His critical essays attacked the literary programme of the 1880s in Sweden, which he considered too parochial. He lived in exile for most of his life, finally settling in Berlin with his German wife, Laura Marholm Hansson. As a result, he is not today very well known in his own country. His 1892 work *Ung Ofegs visor* illustrates his adherence to Nietzschean philosophy and was translated by Egerton in 1893. In 1887 he published his best-known work, a collection of short stories, *Sensitiva amorosa* which constituted an exploration of the erotic, in its many forms. This work caused controversy at home and abroad, particularly because of its depiction of homoerotic experience. Laura Marholm Hansson later included a figure of George Egerton in her collection *Modern Women: Six Psychological Sketches* (1896). See also Alrik Gustafson, *A History of Swedish Literature* (Minneapolis: Minnesota University Press, 1971), pp. 281–293

22. In *Pan* (1894), Hamsun depicts a hunter who lives out his life away from human company, until the rhythms of nature all around him become entwined with the pulse in his own veins. Characters in some of Egerton's tales take on a similar pantheistic faith, and similarly believe in a holistic continuity in all things. Lines from 'The Regeneration of Two' suggest this confluence between the individual and the natural world: 'The sun-filled air, the music, water, all the thrumming sounds of summer seem to fuse into a gigantic gold-green disc, that revolves first quickly, then with ever-slackening turns around her, until she loses herself in the slow swirl' (181). However, Egerton's work, unlike that of Hamsun, treats of the developing consciousness of individual *women*. In 'A Psychological Moment at Three Periods' Egerton sketches an early attempt at psychological realism by describing the development of a young girl.

23. George Egerton, 'The Regeneration of Two', in *Discords* (London: Elkin Mathews & John Lane, 1894), p. 167

24. George Egerton, 'A Shadow's Slant', in *Keynotes* (London: Elkin Mathews & John Lane, 1893), p. 140

25. Egerton, 'A Shadow's Slant', p. 145

26. The best-known author of the 'dialect novel' was 'Fiona MacLeod' [William Sharp] (1855–1905), whose novels were set in the Strathclyde area. His main works were *The Dominion of Dreams*, 1899; *Iona*, 1910; and *The Winged Destiny*, 1910.

27. Rider Haggard's 1887 novel, *She,* was one of the best sellers of the 1880s; Joseph Conrad's *Heart of Darkness* (1902); H. G.Wells's novel, *The Island of Dr. Moreau,* (1896); and Perkins Gilman's *Herland* (1915), are some other examples of novels in this genre.

28. George Egerton, 'The Regeneration of Two', in *Discords* (London: Elkin Mathews & John Lane, 1894), p. 202

29. Terence de Vere White, p. 23

30. George Egerton, 'The Spell of the White Elf', in *Keynotes* (London: Elkin Mathews & John Lane, 1893), p. 70

31. Scott McCracken, 'George Egerton's *Wheel of God*', in Tadhg Foley *et al* (eds), *Gender and Colonialism* (Galway University Press, 1995), pp. 139–157

32. Terence de Vere White, p. 138

33. Katherine Tynan gives the precise date of 14 Dec. 1860, whereas White says 1859. Cf. entry on Egerton in *The Cabinet of Irish Literature*, vol. 4 (London: Gresham, 1902)

34. Katherine Tynan, Entry on Egerton in *The Cabinet of Irish Literature*, vol. 4, p. 297

35. Terence de Vere White, p. 12

36. Linda Dowling, 'The Decadent and the New Woman in the 1890s', *Nineteenth Century* vol. 33, 1979, p. 47

37. George Egerton, 'The Child', in *Discords* (London: Elkin Mathews & John Lane, 1894), p. 4

38. Egerton, 'The Child', p. 7

39. When *Keynotes* was first published, the identity of its author was a mystery. Many supposed the (male) author to be Scandinavian, given that the writing style was similar to that being produced in the North and the locations for many of the stories were distinctly Nordic.

40. George Egerton, 'A Cross Line', in *Keynotes* (London: Elkin Mathews & John Lane, 1893), p. 6

41. Egerton, 'A Cross Line', p. 18

42. Egerton, 'A Cross Line', pp. 19–20

43. George Egerton, 'Gone Under', in *Discords* (London: Elkin Mathews & John Lane, 1894), p. 82

44. Egerton, 'The Child', pp. 6–7

45. George Egerton, 'The Girl', in *Discords* (London: Elkin Mathews & John Lane, 1894), p. 12

46. Egerton, 'The Girl', p. 13

47. Angela Bourke, *The Burning of Bridget Cleary: A True Story* (London: Pimlico, 1999), p. 60

48. George Egerton, 'The Spell of the White Elf', in *Keynotes* (London: Elkin Mathews & John Lane, 1893), p. 78

49. Egerton, 'The Spell of the White Elf', p. 80

50. Egerton, 'The Spell of the White Elf', p. 79

51. Egerton, 'The Spell of the White Elf', p. 81

52. Egerton, 'The Spell of the White Elf', p. 82

53. Bridget Elliott, 'New and Not So New Women on the London Stage: Aubrey Beardsley's *Yellow Book* Images of Mrs. Patrick Campbell and Rèjane', *Victorian Studies* vol. 3.1, 1987, p. 34

54. This comes across very strongly in a much later story by Egerton, 'The Marriage of Mary Ascension' from *Flies in Amber*, where Egerton details the participation of locals in pre-Christian ritual, such as 'paying rounds' at Saint Gobnait's well in Ballyvourney.

55. Bourke, p. 37

56. Bourke, p. 28
57. Egerton, 'The Spell of the White Elf', p. 72
58. Egerton, 'The Spell of the White Elf', p. 80
59. W. Harris, 'John Lane's Keynotes Series and the Fiction of the 1890s', *PMLA* vol. 83, 1968, pp. 1407–13
60. de Vere White, pp. 41–42
61. de Vere White, p. 43
62. *Punch* Dec. 1895, front cover
63. Bourke, p. 38
64. George Egerton, 'The Well of Truth', in *Fantasias* (London: John Lane, 1897) pp. 141–42

The Art of Politics in Somerville and Ross's Fiction

1. Edith Somerville and Martin Ross, *Collection of Irish Anecdotes, 1885–1945*, no. 881, Special Collections, Queen's University Library, Belfast
2. Susan Mitchell, quoted in Hilary Pyle, *Red-Headed Rebel: Susan L. Mitchell, Poet and Mystic of the Irish Cultural Renaissance* (Dublin: Woodfield Press, 1998), p. 191
3. E. Œ. Somerville, 'Hunting in Ireland', *Irish Travel*, Oct. 1927, p. 295
4. Maurice Collis, *Somerville and Ross* (London: Faber & Faber, 1968); Gifford Lewis, *Somerville and Ross, The World of the Irish R. M.* (1985; London: Penguin, 1987) and *Edith Somerville, A Biography* (Dublin: Four Courts Press, 2005)
5. Roz Cowman, 'Lost Time: The Smell and Taste of Castle T', in Eibhear Walshe (ed.), *Sex, Nation and Dissent in Irish Writing* (Cork University Press, 1997), pp. 87–102. Vera Kreilkamp, 'The Big Houses of Somerville and Ross', in Vera Kreilkamp, *The Anglo-Irish Novel and the Big House* (New York: Syracuse University Press, 1998), pp. 112–40
6. Recognition of Somerville and Ross's fiction is neglected in *The Field Day Anthology of Irish Writing: Irish Women's Writings and Traditions*, vols. IV and V (Cork University Press, 2002) in favour of the works of less well known Irish women writers. An excerpt from Edith Somerville's memoir, *Irish Memories*, and criticism by Roz Cowman, first published in *Sex, Nation and Dissent in Irish Writing* have been included to offer a biographical or sexual reading of the writers.
7. Otto Rauchbauer (ed.), *The Edith Œnone Somerville Archive in Drishane House* (Dublin: Irish Manuscripts Commission, 1995); Declan Kiberd, 'Tragedies of Manners–Somerville and Ross', in Declan Kiberd, *Inventing Ireland* (London: Jonathan Cape, 1995), pp. 69–82, and 'Somerville and Ross: The Silver Fox', in Declan Kiberd, *Irish Classics* (London: Granta, 2000), pp. 360–78
8. Somerville and Ross's interest in landscape (including Edith Somerville's landscape paintings), children's literature, and French culture was emphasized in the Somerville and Ross Exhibition in Trinity College Library, Dublin. See Julie Anne Stevens, *Writing and Illustrating Ireland: The Somerville and Ross Exhibition Catalogue*, Trinity College Library Dublin, November to December 2002 (Dublin: Paceprint, 2002)
9. *Observer*, Sep. 1889, from Edith Somerville's first scrapbook, private collection.
10. *Graphic*, Sep. 1889, n. p.
11. *Old Saloon*, Nov. 1889, pp. 702–05; p. 704
12. *Old Saloon*, p. 704

13. *Daily Graphic*, 5 Oct. 1891; *Black and White*, 19 Dec. 1891; *Saturday Review*, 21 Nov. 1891

14. *Daily Express*, 2 Nov. 1891

15. *Graphic*, 20 Oct. 1894; *Liverpool Mercury*, 23 May 1894; *Athenaeum*, 9 Jun. 1894

16. *Westminster Gazette*, n. d., n. p.

17. *Lady's Pictorial*, 19 May 1894

18. Martin Ross, 'The Terror in Ireland', *World*, 5 Apr. 1893, pp. 22–23; p. 22

19. E. Œ. Somerville and Martin Ross, *The Silver Fox* (1898; London: Longmans, Green & Co., 1918); Bram Stoker, *Dracula* (1898; New York: W.W. Norton, 1997)

20. James Frazer, *The Golden Bough* (New York: Macmillan, 1947), pp. 656–57

21. Angela Bourke, *The Burning of Bridget Cleary: A True Story* (London: Pimlico, 1999). As Angela Bourke points out, Bridget Cleary's murder brought into sharp focus the confrontation of two radically different ways of perceiving the world in late nineteenth-century Ireland; modern systems of order faced the deep-seated traditions and ways of apprehending reality of the Irish country people. Somerville and Ross address the same theme in *The Silver Fox* and give precedence to Irish folk traditions. More to the point, the writers adapted these traditions as their own. Edith Somerville believed in fairies and owned a fairy shoe. See Somerville and Ross, *Collection of Irish Anecdotes*, book one, QUB

22. Somerville and Ross, *The Silver Fox*, p. 117

23. Somerville and Ross, *Dan Russel The Fox* (London: Methuen, 1911), pp. 233–34

24. Geoffrey Chaucer, 'The Nun's Priest's Tale', *The Canterbury Tales*, trans. Nevill Coghill (Baltimore, Maryland: Penguin, 1952), p. 244. Nevill Coghill was Somerville's nephew.

25. The political potential of Dan Russel is indicated in Chaucer's naming of his fox as 'daun Russel' (Sir Russel), which suggests to J. Leslie Hotson a possible dig at the sly evasions of Sir John Russel (a pretence of madness to avoid execution) upon the return of Henry IV to England. 'Colfox vs. Chauntecleer', in Edward Wagenknecht (ed.), *Chaucer: Modern Essays in Criticism* (New York: Oxford University Press, 1959), p. 112

26. Edith Somerville wrote *The Story of the Discontented Little Elephant* (1912) in 1911 and in the same year hoped to interest publishers in an adaptation of Southey's 'Crocodile King' as an illustrated children's book. See her letter to James Pinker, 18 Nov. 1911, no. 3330–1, Manuscripts Department, Trinity College Library, Dublin. Edith Somerville was alert to the political significance of the fox figure. In a later essay called 'Dan Russel The Fox,' she points out that English hunters of the past called their prey 'Charlie' after Charles James Fox. *The Sweet Cry of Hounds* (London: Methuen, 1936), p. 51

27. Edith Somerville, *Growly-Wowly of the Story of the Three Little Pigs*, private collection. See Stevens, *Writing and Illustrating Ireland*, p. 31 for a full description.

28. Edith Somerville, *Little Red Riding-Hood in Kerry* (London: Peter Davies, 1934)

29. Thomas J. Arnold, 'Introductory Letter,' in *Reynard the Fox, After the German Version of Goethe*, illustrated by Wilhelm Von Kaulbach and Joseph Wolf (London: John C. Nimmo, 1887), p. xxiii

30. For instance, Somerville and Ross record a story told by Thady Hennessy of Castletownshend about a beast, half dog and half cat, with a bark like the 'squeal of a seagull' living in the woods. QUB Ms 17/1–4/B. Transcribed by June Hilary

Berrow, in appendix c: Folk material, 'Somerville and Ross: Transitional Novelists', Ph. D. thesis, UCD, Jan. 1975

31. Charles Baudelaire, '*De l'essence du rire*,' *Oeuvres Complètes*, vol. 2, ed., Claude Pichois (Paris: Editions Gallimard, 1976), p. 541

32. Philip Bull, *Land, Politics and Nationalism: A Study of the Irish Land Question* (Dublin: Gill & Macmillan, 1996), pp. 123–25; L. P. Curtis Jr., 'Stopping the Hunt, 1881–1882', in C. H. E. Philpin (ed.), *Nationalism and Popular Protest in Ireland* (Cambridge: Past and Present Society, 1987); Somerville and Ross, *The Silver Fox*, pp. 72–74 and *Dan Russel The Fox*, pp. 238–42

33. Susan Mitchell, quoted in Hilary Pyle, *Red-Headed Rebel*, p. 191

34. Daniel Corkery, *Synge and Anglo-Irish Literature* (Cork: Mercier, 1966), p. 13

35. F. S. L. Lyons, *Ireland Since the Famine* (London: Fontana, 1971), p. 219; Philip Bull, *Land, Politics and Nationalism*, pp. 152–53

36. As Simon Schama points out in *Landscape and Memory* (London: Fontana, 1995), p. 15, 'landscapes can be self-consciously designed to express the virtues of a particular political or social commentary'. Declan Kiberd has argued that Somerville and Ross's treatment of the Irish hunt in *The Silver Fox* demonstrates the authors' sympathetic understanding of the Catholic Irish peasantry that admits to the failure of English and Anglo-Irish dealings with Ireland. 'Somerville and Ross: *The Silver Fox*', *Irish Classics*, p. 375. My treatment of Somerville and Ross's later short fiction argues that while the women writers may have included Catholic participants in the Anglo-Irish hunt, the country always remained a Protestant Ascendancy terrain.

37. Somerville and Ross, *The Irish R. M.* (London: Abacus, 1992), p. 567

38. Somerville and Ross, *The Irish R. M*, p. 442

39. Maurice Collis, *Somerville and Ross*, p. 148. Violet Powell, *The Irish Cousins* (London: Heinemann, 1970), p. 166. Lady Gregory was Mrs Martin's cousin

40. Arnold, *Reynard the Fox*, p. xxv

41. Arnold, *Reynard the Fox*. I have concentrated on the first half of Arnold's treatment of Goethe's version.

42. Somerville and Ross, *The Irish R. M.*, p. 453

43. Somerville and Ross, *The Irish R. M.*, p. 472

44. Roger H. Stephenson argues that Goethe's treatment of the beast fable is not a straightforward attack of the French Revolution–as is often argued–but a wider discussion that includes a satire of the corruption of the *ancien régime*. 'The Political Import of Goethe's Reineke Fuchs', in Kenneth Vartry (ed.), *Reynard the Fox: Social Engagement and Cultural Metamorphoses in the Beast Epic from the Middle Ages to the Present* (New York: Berghahn, 2000), pp. 191–207

45. Robert Martin, *Bits of Blarney* (London: Sands, 1899), p. 18

46. Terry Eagleton, *Heathcliff and the Great Hunger* (London: Verso, 1995), p. 191

47. Eagleton, *Heathcliff and the Great Hunger*, p. 192

48. Bram Stoker, *Dracula* (1898; New York: W. W. Norton, 1997), p. 255

49. Stoker, *Dracula*, p. 278

50. Stoker, *Dracula*, p. 255

51. Eagleton, *Heathcliff and the Great Hunger*, p. 215. Bruce Stewart cautions against reading *Dracula* as 'an allegory of the landlord-tenant relations' which sees the vampire as a 'portrait of the Anglo-Irish landlord'. Bruce Stewart, 'Bram Stoker's *Dracula*: Possessed by the Spirit of the Nation?', *Irish University Review* vol. 29.2,

autumn/winter 1999, pp. 238–55. My own findings with regard to Somerville and Ross lead me to agree with Stewart's conclusions.

52. Patrick Maume has mentioned this story a number of times to me as an example of Somerville and Ross's politics, which might be understood better by considering Robert Martin's stories. I am grateful to him for emphasizing the significance of Robert Martin's work although I argue that Somerville and Ross exploit rather than merely repeat the older brother's point of view.

53. Sir John Pentland Mahaffy, 'Who Wants Home Rule?', *Blackwood's Magazine* cxciii. mclxviii, Feb. 1913, pp. 245–53

54. Julian Moynahan, *Anglo-Irish* (New Jersey: Princeton University Press, 1995), p. 196

55. Joseph Devlin, 'Comedy and the Land: Somerville and Ross's Irish R. M.' *Studies in Anglo-Irish Fiction and Balladry*, Working Papers in Irish Studies, 94–1 (Fort Lauderdale, Florida: Nova University, 1994), p. 21

56. Somerville and Ross, *The Irish R. M.*, p. 442

57. Somerville and Ross, *The Irish R. M.*, p. 447

58. Geraldine Cummins, *Dr. E. Œ. Somerville* (London: Andrew Dakers, 1952), p. 30

Index